D0344578

we is got him

we is got him

THE KIDNAPPING THAT CHANGED AMERICA

Carrie Hagen

THE OVERLOOK PRESS
NEW YORK, NY

This edition first published in the United States in 2011 by
The Overlook Press, Peter Mayer Publishers, Inc.

141 Wooster Street
New York, NY 10012
www.overlookpress.com

For bulk and special sales, please contact sales@overlookny.com

Copyright © 2011 by Carrie Hagen

All rights reserved. No part of this publication may be reproduced
or transmitted in any form or by any means, electronic or mechanical,
including photocopy, recording, or any information storage and
retrieval system now known or to be invented, without permission
in writing from the publisher, except by a reviewer who wishes to
quote brief passages in connection with a review written for
inclusion in a magazine, newspaper, or broadcast.

Library of Congress Cataloging-in-Publication Data

Hagen, Carrie.
We is got him : abduction, murder, and politics in America's Gilded Age
/ Carrie Hagen.
p. cm.
Includes bibliographical references and index.
ISBN 978-1-59020-086-5 (hardback)
1. Ross, Charles Brewster, b. 1870. 2. Kidnapping—Pennsylvania—Case studies.
3. Philadelphia (Pa.)—Politics and government—1865- I. Title.
HV6603.R6H34 2011   364.152'3092—dc23   2011025483

Design and typeformatting by Bernard Schleifer
Manufactured in the United States of America

FIRST EDITION

2 4 6 8 10 9 7 5 3 1

ISBN 978-1-59020-086-5

to a different Charley,
　　　　　who loved this city

and to Jeff,
　　　who loves it now

author's note

THIS IS A WORK OF NONFICTION. ANY DETAIL THAT IS NOT common knowledge to students of this case and culture has a corresponding endnote. Any word within quotation marks is taken from memoir, newspaper report, trial transcript, or family paper. Certain geographical locations of importance to this story have undergone name changes over the past 137 years. Unless otherwise indicated in an endnote, I use the location names known to 1874.

contents

major personalities

CHARLEY AND WALTER ROSS

Brothers, ages 4 and 5, kidnapped from their front yard on July 1, 1874. The same evening, Walter is released and returned home.

CHRISTIAN ROSS

The boys' father, a failing businessman caught between loyalty to his family and obedience to the police. After initially leading the search to find his son, Christian is targeted by the press when Philadelphia's city leaders convince him not to pay the ransom.

THE LEWIS BROTHERS

Christian Ross's neighbors, brothers-in-law, and wealthy merchants. The Lewis brothers represent the family in the investigation when Christian collapses. Frustrated with libel and police incompetence, the brothers disregard the advice of city leaders in November 1874 and negotiate an exchange with the kidnappers on their own terms.

WILLIAM McKEAN AND THE ADVISERS

A powerful group of Philadelphia council and businessmen, leaders of Philadelphia's chapter of the "Republican Ring." Eager to promote the Centennial Exhibition and determined to retain their offices in the November 1874 election, these men do what they can to keep news of Charley's kidnapping from the press. One well-known member is William McKean, editor of the Philadelphia *Public Ledger*.

MAYOR STOKLEY

Philadelphia mayor and figurehead of the city's Republican Ring. Responsible to the Republican advisers, Stokley is concerned with his public approval ratings once his constituents blame him and his force for running an incompetent investigation.

WILLIAM MOSHER

One of the two kidnappers, a forty-something river pirate and career criminal. Raised in Brooklyn, Mosher lives in Philadelphia with his wife and three sons under the name of Henderson. While on a "peddling" trip to Germantown, Mosher and his criminal apprentice Joseph Douglas see the Ross boys. Assuming the boys' father is a wealthy man and will immediately pay any ransom amount, they take the children.

JOSEPH DOUGLAS

The second kidnapper, a younger man of twenty-eight. After serving a prison sentence for burglary, Douglas works as a streetcar conductor in Manhattan until Mosher finds and entices him to move to Philadelphia. Less conspicuous and more emotionally stable than his mentor, Douglas seeks to cut ties with Mosher once newspapers print their descriptions and Christian Ross refuses to pay the ransom.

WILLIAM WESTERVELT

Brother-in-law of William Mosher and a former police officer. In July 1874, bartenders in New York's Five Points neighborhood notice Westervelt meeting with two men that fit newspaper accounts

of Charley Ross's kidnappers. Westervelt becomes a police informant early in the investigation, but unbeknownst to the NYPD,
he also acts as a double agent, informing the kidnappers of police
activity.

SUPERINTENDENT GEORGE WALLING

A career officer and head of the New York Police Department.
Walling assumes a main role in the case soon after Mayor Stokley an-
nounces Philadelphia's $20,000 reward for information, when Gil
Mosher, William's brother, arrives in his office with suspicions of his
brother's involvement. When Walling realizes the connection between
his former officer William Westervelt and William Mosher, he offers
Westervelt his old job back in exchange for spying on his brother-in-
law's activities.

CAPTAIN HEINS

One of the first Philadelphia officers put on the case. Heins's loyalty
to the Ross family irritates Mayor Stokley and the Republican advisers,
who suspect Heins is withholding information from them. The captain
closely communicates with Walling throughout the summer of 1874,
until he suspects William Westervelt's intentions and warns the superintendent against working with the informant. In the spring of 1875,
Heins demands that Walling turn Westervelt over to the Philadelphia
Police.

THE RANSOM NOTES

The voice of the kidnappers. Appearing in excerpts throughout the
first two sections of the narrative, these notes direct Christian Ross to
communicate his plans through personal advertisements; once this
occurs, the chronological placement of the letters and the ads creates a
conversation between the criminals and the family.

THE NEWSPAPERS

The voice of the public. The narrative integration of excerpts from the *New York Herald*, the Philadelphia *Public Ledger*, the *New York Times*, the Philadelphia *Evening Bulletin*, and the Philadelphia Inquirer reflects the American temperament from July 1874 through September 1875.

PART ONE:

"we is got him"

(JULY 1874)

we is got him

Horses stumbled up and down Germantown Avenue in 1874. Their shoes got caught between layers of cement and broken cobblestone and slid on uneven gravel. Travelers had complained about the road between central Philadelphia and Germantown since 1700, nearly twenty years after William Penn purchased the woods northwest of Philadelphia from the Delaware Indians. Through an agent, he offered the land to victims of religious persecution in Europe, and in 1683, thirteen families of Germans arrived. They lived in caves while they built homes along an Indian footpath, a trail leading eight miles uphill from the Schuylkill River. Settling toward the top of the ridge, the immigrants established themselves in their family trades as weavers, shoemakers, and tailors. By the turn of the century, Philadelphia's society recognized the people of "German Town" as gifted artisans, and the community earned enough money to establish financial independence from Philadelphia earlier than other settlements. The townspeople's pride, however, was frustrated by a common grievance: There were too many holes in the trail leading directly through town.

Over the next two centuries, the former Indian footpath evolved from a trail into a route, a road, and then an avenue. As each generation tried and failed to fill its holes, the thoroughfare became a historical marker. During the winter of 1688, a group of Quakers and Mennonites met along it to sign the nation's first document condemning slavery. In 1777, General Howe's men marched Washington's troops down it following the British victory at the Battle of Germantown. Before the Civil War, runaway slaves found their way to it, resting at the Johnson house, Philadelphia's only documented stop on the Underground Railroad. And in July 1874, two river pirates turned onto it after kidnapping two little boys from their father's front yard, initiating the first recorded ransom kidnapping in American history.

Germantown's neighborhoods branched off a two-mile stretch of the avenue called Main Street. Every weekday, hundreds of commuters passed these residential streets on their way to and from the city. After Philadelphia absorbed Germantown into its city limits in 1854, the state of Pennsylvania built a turnpike north of its boundaries, making Germantown Avenue an even more important connection between Philadelphia, its northwestern suburbs, and central Pennsylvania. Often, salesmen and charlatans turned off the avenue onto quieter streets to peddle contraband or homemade products at the doorsteps of Victorian mansions, colonial houses, and Gothic cottages—homes of the middle class and summer retreats of Philadelphia's elite. In the early summer evenings of 1874, light winds rustled the trees and carried the scents of lilies and clover up to Main Street. Nurses bathed children, cooks prepared dinner, and groundskeepers tended symmetrical flower beds.

Washington Lane was one of six roads connecting Germantown to other neighborhoods, and on Wednesday, July 1, Peter Callahan groomed at least one property there. Earlier that day, local churches and clubs had hosted a picnic outing for children from the city's poorest neighborhoods. Laughter had echoed through the streets around lunchtime, but before the dinner hour, only two little children could be heard playing outdoors. Just after 5:00 P.M., a black wagon turned onto what is now East Washington Lane. It was drawn by a brown horse with a rusted harness and a white spot on its forehead. Peter Callahan noticed the two men sitting in the wagon. The driver's face was partially hidden by oversized eyeglasses and a sandy mustache. He looked about thirty, and he was a redhead. He wore a gray coat, a gold vest chain, and a tall, dark-colored straw hat. The passenger drew more attention to himself, mainly because he held a red handkerchief over his face. His hair was dark, and he was shorter and older than the driver.

When the wagon reached a brick wall about three feet high, the driver pulled the reins. Peter Callahan knew the children were playing on the other side of the wall that marked the front boundary of a family's property. The passenger jumped from the wagon and dropped his red handkerchief. Callahan saw his face—a dark mustache, stray whiskers sprouting from his square jaw, a deformed nose. Callahan wasn't sure what was wrong with it, but the tip of the man's nose appeared to point toward his forehead. The man began talking to the two little boys, and a few minutes later, the brothers followed him into the wagon. The older boy sat between the two men. The younger sat on the passenger's lap. As the horse began to trot up Washington Lane, the men spread a ripped, dirty lap cover with a red stripe across the children.

Callahan went back to work on the garden. He didn't say anything. Groundskeepers were used to seeing strangers roaming the residential streets.

you wil have two pay us

BEFORE THEY WENT OUT TO PLAY, FIVE-YEAR-OLD WALTER ROSS and his four-year-old brother Charley had taken a bath. Christian Ross, their father, was due home from work at six, and both boys anticipated the treat he would have for them. Walter and Charley asked their nurses if they could play outside as they waited. The women agreed. Charley had light brown hair that was parted on the left and curled in ringlets to his neck. He wore a pink ribbon around his head to keep his hair out of his eyes. Although Walter was only slightly taller than his younger brother, Charley looked up to him and put Walter in charge of his trinkets and toys. Charley loved to hug his six brothers and sisters, but he was very shy around strangers. If somebody he didn't know approached him, Charley covered his face with his right arm.

Neither boy shied away from the man with the odd nose when he jumped over the brick wall. They walked toward the candy in his hand, and Charley asked if the man could take him to buy some firecrackers. When the man pointed out the wagon, Peter Callahan saw the driver scan the street.

The horse turned right once they reached Main Street. Walter asked why they weren't turning left to buy firecrackers at a popular shop.

"No, we will take you to Aunt Susie's, who keeps a store, and will give you a pocketful for five cents," the passenger said. Walter saw his nose clearly from his seat between the men. The cartilage separating his nostrils had worn away.

Walter soon realized that the horse turned at intersections in the road frequently. He asked the men to identify features in the landscape as they passed farms, stables, and watering holes. They answered his questions. As the wagon took him farther and farther from home, Charley began to whimper. He rarely cried aloud. If somebody snapped at him or spoke in harsh tones, Charley's eyes brimmed with tears until they spilled onto his cheeks. The men quieted him with candy and promises to buy all the firecrackers he wanted once they reached the store.

"Faster, faster!" the passenger called as the horse climbed hills. Twice the men stopped at water pumps and told Walter to fill an empty bottle. The passenger added liquor to it from a flask as he balanced Charley on his lap. The forefinger on his left hand had shriveled to a sharp point around his nail. He wore two rings on the middle finger of his right hand; both were gold, one a plain band and the other set with a red stone.

"Slower, slower!" the passenger called as the horse ran downhill. The wagon turned again, again, and again before reaching Kensington, a neighborhood in northern Philadelphia. At the intersection of Richmond and Palmer Streets, the men saw a tobacco store down Richmond Street with a window display of firecrackers and torpedoes. The passenger handed Walter twenty-five cents and told him to go inside and buy his brother some toys and himself some candy. Walter obeyed.

John Hay, a young tobacconist, saw Walter at the counter and asked what he wanted.

"Firecrackers." Walter pointed to some large ones.

Hay paused. Neighborhood boys usually bought as many small firecrackers as they could get for their money; it didn't make sense that Walter asked for fewer, larger ones. He told the boy to come back when he was sure he knew what he wanted. Walter left, went back to the buggy, and soon reentered the store.

A few minutes later, he walked back outside with two packs of firecrackers and one of torpedoes. He stopped. The wagon, the men, and Charley had disappeared. Walter ran to the intersection and looked back and forth. Then he screamed.

As expected, Christian Ross rode up Main Street before 6:00 P.M. He was a tall and skinny man, fifty years old, the father of seven chil-

dren, and a Sunday-school teacher at the local Methodist church. He
had a receding hairline, a large nose and a full, carefully groomed red
beard that almost covered his lower lip. Christian commuted ten miles
from his home to his wholesale dry goods company on Third and Market streets. It was a difficult time to own a small business. The Panic
of 1873 had hit Philadelphia the year before, when the Jay Cooke Bank
closed. This New York-based bank had heavily financed railroad construction, but the pace of westward expansion depleted funds, and the
bank folded under rising costs of labor. Philadelphia's commercial and
industrial communities were funded by local family-owned banks, so
they did not suffer like others in the East. Smaller businesses like
Christian's, however, took a hit as consumers lost or conserved expend-
able income. Christian's wife, Sarah, had recently taken a trip to
Atlantic City, causing neighbors to wonder whether she was struggling
to cope with financial stress at the Ross home. The family said she was
recovering from an illness.

Christian looked forward to seeing his two youngest sons that
evening. The boys had been complaining because they were stuck at
home while their older sister Sophia vacationed with their mother and
their two older brothers visited their grandmother in central Pennsylvania. Walter and Charley knew they would switch places with Sophia
in mid-July, but in the meantime, the household—including two nan-
nies, a cook, groundsmen, an older and a younger sister—was quieter
than they liked. With the approach of Independence Day, the boys had
seen children in town playing with fireworks. Germantown and
Philadelphia ordinances banned fireworks and firecrackers from residential areas, yet children could easily purchase them in corner stores.
That morning, Walter and Charley had followed their father to the
stables, asking him for money to buy firecrackers. Christian said they
needed to wait until he came home with a cartload of sand to muffle
the sound.

Christian turned onto Washington Lane and headed downhill to his
house. Between one and ten acres separated the residences on either
side of the street. Christian's brother-in-law Joseph Lewis lived on a
large property at the top of the hill, close to the train station. Christian
owned a smaller plot farther down the street. As he approached his

drive, he was surprised that the boys weren't waiting for him. He walked through the garden up to his sheltered front porch and asked the nurses for his sons; the women said they had been playing outside with other children for close to two hours. Christian walked to the front gate and listened for the boys—when he didn't hear them, he decided to wait on the front porch with a newspaper. An hour later, the cook served dinner. Assuming his sons had wandered off with a friend, Christian sent a servant to find them. Only when they didn't return during the meal did he become concerned. Christian went back to the street, followed by members of his household, who divided into small search parties. As Christian walked in front of his house, his neighbor Mary Kidder called to him.

"Are your boys likely to ride with strangers?"

Christian stared at her. Four days earlier, Walter had run up to him with a white braided stick of candy about four inches long. He said a man in a wagon had given one to him and one to Charley. Christian had asked both boys if they had spoken to the strangers. "No, sir," Walter had answered. Later, Christian remembered feeling touched by the encounter, glad that men took the time to notice children.

Mrs. Kidder hurried across her lawn. Her husband, Walter, followed. She told Christian that she had looked out of her window earlier and noticed his boys talking to a man. Shortly thereafter, she saw them ride away with him in a wagon. Mrs. Kidder had thought the scene odd, but with the exception of petty robberies and corner lounging, crime didn't threaten the people of Germantown. That week, a local paper had addressed the town's biggest complaints: the shabby condition of Germantown Avenue, cooks who threw kitchen trash outdoors, women who visited saloons, and police officers who allowed bartenders to illegally sell oysters. As of 1874, kidnapping in America was a misdemeanor, not a felony, and certainly not anything parents in Germantown had ever feared. Walter Kidder walked up the hill with Christian to Main Street and the police station. It was 8:00 P.M.

The Fourteenth Precinct was located at the town hall on Germantown Avenue. Before they reached the precinct station house, Christian saw a man walking next to a child in the distance. He recognized Walter and rushed to him.

"Where have you been, Walter?" he asked.

The little boy rubbed his red, swollen eyes. In his hand, he held firecrackers. "Walter, where is Charley?"

Walter looked confused. "Why, he is all right. He is in the wagon." Walter had assumed that Charley had returned home and he was the one lost.

The man standing next to him identified himself as Mr. Henry Peacock. He told Christian that on his commute home from work, he had seen and heard a terrified Walter talking to women on a street corner in Kensington. When he heard "a man had put him out of a buggy and had then gone off and left him," Mr. Peacock offered to take Walter to the police station. The little boy, he said, then burst "into a frantic fit of crying." Walter was able to tell Henry Peacock where he lived, but he only mentioned one man as being in the buggy, and he didn't say anything about a brother.

Christian wrote down Mr. Peacock's address and asked him to walk Walter home. He and Mr. Kidder continued to the police station.

Germantown's Town Hall stood at the corner of Germantown Avenue and Haines Street. From a distance in any direction, townspeople could see a four-sided clock positioned on the roof, the rotunda above it, and a narrow tower rising from the rotunda into the sky. Six pillars supported the front entrance of Town Hall. It had served as a makeshift hospital during the beginning of the Civil War, but now the building remained fairly empty, except for twelve police officers, any disorderly drunk locked up in a basement cell, and the occasional audience gathering to see a traveling entertainer or politician. Christian and his neighbor walked up the steps. They found Lieutenant Alexander Buchanan, the commanding officer on duty, and asked him to wire a telegraph inquiring about a lost child to central police headquarters. The central office dialogued with each of its precincts via telegraph, which often meant that a network of bells transmitted important communications between offices. Buchanan, a large thirty-eight-year-old Irishman with thick, black eyebrows and an ungroomed moustache, wrote down Charley's name and age.

Thirty minutes later, Buchanan reported that no lost little boys had been found. He said he was sure Charley would show up soon and advised Christian to calm down.

Christian asked what else the police could do.

Buchanan said he couldn't do anything else.

Christian persisted.

Buchanan advised him to contact a Captain William Heins at central police headquarters on Chestnut Street.

Walter Kidder walked Christian back to Washington Lane and returned home. At the top of the hill, Christian stopped at the house of Joseph Lewis, his brother-in-law.

The Ross and Lewis families had known each other for decades. Both were from central Pennsylvania, and both were descended from successful businessmen and related to state politicians. Christian's grandfather was a German immigrant who served in the Revolutionary War and later operated a popular mercantile store in Harrisburg. His daughter Catherine married Joseph Ross, another dry-goods shopkeeper, and the couple raised seven sons in a suburb of Harrisburg called Middletown. Christian was the oldest boy. After working in his father's shop, Christian moved to Philadelphia in his mid-twenties, taking his younger brother Joseph with him. At a Methodist church in Philadelphia, Christian met Sarah Ann Lewis, the younger sister of four brothers who ran a local clothing business. The couple married nine years later, when Sarah was 28 and Christian was 38. A year after their marriage in 1863, Christian's father, Joseph, died and left Christian an inheritance that he used to open his own clothing store—Ross, Schott, & Co. By 1874, as Christian's business faltered, the Lewis brothers owned three successful dry-goods stores in town, and Joseph Lewis owned more property than any other resident on Washington Lane.

Joseph and his son Frank Lewis listened to Christian talk about the events of the past few hours. Joseph then advised Christian to follow Lieutenant Buchanan's suggestion and visit Captain William Heins at police headquarters. He sent his son Frank with him. The men took a streetcar down Germantown Avenue, changing cars once at the Ninth Street depot before they reached Independence Hall—home of the central police station, city council chambers, the courthouse, and the mayor's office. As they walked towards the station Christian and his nephew passed the windows of colonial storefronts. Few lights reflected in them. Christian noticed how unusually quiet the city seemed.

The men arrived around 11:00 P.M., just after Captain Heins had left for the night. The detective on duty listened to Christian's story and told him drunks must have taken Charley. He said the men would eventually sober up, realize their folly and drop Charley off.

Christian asked what else the police could do.

Nothing, the detective answered.

Christian and his nephew disagreed. They took a streetcar to Kensington and walked to the local police station. The officers on duty there said they had heard nothing about a missing child or Lieutenant Buchanan's wire. Christian and Frank found the intersection where Walter had been crying and knocked on the door of a nearby store. A druggist answered. He listened to Christian's questions but said he couldn't help him. The men walked two blocks to Mr. Peacock's house, awoke him, and asked again where the men had abandoned Walter. Peacock took them to a different shop. Nobody answered this door. Peacock then led the men around the neighborhood for two hours, answering whatever questions he could. By the time Christian and Frank left Kensington, no streetcars were running, and they had to walk six miles before finding an open stable on Germantown Avenue. It was 5:00 A.M. when they arrived home.

Christian woke Walter two hours later. He emptied the pockets of his son's clothes from the day before and found five-cent pieces, copper coins, and unopened candy. As soon as Walter had eaten breakfast, he went to his Uncle Joseph's house with Christian and recounted what he could of Charley's disappearance. Afterward, Christian and Frank returned to police headquarters in search of Captain Heins. They found him and told their story once again. Other officers on duty repeated their belief that drunken fools had taken the child; Heins, however, took Christian's concern more seriously. He assigned an Officer Etwein Joyce to accompany Christian back to Kensington on a search for more information.

A thunderstorm loomed over the city that Thursday, July 2, but there wasn't much rain. One man referred to the humid, cloudy day as "head-aching weather." Outside of John Hay's tobacco shop on Richmond Street in Kensington, men often gathered to sit, smoke, and talk about boat races or their jobs at the shipyards down the road. Christian and Officer Joyce entered the store and introduced themselves to Hay. He remembered selling firecrackers to Walter the night before. He said he had assumed Walter was a neighborhood boy and didn't think anything much about him.

In search of eyewitnesses, the men walked outside to interview pedestrians, several of whom recalled seeing Walter crying on the corner. Only one person could place Charley in the wagon at the scene. A little girl said she saw the buggy with the little boy drive away as she stood on the sidewalk.

By now, Officer Joyce was suspicious. He left instructions with the Kensington Police to search for Charley and took Christian and Frank Lewis to the nearest ferry stop along the Delaware River. Joyce asked the driver if he had seen a child matching Charley's description. The man said no. Joyce decided to take Christian back to Germantown. He determined that if the men had followed Germantown Avenue directly to Kensington, somebody would have seen the children in the wagon. The men stopped at feed stores, stables, hotels, and watering holes along the Avenue. They asked if anybody had observed a horse and wagon pulling two men and two young boys the day before. Nobody had. A few hours later, Walter sat between his father and the officer on their way back to Kensington. This time, the men asked Walter to try piecing together his journey from the day before. His memory shocked both men. Based on his recognition of landmarks that the kidnappers had identified, Walter remembered a route involving eighteen different turns over the course of eight miles. His recollection was verified by eyewitnesses at feed stores, stables, and hotels along the more residential second half of the route.

Christian took Walter with him to headquarters, where he drafted a newspaper advertisement. Only one paper, the Philadelphia *Public Ledger*, agreed to print the ad the next morning on such short notice. Meanwhile, word of Charley's disappearance had spread quickly in Germantown. That night, the community gathered to pray at the Ross home.

The next day, more eyewitnesses stepped forward. A local doctor reported that on the morning of Tuesday, June 30, the day before the kidnapping, he had seen two men in a dirty, dusty buggy near the Ross property. He had noticed the wagon because it was parked in the sun, not in nearby shade that would have kept the horse cooler. As one man sat in the driver's seat, the doctor noticed another jumping from behind a wall adjacent to the Lewis property. The jumper paused to clear his forehead from sweat, then sat next to the driver in the sun. They noticed the doctor's gaze, and as he passed them on the street, they pulled a curtain over the back of the carriage. The doctor wasn't sure if the men were thieves or gas men, but as he didn't see a policeman nearby, he continued on with a house call.

A handyman remembered that on Monday, June 29, he'd heard a stranger offering candy to the Ross boys and talking to them on the street. A couple of people in town said that on Sunday, June 28, strangers in a wagon had waved to Walter and Charley as they left church. Mr. Johnson, another neighbor of Christian's, said he had seen a man with three-inch long whiskers offer the children candy the previous Saturday, June 27. After listening to his neighbors, Christian realized that the day of the kidnapping was the fifth day in a row that the kidnappers had made contact with his children in broad daylight. Sarah Ross, still in Atlantic City, had no idea of her son's disappearance.

Readers of the Philadelphia *Public Ledger*, the city's most popular daily, opened up their papers on the morning of July 3. In the "Lost and Found" column, they read about a missing breastpin marked with a topaz stone. They read of misplaced gold spectacles, a missing gold charm bracelet, and a striped gray cat named Dick whose owners wanted him in exchange for a "liberal" reward. And then, underneath a request for a gold double-drop earring, they read about a missing child.

> Lost—A SMALL BOY, ABOUT FOUR YEARS of age, light complexion and light curly hair. A suitable reward will be given by returning him to EL JOYCE, Central Police Station.

At the time of the advertisement, Charley had been missing for thirty-six hours. Neither Charley's nor Christian's name was printed in the ad because Christian feared disturbing Sarah should she read the *Ledger* in Atlantic City. Early on the morning of July 3, he took the train back to central headquarters on Chestnut Street. By then, Officer Joyce had convinced his peers that while drunken men may have taken Charley Ross, they did so with a motive. The police asked Christian and Frank to tell their story once again. This time, they took notes. With them were Philadelphia's mayor William S. Stokley, the district attorney, the chief of police, Captain Heins, and a number of detectives.

The men asked Christian several questions directed at identifying possible kidnapping motives. They then asked him to direct their first move. Christian suggested they look for the horse and wagon. Police Chief Kenneth Jones told his lieutenants to dispatch plainclothes officers to each district in the city and to search any place that housed or hired horses. Each officer was instructed to observe all "suspicious persons" and to question their contacts in the criminal community. Two detectives took Frank Lewis to get his little cousin Walter back in Germantown so the boy could identify the kidnappers' route once again. Meanwhile, Christian continued to answer detectives' questions at the station. They asked him to explain any troubles he'd had with family members or servants; which servants he had fired; if any creditors wished to collect payment by taking Charley; what arguments he had had recently and with whom; whether he had ever served on a jury. At the end of Christian's testimony, the detectives had the names of a few fired servants and one convicted felon. All were located, interviewed, and dismissed.

Plainclothes officers learned no new information until the afternoon. The first lead came from Germantown. Residents had told Lieutenant Alexander Buchanan at Town Hall that they had seen a gypsy band traveling with a crying child along Washington Lane. Buchanan's message rang through the bells of the telegraph system in each of the city's precincts. At 10:00 P.M., the sixteenth ward, in West Philadelphia reported that a gypsy party camped in nearby woods. Three officers and Joseph Lewis went to identify the child.

Several women were watching two men fight when the search party arrived. After the police broke up the struggle, one man was bleeding from a cut in his face. The gypsies appeared to be traveling with several horses and two wagons full of trinkets and chests. They denied having a strange child, and the bleeding man threatened to shoot any officer who further disturbed his people. Officers climbed into the wagons, opened each chest, and ripped through its contents—scattering clothes, weapons, and jewelry onto the ground. The two men were arrested on charges of property theft and released from custody the next morning.

While Christian and Frank Lewis awaited the news from West Philadelphia, they wrote a second advertisement at the central station. This one offered money for the lost boy's return to the Philadelphia *Public Ledger* building at Number Five North Sixth Street. Once again, Charley's name was withheld.

be not uneasy

ACROSS CHESTNUT STREET FROM INDEPENDENCE HALL, A statue of Benjamin Franklin stood on a corner podium of the *Ledger* building on Sixth Street. On the morning of July 4, while scattered showers kept some off the cobblestone streets, newsboys sold two-cent papers underneath the eyes of the Philadelphia hero. The *Ledger* headlines reviewed Philadelphia's Independence Day activities, lightning storms in Maryland, and the president's vacation plans. At the top of the front page, the editor had posted a notice under the title "Too Late for Classification."

300$ REWARD WILL BE PAID TO THE person returned to No 5 North Sixth Street, a small Boy, having long, curly, flaxen hair, hazel eyes, clear, light-skinned round face, dressed in a brown linen suit with a short skirt, broad buttoned straw hat and laced shoes. This child was lost from Germantown on Wednesday afternoon. 1st lost, between 4 and 5 o'clock.

Christian Ross had spent the previous night at police headquarters. Early the next morning, he walked across Sixth Street, hoping that the detectives were right and a reward had prompted Charley's return. If and when a reader of the morning's *Ledger* brought Charley to the news building, Christian wanted to be there before his little boy arrived. He waited until 9:00 A.M.

Back at Independence Hall, Mayor William Stokley entered the City Council chamber. One of Philadelphia's longest-running mayors,

Stokley took great pride in the power he held over the second largest city in the country. His constituents numbered close to 800,000, more than 20 percent of whom worked in the 8,000 factories contained within the city's 120 square miles. Manufacturing defined Philadelphia during industrialization, but so did its Republican majority: almost five times as many Republicans held councilmen positions as did Democrats, and in 1872, Ulysses S. Grant accepted the Republican nomination for president at the city's Academy of Music.

William Stokley had also been the figurehead of the police department since 1871, when he won the mayoral election on a platform against urban violence. Fights between independent fire companies were among the many that flared on the streets, and Stokley, a former volunteer fireman, knew the city had to intervene. His first political act was to establish a paid fire department, a decision that curbed firehouse feuding but failed to address the two main sources of street violence: ethnic tension and unemployment. By the first years of Reconstruction, the immigrant community in Philadelphia had grown to one third of the city's population, and as industrialization absorbed artisan jobs, native sons blamed the factories and the foreigners for destroying their family businesses. Craftsmen organized themselves politically, neighborhoods organized themselves socially, and resentment fueled riots among blacks, whites, Italians, Irish Catholics, Whigs, and Democrats. City leaders took sides, and the police often joined the fights.

The press accused Stokley's force of ignorance and underperformance. Aiming to improve his officers' images and prove his leadership skills, the mayor began surprising them on the job. He immediately fired those who appeared drunk, unkempt, or lazy. The public excoriations promoted Stokley as a disciplinarian, but more professional-looking officers didn't change the social temperature. Matters became worse in the economic recession that began as the Panic of 1873: most factory workers remained employed, but other city wages dropped 10 percent, and thousands of railway workers were jobless during the winter of 1873 to 1874. As bread lines grew longer, the press criticized police for honoring capitalist wishes by failing to protect the working class. Stokley's solution was to hire more officers. Five days before July 4, he added 200 men to the force.

Mayor Stokley had heard about Charley Ross's disappearance on July 3, and he knew many of his new hires were looking for the kidnappers' horse and wagon. On the morning of the fourth, however, Stokley had bigger things to do than worry about a missing child. In two years, Philadelphia would host America's Centennial celebration, and he had a party to plan.

The nation's leaders wanted the Centennial to honor America's history. When the founding fathers signed the Declaration of Independence in 1776, four million Americans had settled the country's thirteen states. One hundred years later, the nation had grown into 40 million people and thirty-eight states. Great pride and great cost had fostered such progress. Most notably, a Union victory had ended the Civil War nine years before the disappearance of Charley Ross. The states formed one country, but 600,000 soldiers had died, and freed slaves struggled to find work even in the North. Capitalists had channeled the nation's resources into wealth, but bad investments had bankrupted small businesses and industrial growth sparked ethnic riots. So as much as the nation's leaders wanted the Centennial to honor America's history, they needed it to secure America's future. Americans had to feel united in order to produce a sustainable economy in the aftermath of war. By showcasing inventions and art forms, the Centennial could appeal to their cultural heritage, spark their patriotism, and thus encourage their acceptance of future government initiatives.

Stokley greeted his honored guests inside the city council chamber. The men—councilmen, Centennial commission members, highway commissioners—wore blue ribbons on their jackets. Together, they exited the rear of the building and marched toward eight carriages a block away on Walnut Street. Seven of the carriages turned right and took a scenic route through the central district to the east banks of the Schuylkill River. The mayor's carriage went directly to the Centennial excavation grounds on the opposite side of the river. There, as he approached the park's west entrance, Stokley entered a pastoral scene.

Trees lined both riverbanks, and across the Schuylkill, promontory rock formed natural cliffs that hid a railroad and passing freight trains from walkers and horseback riders who meandered along the river's edge. In the middle of the water, small falls toppled through the Water-

Works purification facility, a Greek Revival edifice engineered in the 1790s to cleanse the city from yellow fever. Stokley's carriage followed the river's curves. He arrived at the excavation site before 10:00 A.M., joining workmen who stood in the midst of shovels, tools, and carts. Stokley accepted an offered spade and dug into the ground. Workmen erupted into three cheers. When the mayor left, they would begin the work of transforming 450 of the park's nearly 3,000 acres into an international showcase celebrating America's first century of independence.

Stokley paraded a short distance from the west end of the new Girard Avenue Bridge, a structure one thousand feet long and one hundred feet wide. Engineers of the day believed it to be the widest bridge in the world, and most of the Centennial's 10 million visitors would trek across it. The seven carriages full of men in blue ribbons turned onto the east side of the bridge and aligned themselves side by side before they slowly and simultaneously paraded across. From a footpath on the pier, invited guests applauded and whistled. Those not invited watched the procession from the riverbanks.

Christian waited at the *Ledger* building until mid-morning. Frustrated and defeated, he returned to the station. As he opened the door, a man yelled, "I have it! I have it!" It was the voice of one of his brothers-in-law. He handed Christian a letter that had been delivered to Ross, Schott, & Co. that morning. Officers in the station gathered around Christian.

July 3—*Mr. Ros:* be not uneasy you son charley bruster be all writ
we is got him and no powers on earth can deliver out of our hand. you
wil have two pay us before you git him from us, and pay us a big cent to.
if you put the cops hunting for him you is only defeetin yu own end.
we is got him put so no living power can gets him from us a live. If
any approach is maid to his hidin place that is the signil for his instant
annihilation. if you regard his lif puts no one to search for him yu mony
can fech him out alive an no other existin powers. don't deceve yuself
an think the detectives can git him from us for that is imposebel. You
here from us in few day.

Christian finished reading. Nobody spoke.

The eight carriages carrying Stokley and his guests drove back into the center of town around noon to witness the day's third event: the dedication of City Hall's cornerstone at Broad and Market Streets. William Penn had envisioned a municipal building on this very location, but the establishment of river communities and suburbs had delayed his plans for 180 years.

Five thousand attendees pushed toward the cornerstone site when Stokley arrived. Underneath an enclosure at the north end, thirty-seven paintings representing each state hung from thirty-seven poles. The mayor and his guests sat inside of a semicircle framed by the poles; small flags, streamers, and the city's coat of arms decorated the cornerstone in front of them. The local Order of Masons called the ceremony to order, and after a few guest speeches, the Masons presented artifacts including copies of the Pennsylvania state constitution, the city charter, plans for City Hall, the annual message of the mayor, and the newspapers of July 4, 1874. As Stokley watched, the objects were placed inside the vault, which was then covered with marbleized slate and cemented with a stone cap. The cornerstone was sealed.

Benjamin A. Brewster, Pennsylvania's attorney general and the future U.S. attorney general, gave the keynote address. In it, he remembered William Penn's plan for the city and praised its ethnocentric pride:

"We have a manly local pride of citizenship; other seaboard cities are provincial or filled with strangers from other parts of the nation and from other countries, and Western cities are like New York, the homes of new men from old places. If a foreigner were to ask me where will I find a real American untouched in his character and nationality by the ever-drifting tide of emigration, domestic and foreign, and with no taint of provincial narrowness, I would say go to Philadelphia, and there you will find just such men and women by the hundreds of thousands."

Newspapers declared the morning's ceremonies a success and praised Mayor Stokley for his planning commission's attention to detail. Over the next two years, the press would weigh Philadelphia's civic issues with her Exhibition plans, reminding both citizens and politicians that the country's international reputation depended upon Philadelphia's hosting abilities. Congress expected the 1876 Centennial Exhibition to illustrate the state of America on the brink of her second century. And it would—by celebrating history, showcasing industrial progress, and assuring the world that the Civil War had not demoralized patriotism. This portrait, however, would be incorrect.

As Mayor Stokley stood at the end of the dedication ceremony, he didn't realize that freshly buried in front of him, underneath the sealed cornerstone, was the beginning of a different story that would carry his name across the globe. It would be this narrative, and not the Centennial displays, that would honestly depict the American character during Reconstruction.

Stokley returned to Independence Hall that afternoon. When he entered central police headquarters, officers handed him an odd-looking letter. It told the mayor about a new crime: one that had developed under his watch, and one that would change the authority of his office. No longer the master of ceremonies, Mayor William Stokley found himself at the head of an investigation to solve the first recorded ransom kidnapping in American history.

And the world was making plans to visit his city.

yu be its murderer

CHRISTIAN LEFT POLICE HEADQUARTERS ON THE AFTERNOON of July 4. He directed his horse-drawn carriage past businesses on Market Street and piers along the Delaware River. Much of the city's working class lived in row homes constructed around shipyards, textile mills, and railroads; less fortunate workers lived in shacks and slums near woodworking houses and clothing sweatshops in the south of the city. Although standardized development had chafed the town's colonial charm, it had earned Philadelphia a reputation among urban planners as a model of affordable housing.

Christian turned onto Germantown Avenue. He knew he could not keep a ransom note from his wife, and he wanted Walter to go with him to Atlantic City.

On a normal weekday, shoppers strolled along Main Street. Storekeepers pampered their rich patrons, at times taking merchandise outside for those too busy, privileged, or lazy to leave their carriages. Jimmy Jones, a short man with a small, pointed beard and half-lens glasses, whisked fabrics under the noses of such women, and Mr. Jabez, the grocery-store proprietor, delivered and recorded their food orders in an account book. While they waited for their mothers and grandmothers to shop, children ran to buy doughnuts from Mrs. Fox, paper dolls from Mr. Betchel's stationery shop, and jacks or lemon candy from Mr. Lutz's general store. Customers had to enter Old Mrs. Potterton's shop if they wanted to search for favorite china patterns. Plates, saucers and teacups in a variety of shapes covered her store from floor to ceiling.

But as Christian drove toward home, storekeepers celebrated the holiday away from work. Families picnicked next to large tubs of ice water and lemonade on wooded hillsides next to the rivers. Weeping willows cast shade over old Indian trails that led walkers past vine-covered arbors and patches of daffodils. Even though parents had heard of Charley Ross's disappearance, they still agreed with the initial opinion of the police: whoever took the little boy would eventually return him. In their minds, the kidnapping was an unfortunate incident. They told their children to stay closer to home, but siblings continued to chase each other east of Germantown Avenue, down the hills leading to the Wingohocking Creek, and west of the Avenue, through the valley that rolled along the Wissahickon River.

Because the police had respected Christian's wish to withhold details, the press had not demanded statements from him or the police. Christian's cooperation helped the police withhold news of the ransom letter, but his silence kept the public from realizing the new threat to its children at a time when nobody knew if the kidnappers intended to take more victims. Germantown's children were used to treating the whole town as their backyard. Boys and girls played tricks on their neighbors by putting on old clothes and begging for food at back doors. They attached twine to doorbells and hid in the tall grass between residences, stifling giggles when bewildered neighbors opened doors to phantom callers. They chased one another down bridle paths, hid from one another underneath bridges, and tried to catch bullfrogs in the small water runs that connected rivers, creeks, ponds, dams, and hollows. Daredevils climbed high rocks in the quarry and jumped into the Wingohocking, fearless of sharp rocks hidden in the deep waters. Sometimes the children encountered strangers. Beggars often walked through the fields, and so did an eccentric musician who played a small wooden instrument. Once a wandering artist sat with a group of siblings and entertained them with stories of the Indians. At the end of their afternoon together, he told the children where they could meet him again, as long as they didn't mention the conversation to their parents.

Germantown's urban legends played a part in the children's games. In the seventeenth century, monks had awaited the second coming of Christ in caves along the Wissahickon, and according to folklore, two men with bushy beards still roamed the area; children who feared the apparitions made sure not to run through the woods alone. They also stayed together when they passed a group of black oak trees next to an old mill—a pile of bones had been unearthed under the trees, prompting boys and girls to shriek, "See the ghost! See the ghost!" when they ran by. Some believed another ghost in a white robe haunted the Civil War memorial on Main Street, and others suspected Old Lady Fox of having secret contact with the dead, even though she sent her butler to give the children lemonade and cakes with white icing. The children's stories were harmless enough, but on Washington Lane, one little boy was haunted by visions of real spooks who had visited his front yard.

Christian told his maids that he and Walter would spend at least one night with Sarah in Atlantic City. They quickly made preparations, and soon the five-year-old sat alone in the passenger's seat as the wagon pulled out of the Ross property.

Sarah Lewis Ross had given birth to eight children in the eleven years that she had been married to Christian. She had met him at church when she was eighteen. He was almost ten years her senior, a friend of her four older brothers. The two didn't marry for nearly a decade—perhaps because Christian needed the time to build his business and his income; Sarah came from a wealthy family. After settling down the street from Sarah's older brother, they had their first child. The baby, a boy, died in infancy. Now, three days after her youngest son had been taken, Sarah had no idea of his disappearance. Christian told the police that he had withheld Charley's name from the advertisements because, on the off chance that his wife read a Philadelphia paper in Atlantic City, he didn't want to worry her. Although people would later criticize this choice, it is more puzzling that Sarah was away from her Germantown home in the first place.

Nineteenth-century society valued a woman foremost as a mother. Most women identified themselves according to their role in their households. A mother's work, then, was to take pride in protecting the morality of her family, to bring up her children as Christians, and to foster a safe, welcoming home. It was not normal for a woman to leave her children, even under the care of nurses and her husband, for weeks on end. Unless, of course, she was ill. Christian had given illness as the reason for Sarah's trip to Atlantic City with their daughter Sophia. Both parents, though, had planned for Charley and Walter to change places with Sophia in mid-July, and the presence of a four and a five-year-old would have made it difficult for Sarah to recover from whatever illness required her departure from her family. Christian's neighbors suspected that marital stress—provoked by Christian's business losses—had led to the separation. But regardless of Sarah's reasons for being in Atlantic City, Victorian society would attribute whatever harm came to Charley to the absence of her motherly virtue.

Christian and Walter drove through heavy rains. They arrived in Atlantic City at 8:00 P.M. Sarah welcomed them along with Sophia.

"Why did you not bring Charley with you?" Sarah asked. "Is he well?"

Christian led his wife into her room.

"Charley is missing," he said.

Christian told Sarah that the situation could be much worse. He gave her an account of the past three days and promised they would soon have their son back.

Two days later, Sarah, Sophia, and Walter took the train back to Germantown.

Christian drove directly to his office from Atlantic City. The streets were crowded after the holiday weekend. As Christian made his way through traffic, he passed dozens of handbills that informed the public of Charley's kidnapping. Detectives had printed the flyers in his absence; officers were busy attaching them to every public place in Philadelphia and its surrounding towns and mailing them to police stations in New York and northern New Jersey. The police had also begun to more actively pursue suspects: they arrested another entire gypsy tribe for questioning, and after one officer said the kidnappers' handwriting looked Italian, they took an innocent immigrant into custody.

Christian's nephew Frank Lewis and Captain Heins had continued to investigate the kidnapping route. They covered a radius of at least ten miles around the kidnapping site, repeatedly driving through Kensington and other villages to the north of the city, searching for more eyewitnesses at taverns, blacksmith shops, and watering holes. Frank

Lewis had also helped an officer write a third newspaper ad in Christian's absence. It appeared on July 5 in the Sunday *Public Ledger* and once again offered $300 for Charley's return. Other papers would print it throughout the week.

When Christian arrived at his office on July 6, he didn't have to wait long to ask for developments in the case. His brother Joseph Ross hurried toward him with another envelope. He had already opened and read it. "No harm has come to Charley," he said, "but $20,000 is demanded for his ransom."

"Surely you have not heard rightly," Christian replied. He scanned the letter and saw the number himself. The kidnappers had mailed it from Philadelphia that day. Christian took the note and walked out of his office.

> PHILADELPHIA, July 6—*Mr. Ros:* We supos you got the other
>   leter that teld yu we had yu child all saf and sond.
>   Yu mite ofer one $100,000 it woud avale yu nothing. to be plaen
> with yu yu mite invok al the powers of the universe and that cold not
> get yu child from us. we set god—man and devel at defiance to rest
> him ot of our hands. This is the lever that moved the rock that hides
> him from yu $20,000. not one doler les—impossible—impossible—
> you cannot get him without it. if yu love money more than child yu
> be its murderer not us for the money we will have if we dont from
> yu we be sure to git it from some one els for we will mak examples of
> yure child that others may be wiser. We give yu al the time yu want
> to consider wel wat yu be duing. Yu money or his lif we wil hav—
> dont flater yu self yu wil trap us under pretens of paying the ransom
> that be imposible—d'ont let the detectives mislede yu thay tel yu thay
> can git him and arest us to—if yu set the detectives in search for him as
> we teld yu befor they only serch for his lif. for if any aproch be made
> to his hidin place by detective his lif wil be instant sacrificed. you wil
> see yu child dead or alive if we get yu money yu get him live if no
> money yu get him ded. wen you get ready to bisnes with us advertise
> the folering in *Ledger* personals (Ros. we be ready to negociate). we
> look for yu answer in *Ledger.*

his lif wil be instant sacrificed

ALTHOUGH THE PHILADELPHIA POLICE DEPARTMENT WAS headquartered three blocks away from Christian's office, he went home to Germantown to read the letter. Sarah asked to see it. Christian refused, left the house, and rode the ten miles back to police headquarters. But the police were no longer in charge.

Soon after the $20,000 demand arrived, a group of the city's political advisers became involved in the case. From the local police station to the state senate, politics and power in Pennsylvania were deeply rooted in Republican government. This was largely due to the efforts of Simon Cameron, a senator who orchestrated Pennsylvania's "Republican machine" around 1860. Cameron encouraged his fellow politicians to strengthen party power by emphasizing the importance of local elections; the strategy worked so well that the senator himself capitalized on Pennsylvania's Republican stronghold to orchestrate a deal with Lincoln's advisers. In exchange for a position in the future president's cabinet, Cameron guaranteed Pennsylvania's convention votes at the 1861 Republican convention. The advisers agreed, Pennsylvania became a swing state, and Lincoln won the nomination. By 1874, halfway through Grant's second term, Republicans in Pennsylvania had occupied the gubernatorial office for thirteen consecutive years.

Under Cameron's leadership, congressmen campaigned and fundraised for smalltown candidates, who in turn pledged their loyalties by manipulating elections. Prior to the Uniform Elections Act of 1874, any party worker could rig results by allowing and encouraging repeat voters, submitting ballot cards for the deceased, and destroying votes he didn't like. The success of the machine demanded party loyalty from incumbents of every echelon of state government, from senator to city councilman. And as 1874 was an election year, Mayor William Stokley needed to do what he could to ensure his place among the brotherhood.

Even though Stokley was the face of city leadership, he himself answered to a group of Republican advisers who controlled the longevity of his tenure, and it was this group that took control of the Ross investigation as soon as the ransom note arrived. As Christian would later say, "There was no plan of any importance adopted without their judgment and approval, and whatever measures they proposed were carried out." The press identified neither the number of this group nor all of its individuals, but it included members of Philadelphia's town councils and wealthy citizens. Publicly, these counselors were consultants and promoters of civic progress; privately, they exercised an authority over all decisions made by city officials, including the police.

When these "city authorities" saw the ransom amount, they realized the implications of paying it. The kidnappers wanted $20,000 for this single criminal act—the annual salary for the president of the United States was only $5,000 more. If satisfied, the kidnappers could, and most likely would, strike again. City planners were pouring hundreds of thousands of dollars into civic improvements for their Centennial celebration. Already, they had gone into debt with the hope that tourists would generate more than enough income to pay the bills. But parents wouldn't come to Philadelphia if they feared that kidnappers would snatch their children and sell them back for $20,000.

The arrival of the second letter pushed Christian closer toward paying the ransom. The kidnappers had marked him as a wealthy man, but his personal fortune had been depleted by the Panic. Yet, while Christian didn't have enough money to cover the ransom, his brothers-in-law did. Christian had involved the Lewis brothers in every step of his search for Charley. Furthermore, there was nothing the police knew that they didn't know. In fact, from the moment Christian reported Charley's disappearance, the police had relied upon the family for investigative ideas. The city advisers, however, understood the danger of allowing the Ross/Lewis family to have authority in the investigation.

If Christian Ross paid the $20,000 ransom and the details of the transaction got out, panic would threaten all the efforts of the Centennial planning commission.

But if the ransom were not paid, the authorities could perhaps contain the city's fears while promoting Philadelphia as a tourist destination. The Ross family, fearing that the kidnappers would carry out their threats, would hesitate to talk to the press, and parents would be more focused on finding the Ross child than fearing for their own. The advisers reached the decision that no ransom could be offered. The family needed to be marginalized. The advisers asked Christian to meet with them.

The kidnappers only want money, they told him. Don't worry. They won't hurt him. If you don't give them the money, they'll give up. They'll abandon the boy by the side of a road. Somebody will find him. The city is looking for him.

By now, Police Chief Kennard Jones had asked officers in each district to identify civilian men to lead search parties. Appealing to the "manly local pride" that Benjamin Brewster extolled on July 4, the authorities summoned citizens to target "suspicious-looking" people and places. Shopkeepers, artisans, factory workers, and children soon became amateur detectives, setting their gaze on the unknown and unfamiliar. Wherever they went—to ships on the Delaware, factories, ferries, woods, railroad depots, stables, shacks, farms, bars, henhouses, and tree houses—they were told to act as policemen, given permission to spy, trespass, interrogate.

While the city searched, a wealthy Philadelphian whose name Christian kept anonymous offered to free him from his worries. The man was socially connected with the city advisers, but he met with Christian privately. He asked if anybody knew the extent of his financial problems.

"No one outside of my own and my wife's family," Christian replied.

"If you will tell me your real condition, I may be able to assist you," the man offered.

Christian told him about his failing business.

"Do you wish to pay the ransom, and run the risk of getting the child in five hours?" the man asked. "If you do, I will give twenty thousand dollars, and never ask you to return one cent."

Christian stared at the man. "I thank you, sir," he said. "I cannot accept your generous offer; for having taken the position that I would not compound the felony, I prefer continuing to make efforts to find the criminals. Hoping, if successful in getting them, that I will recover my child and probably prevent a repetition of child-stealing for a ransom."

The man asked Christian what his wife would think. Christian said that Sarah was a patient woman. This decision was somewhat curious. Although Christian had agreed not to pay the ransom, and his justification for withholding it was a noble one, he was still a heartbroken father who couldn't afford the price of his son. Christian was a third-generation businessman—organized, somewhat savvy, goal driven. Even though he followed the advice of the city leaders, he had to have realized that their strategy was not foolproof. This donor presented a backup plan. Christian could have asked for time to consider the proposition, or accepted the money in case an immediate exchange presented itself. If his pride were a factor, the unconditional offer of a compassionate public figure would have been more agreeable than a loan from his in-laws. After all, wasn't his goal to get his son back? Christian's dismissive response lent itself to three possibilities: he believed wholeheartedly that rejecting the ransom was ethically appropriate—even though such a decision could lead to Charley's endangerment; he feared disagreeing with the city leader; or he knew more about the kidnappers than he reported.

In response to the second letter, the advisers encouraged Christian to withhold publishing the letters and to give them the responsibility for writing any further personal advertisements. Concerned for Sarah's health, Walter's privacy, and Charley's safety, Christian agreed. The advisers then began an interrogation that pushed Christian for details on his private, social, and business lives. Recognizing that they were searching for a kidnapping motive, Christian answered every question.

The authorities responded to the second ransom note according to the kidnappers' directions. A personal ad in the next morning's *Public Ledger* read, "Ros, we be ready to negociate."

The third letter arrived at the Ross home. Shaking, Christian studied the envelope. He noticed the stamp. For the third time, it was
placed in the lower left-hand corner of the envelope, and it looked like
it had been used before. The letter was folded in the same way as the
others: the writer had turned the left side lengthwise into the center,
and then the right before folding the paper down to fit inside the
envelope.

> PHILADELPHIA, July 7—*Mr. Ros:* We se yu anser in *Leger* the
> question with yu is be yu wilin to pay for thosand ponds for the ran-
> som of yu child. without it yu can never get him alive if yu be ready
> to come to terms say so. if not say so. and we wil act acordinly. the
> only answer we want from yu now is, be yu wilin to pay
> $20,000 to save Charley. if yu love yu mony more than him his blood
> be upon yu and not us fo wil show him up to yu either dead or a live (it is
> left with yu) anser the folering in *evnin herald* or *star. Ros.*—wil come
> to terms. *Ros.*—wil not come to terms. omit either line yu pleas
> try the experiment.

Christian knew he was risking his son's life by failing to borrow and
deliver the money as quickly as possible. But if he paid, was he sure to
see Charley alive again? Probably. In 1874, human history suggested
two motives for people-snatching: kidnapping for human trafficking
and kidnapping for ransom. The former usually resulted in a permanent
disappearance; the latter, if paid, usually resulted in a return.

Jewish communities in the Middle Ages were familiar with the
practice of exchanging money for life; Italians and Turks "kidnapped"
wealthy Jewish merchants as they moved between Venice and Con-
stantinople, holding them until families or colleagues paid for their
return. But the term "kidnapping" wasn't coined until 1682, when it
first referenced the taking of a British child to work on a Jamaican plan-
tation. One hundred years later, the definition had evolved to include
any "man, woman or child" who was stolen "from their own country"
and sold "into another." Human trafficking crimes served imperialism
in the seventeeth and eighteenth centuries. To populate and develop
the New World, many European slave traders stole Africans, and others

snatched their own laboring countrymen. Children also fell victim to migrating gypsy tribes, who would torture them beyond recognition and then sell them to traveling circuses.

In the eighteenth and nineteenth century, both Europe and America saw the numbers of missing children spike during wartime, when hundreds of "street urchins" disappeared during the French Revolution and the American Civil War. Whether these boys and girls were absent due to military service, malicious villains, a caregiver's death, or the saving efforts of the church, most were victims of adult ambition. Victorian literature romanticizes tales of these helpless innocents who fall into the grasp of highway robbers, Native American captors, or urban con artists.

Just prior to Charley's disappearance, American newspapers had discussed kidnapping as a solely Italian problem, alluding to stories of Jewish children captured by the Catholic Church and forced into Christianity. According to scholars, the Charley Ross abduction was the first recorded ransom kidnapping in American history. Christian may have had history to study, but there was no precedent for him to follow in a case such as this one.

The kidnappers were trying their hand at a new crime in America: if they took the money and kept or killed the boy, they would only gain $20,000. If they returned him safely, they would gain $20,000 and establish a reputation for keeping their word, which would improve the success of future ransoms. Both potential outcomes burdened Christian. He wanted his child, yet he also felt a responsibility to thwart copycat crimes. With the arrival of each new ransom note, Christian began to understand that his choices would influence whether the kidnappers became failures or models. Following the advice of the advisers, communicated through the police, wasn't exactly a "tried and true" option. The problem wasn't so much that the authorities had never handled a ransomed kidnapping before—it was that the police hadn't been around that long.

When Christian and his brother Joseph had arrived in Philadelphia over thirty years before, there was no organized police force. Robbery victims hired "thief catchers" to recover stolen property by negotiating with thieves, and neighborhood watches quieted noise, arrested criminals, and reported fires. City neighborhoods multiplied in 1854, when more than eighty thousand acres were incorporated into the city limits. To prioritize public safety and crime prevention, the city government established a police tax and hired a paid, uniformed "reserve corps." The corps' initial efforts to suppress street violence were so ineffective that the public asked to exchange the police tax for the old neighborhood watch. Many officers profited from lucrative side businesses as thief catchers, and citizens mocked their disrespect for the law as well as their blue uniforms.

Between the 1850s and the 1870s, police responsibilities centered on protecting the innocent; crimes that didn't threaten public safety, such as burglaries and vandalism, were often ignored. It made sense then that the *Evening Bulletin* challenged the police to prove their professionalism through their handling of this one, single case: "The detective force of Philadelphia is now upon trial before this community ... For a long time, an impression has prevailed perhaps unjustly, that the detective force achieves its successes only under the impetus given by large pecuniary inducements; and that it possesses no special skill in the business of rogue catching. The success or failure of the present undertaking will remove this opinion or confirm it."

The kidnappers' directions in the third letter asked Christian for one of two responses: "Ros.—wil come to terms" or "Ros.—wil not come to terms." They told him to publish his answer in either the *Herald*, the *Evening Herald*, or the *Star*. Advisers insisted on communicating through the *Public Ledger*. A conversation of sorts had begun between the Ross camp and the kidnappers. One voice spoke through a letter to the Ross home, another through the newspaper personals.

The Philadelphia *Public Ledger*. July 8.
"Ros wil come to terms to the extent of his ability."

PHILADELPHIA, July 9—Ros. we is set your price. We ask no
more. we takes no les we no the extent yu bility. how mucht
time yu want to obtain this money. yu is only in part answered our
question. the only question for yu to answer is is u got it and be wilin
to pay it then we wil proceed to bisiness at once. this anser or omition
it satifies us.

The Philadelphia *Public Ledger*. July 9.

"Ros is willing. Have not got it; am doing my best to raise it."

The Philadelphia *Public Ledger*. July 13.

"Ros is got it, and is willing to pay it."

PHILADELPHIA, July 13—*Ros:* in 5 ours after we receve the mony and find it correct, yu wil se yu child home saf. Aft we gets the mony we has no further use for the child, an it is our interest then to restor him home unharmed, so that others will rely on our word. if we don't get the mony from yu the child's life wil an shall be sacrificed. be you redy to pay it as we dictate. if so, have the $20,000 in United States notes. in denomination not excedin "tens." have yu money were yu can git it any moment wen cal for, the detectives, wen they read this, wil tel yu they have now got the key that opens the secret, but don't be misled by them (we alone hold the lock wich is yu child, if they open the dor for yu it wil only revele his (ded body) consider wel, an if these terms agre with yu anser the folerin. Ros, it is redy, yu have my word for it. we look for the answer in the *Evenin Star*.[1]

The Philadelphia *Public Ledger*. July 14.

"Ros, Came too late for *Evening Star*. It is redy: you have my word for it."

---

[1] Most ransom letters are abridged. The responses of Christian Ross and his advisers are not abridged.

THE CITY ADVISERS PLANNED TO FOOL THE KIDNAPPERS WITH marked bills. Christian did not like the idea. "I felt that it was a fearful risk, involving the life of the child," he later said. When they read that the kidnappers wanted Christian to keep the money on his person, the police assigned an officer to protect him around the clock.

Christian was also frustrated because communication with the kidnappers was slowing down. In the first days after Charley's disappearance, the kidnappers had responded to newspaper messages within twenty-four hours. Between the fourth and fifth ransom letters, however, four days had passed. Christian faulted the advisers twice for this: for one, they were intentionally stalling for time as they figured out how to negotiate under false pretenses. He was also insecure with their insistence on communicating through the *Ledger* instead of the *Herald* or *Star* as the kidnappers had asked. Increasingly obsessed with the kidnappers' threats to take Charley's life, he didn't sleep, and he rarely ate.

Meanwhile, Police Chief Jones was angry with reporters. He had of course reached out to the community for help. After authorizing public citizens to form search parties, he had also called upon clergy to release approved information—on July 12, pastors read police statements that described the kidnappers, the wagon, and the horse. But by now, the Rosses' Germantown neighbors had repeated numerous versions of the kidnapping story and the eyewitness accounts. These stories, along with the increasing presence of the "LOST" flyers, attracted the interest of reporters from the city's numerous dailies—some of whom began paying special attention to the *Public Ledger*. Without knowing about the ransom letters, close readers had noticed odd statements in the classifieds: "Ros we be redy to negociate"; "Ros wil com to terms to the extent of his ability"; "Ros is willing. Have not got it; am doing my best to raise it." This third message alerted the press and the public to the possibility that the kidnappers wanted money, and it assured them that the kidnappers read the *Ledger*. After contacting sources within the police department, the *Philadelphia Inquirer* reported that authorities were constantly watching the *Ledger* building.

Realizing the media was informing the kidnappers of police surveillance, Jones wrote to the city's weekly and daily papers, asking each to withhold any information pertaining to the Ross case. The *Inquirer* ignored his request and ran a story about the police chief's letter on Monday, July 13. The city was outraged. Handbills all over the city had been asking them to help find Charley, and in their minds, they were as much a part of the investigation as their incompetent police force.

And this frustrated the kidnappers. Their continued request for Christian to communicate through a newspaper other than the *Ledger* revealed their nerves. Various dailies had given them a sense of police procedure by reviewing things like the frequency of Christian's visits to headquarters and which mailboxes the police monitored; however, the press had also informed them about the magnitude of the investigation and angry public opinion. Any plans they may have had to keep Charley a short while or to repeat their crime in Philadelphia were frustrated. And on July 14, they learned of a greater problem. That day, the *Inquirer* ran an article that reviewed Christian's business and personal financial losses following the Panic of 1873. The kidnappers must have realized Christian Ross did not have the $20,000 that the *Ledger* ad had promised them. They had kidnapped a child from a wrong family.

the danger lies intirely with yuself

PHILADELPHIA, July 16—*Ros:* The reason we did not respond to yu answer was we had to go a bit out in the country an the blasted old orse give out so we could not get back in time. We went as much as anything to se how Charley was. Yu have our word that he is yet safe—in health an no harm done him thoug he is uneasy to get home with Walter. he is afraid he won't get home in time to go to Atlantic City with his mother when Saly comes back. —as we said befor after we gits the mony we have no further use for the child but we have a big object in restoring him to yu safe and sound. We shall be redy we think by Saturday to efect a change with yu (the child for the money). we wil give you this much incite into our bisiness—that if any arest is made it wil be an inocent person who wil be ignorant of the part he is actin. but it is imaterial with us wether it be an inocent person or one of our own party the moment any arest is made or any clandestine movements in transmiting this mony to us it will be conclusive evidence with us that yu have broken yu faith with us. we want yu to nail this money up in a smal strong ruf box an have it were yu can git it at a minutes notice. mark on it (Drugs for H H H.

IN MID-JULY, A YOUNG WOMAN SETTLED INTO HER NEW APARTMENT in a working-class neighborhood of South Philadelphia. A family named Henderson rented a house on Monroe Street, and they sublet rooms to a few different tenants. In addition to being a landlord, Mr. Henderson worked as a handyman, a peddler, and a salesman; often, his neighbors noticed he would return home from auction houses with used furniture to refurbish, and sometimes, they saw packages of dresses and shawls delivered to the house. After receiving a shipment or finishing a woodworking project, Henderson would load up a wagon and leave home for days to sell his wares in the country.

The new renter was introduced to the Hendersons' three sons: Willie was about seven, Charley about four, and Georgie younger still. Her landlord wasn't home when she moved in, but just as she arrived, the landlady was preparing to give birth. The night before the baby was born, Mr. Henderson showed up with a much younger male friend. The friend was also taller, and he had red hair.

Outside of the Henderson home, searchers walked through alleys and into the bars advertising oyster sales. They moved farther into South Philadelphia, peeping around the shanties and shacks of the increasingly black neighborhoods. Throughout the city, the streets were cleaner than normal—July's frequent storms had washed them. Hunters marched through the indoor markets where farmers leased space to sell their crops. They snuck behind row homes and flats and walked quickly through alley tenements. In the wealthy Rittenhouse square district in Center City, colonial townhomes with faux Victorian fronts did not harbor many hiding spaces, but further east, a few blocks closer to the river, ghosts whispered through the old, squeaky wooden frames of clapboard houses.

Back in Kensington, a stable keeper named C. M. Foulke responded to the flyers posted around the city. Two men who resembled descriptions of the kidnappers had rented a wagon from his livery stable in the days preceding the kidnapping. Foulke didn't like the men—he didn't like how they looked. As someone had recently stolen a wagon from him, Foulke told police, he asked the men for a reference, and they provided one from a nearby restaurant owner. He let them take it out for a few days toward the end of June but didn't like the hours they kept: 8:00 A.M. through 3:00 P.M. didn't seem like a proper workday, and the men didn't seem the type to rent a wagon for reasons other than business. So when they asked at the end of the month if they could rent it for a week straight, he told them only if they made a deposit for the full value of the wagon. They couldn't, and Foulke didn't see them again.

yu child shal die

UNLIKE THE *PHILADELPHIA INQUIRER*, THE *PUBLIC LEDGER* followed Chief Jones's instructions not to publish interviews, stories, or speculation about the Ross case. The paper wasn't always known for its code of integrity; during its first year, 1836, the *Ledger* had had a reputation for favoring drama over fact. Most of Philadelphia's papers printed gossip as truth then, largely because the city's dailies shared reporters who exchanged information and inflated details to create cohesive stories. To gain an audience, the *Ledger* exaggerated more than other papers, attracting libel suits that made the penny paper instantly popular. Its sensationalist journalism began to change in 1837. Having established a readership, the *Ledger*'s editors began to more aggressively compete with their rivals: they hired their own writers, demanded their loyalty, and forced them to find their own stories on the streets. The *Ledger* staff was the first in Philadelphia to enlist newsboys, the first to experiment with a rotary press for quicker printing, and one of the first to use carrier pigeons and a pony express to collect national information quickly. And never had prompt reporting been more in demand than during the Civil War.

Between 1861 and 1865, battlegrounds changed the face of newsrooms. Nearly 3 million men fought in the war, and an estimated 620,000 died. Nobody had expected such large numbers of fatalities. As the war years dragged on, the newspaper went from being the mouthpiece of political parties to the strongest link between families at home and soldiers on the front. This rabid readership elevated journalistic standards: the public's appetite for eyewitness reports, tolerance for graphic details and demand for prompt coverage became insatiable. In an attempt to scoop the competition, every major American city had correspondents on the battlefields; the *New York Herald* alone sent forty. This golden period of print journalism continued after the war ended, when both journalists and readers multiplied around the country.

During the 1860s, the ambition of the Philadelphia *Public Ledger*'s editors attracted a new owner—George W. Childs, a successful businessman and friend to Ulysses S. Grant. It was Childs who constructed the *Ledger* building, considered one of the biggest news offices in the country, across from Independence Hall. Under Childs's leadership, the *Ledger* developed the second-largest circulation in America, boasting a readership of 400,000. In 1874, Childs's chief editor was a man named William V. McKean. McKean wrote a code of reportorial ethics that he insisted his reporters follow, and so, while papers like the *Inquirer* ignored Chief Jones's request, McKean honored his wishes. McKean also obeyed because the details surrounding the abduction were not quite clear, and Childs had told his staff to withhold any story until its facts could be corroborated. There was a third reason why he kept the Ross story out of his paper. McKean was one of the Republican advisers. As an editor, he did not want to print speculation and as a city leader, he wanted to minimize the amount of public attention given to the investigation.

New York papers blamed the *Ledger* and other dailies for endangering the lives of Charley and Philadelphia's other children with their silence. "For what may be done in one instance, and in one place," wrote the *New York Tribune*, "may be done in another instance and in another place." On July 17, the *Ledger* responded to the accusations.

"We have abstained until now, *because it was the expressed wish of the proper public authorities* that as little as possible should be published about the matter, and so we have published nothing." The *Evening Bulletin*, another target of New York's criticism, defended itself by pledging its faith to Philadelphia's police force. "The journalists of this city are well aware that from the day of the perpetration of the crime to the present moment there has been a ceaseless, vigilant and well organized movement on the part of the detective force against the kidnappers." Three days before New York's attack on Philadelphia's press, however, the same *Evening Bulletin* had called police detectives "a particularly useless and expansive body" that "cannot detect" unless it "recovers stolen property by arranging the matter comfortably with the criminals."

Both the *Ledger* and the *Evening Bulletin* cited jealousy, not concern for Charley, as motive for New York's criticism. The Philadelphia press assumed that America, particularly the city of New York, envied the attention their city would likely get during the upcoming Centennial. The planning commission had already expressed surprise with the nation's hesitancy to offer financial support, assistance, and displays, and there was no part of the country Philadelphia liked to blame more than New York City. By the mid-nineteenth century, Philadelphians had felt a shadow fall as New York surpassed their city as the cultural capital of the States. They were only too pleased when the federal government chose Philadelphia over New York as the Centennial location.

New York had tried, and failed, to host such an exhibition before. Inspired by the success of London's Crystal Palace Exhibition in 1851, a Massachusetts auctioneer named Edward Riddle had convinced the city government to replicate the European expo—the first world's fair—on the grounds of Bryant Park. Riddle's efforts were doomed from the start. The centerpiece of London's Crystal Palace was a 900,000-square-foot structure made of iron and nineteen acres of glass. There was no way the U.S. government would finance such a creation: the Southern states were moving toward secession, and their representatives weren't looking to pour money into a fair in New York. Poor funding led to limited advertising and an unimpressive result; even though the city had approved a five-year lease on the land, the exhibition closed after three. Riddle's risk cost the city $340,000, and in 1858, the building burned to the ground. By 1874, Europe had hosted six successful world's fairs—two in London, two in Paris, and another in Vienna. The American Centennial in Philadelphia would be the world's seventh party, and the first for the Americas.

But even the excitement over the Centennial didn't keep the criticism of the New York press from aggravating Philadelphia's inferiority complex. Almost daily, it suggested that Charley would die because of

Philadelphia's impotent police force and unethical parents. City authorities feared this image would prevail. The only way to uphold Philadelphia's honor was to find the little boy and arrest the criminals without
paying ransom.

"There must be no compromise with thieves," the *Philadelphia
Inquirer* said.

In response, the *New York Herald* asked why any parent would
refuse payment if he or she knew the ransom would return a beloved
child. It attacked Christian's integrity and accused him of participating
in the kidnapping.

"No man with any soul in him could have done such a thing,"
responded Christian.

His friends loudly defended his innocence. They decried the
New York Herald article and blamed the paper for further impairing
Christian's health. They encouraged Christian to defend himself by
divulging the ransom letters and explaining the potential copycat consequences of appeasing the kidnappers. Christian refused. He said he
didn't want Sarah to read the letters at all—not at home, and not in the
press. Friends pleaded with him to release a photograph of Charley so
his critics could see he was trying to further the investigation.

"No possible good could result by their being read," the advisers
told Christian.

Christian's friends and neighbors did not understand that the
kidnappers were bargaining with Charley's life. They knew the public
demanded to see the letters, and they believed their friend was innocent of the crime, so it made sense to them for Christian to defend himself by publicizing everything he knew about the investigation. If
Christian were to release the letters, he would be releasing the kidnappers' threats against children in the city. In letter five, the kidnappers
had said, "it is our interest then to restor him home unharmed, so that
others will rely on our word." Thus, they did reveal the intention that
the advisers feared: a desire to repeat the crime after Charley was
returned. Not only could these published words create pandemonium,
but they could also turn the public's concerns away from finding
Charley—because if he were never returned home "unharmed," the
kidnappers' word would be compromised and perhaps they wouldn't

take another child. Christian did worry about angering the kidnappers. Also in letter five, he had read, "if they open the dor for yu it wil only revele his (ded body)." Should he release the letters and a photo of Charley, he would be enabling the citizens of Philadelphia to become detectives themselves and risk provoking the kidnappers. The advisers' decision to pass off counterfeit bills and to ignore the kidnappers' communication directions had made Christian nervous enough; he didn't want to endanger his child's life further by defending himself from petty gossip.

he is yet safe

"ALMOST EVERY MAN HAS BEEN A DETECTIVE IN THE CASE," wrote the *Philadelphia Inquirer* on July 17, "and people on the outskirts have scoured the country in wagons, searching gypsy camps and other places where there might be any likelihood of the child being discovered." Watchers paid close attention to tramps and beggars. "Tramp Acts" were being passed by states during the 1870s, making it illegal for vagrants who didn't have work to move about the country. The laws didn't make a provision for veterans or others displaced by the war.

With so many people on the streets looking for a little boy that matched Charley's description, the papers had many false accounts of the boy's recovery, some of which they reported. Sarah Ross's friends responded to erroneous accounts by running to congratulate her. Sarah told them the papers were wrong. She sought the help of a spiritualist, and after a medium told her that Charley was hidden in a boat, search parties conducted extra investigations of the wharves and boats along the rivers.

As newswires spread the story throughout the nation, strangers showed up at the Ross home. Late one night, two men walked around the brick wall at the front of the property. They climbed the porch steps and rang the doorbell. Sarah rushed to the second-floor landing. Christian ran out of his room, and two police officers hid near the front door. Christian opened the door and saw two strangers. The men asked if they stood at the Ross residence. When Christian said yes, one man handed him a card, and the other said he had information about Charley. The story he told Christian offered no new information; it had been pieced together from articles in the newspapers. Christian said good-bye and the family returned to bed.

Religious fundamentalists visited Washington Lane and blamed Charley's disappearance on Christian's practice of trimming his beard. Another man walked up to the Rosses' barn, opened a prayer book, and began to chant in front of the wagon. Charley's siblings watched him. Walter tried to jump into the carriage, incurring the man's wrath. "Now you have broken the spell," the man said to him. "I cannot bring your brother home." Unsolicited advice arrived by mail from as far away as California. Amateur sleuths offered to help for a nominal fee, and one letter sent to the police advised them to dig up the Ross property in search of Charley's body.

The advisers waited to answer the instructions that arrived in the latest ransom note. The kidnappers had warned against "any clandestine movements in transmiting this mony to us," giving the Ross camp reason to reevaluate their strategy of releasing marked bills. The day after they read the letter, a well-known private detective offered them another reason to postpone a response.

On July 17, Joshua Taggart left his office at Taggart, Lukens and Carlin, a private detective agency. He walked slowly through the dirty streets, past brownstone row houses. Taggart was one of the most experienced private detectives in the city, and in 1874, connected through colleagues to the Philadelphia Police Department. Such an arrangement was not uncommon to the young force. Police detectives earned just as much as patrolmen (about $1,000 a year); the nature of their undercover work, however, required them to spend money— usually at bars—and they weren't reimbursed for expenses. Many of these officers doubled as "thief catchers" to supplement their incomes, negotiating payments for stolen property between victims and thieves. The true "private detective," a job title that held slightly more respect than "thief catcher," was usually employed by an agency registered with the city.

Through the 1870s, police officers could claim part or all of any reward offered for resolving an unsolved crime. So if that police detective also worked as a private detective, he could earn two rewards for one case: as a thief catcher, he could track down a thief, negotiate a price for stolen merchandise, and collect his "finder's fee" from the victim; he could then put on his uniform as a police officer, provide details about the criminal, and collect any reward that may have been offered to the public for information leading to an arrest. The arrangement, well known to the public, caused plenty of ethical dilemmas by fueling competition between investigators both on the force and off. Editorials complained about compromised officers, but authorities turned a blind eye to the practice, and in so doing, condoned it.

In order to be a good thief catcher, Taggart had to protect certain informants—otherwise, they would fear arrest and refuse him information. Yet in order to claim reward money and maintain a relationship with the police, he had to assist in making arrests. For a number of years, Taggart had balanced his relationships with cops and criminals very, very well.

For the last two weeks, Taggart had moved from tavern to clapboard house, picking up undertones of gossip. Somewhere along these muddy streets lurked a man whom he believed could identify the kidnappers. The police trusted the detective's instincts and gave him access to the ransom letters already delivered to Christian Ross. On July 17, Taggart approached a known hangout for crooks—the southwest corner of Fifth and Spruce Streets—without drawing any attention. And then he arrested Christopher Wooster.

For the past twenty years, the authorities had known Wooster, sometimes as Christopher Wooster, sometimes as "Frank Wistar," and sometimes as "Christian Worcester." They knew him most, however, as a con artist. With his criminal pal "Button Joe," he had operated brothels, swindled banks, blackmailed businessmen, and robbed a reverend. Wooster's tall, thin silhouette blended in with the other night-time shadows that haunted the streets. At the time of his arrest, he had a black eye and a thick, rough beard that failed to fill his sunken cheeks or detract from his oddly shaped nose. Recently, he had been released from Moyamensing Prison in South Philadelphia, for blackmail.

The *Inquirer* asked the assistant city solicitor what punishment awaited Christopher Wooster if he was guilty of complicity. According to an act of 1860, kidnapping was a misdemeanor, not a felony. The penalty for taking a person under the age of ten was a maximum fine of $2,000 and a maximum prison sentence of seven years. The reporter wanted to know if the kidnappers would get away with a light sentence.

"Oh no," responded the solicitor. "The punishment can be piled up on them by utilizing what I may call the elasticity of the law. For instance, they can be convicted of having engaged in a conspiracy to extort money, which will add several years to the original sentence. Then again, I do not know but they could be given three years for the robbing of the jacket on the boy, three years for stealing his hat, three years for stealing his shoes, and so on, giving three years for the theft of each individual article of clothing on the lad at the time he was stolen."

"That would be tantamount to an imprisonment for life?"

"Practically, yes."

"When caught, I suppose, the guilty parties will be arraigned speedily?"

"That you may safely depend upon. Let the guilty parties be once taken into custody, and if any criminals ever took the short route to the penitentiary they will be the man."

The assistant solicitor's desire to "pile" punishment through "the elasticity of the law" pointed to a need for new state legislation with greater consequences for kidnappers. But even if his office succeeded in identifying Charley Ross's kidnappers and applying "elasticity" to their charges, the average convict served less time in Pennsylvania prisons than his sentence stipulated.

Christian Ross didn't think Wooster was guilty. His family had already suffered through too many rumors and too much advice to believe an easily accessible criminal like Christopher Wooster was responsible. Nevertheless, he agreed to let Walter attempt identification. The five-year-old didn't recognize him. The *Evening Bulletin* also questioned Wooster's involvement. They called him "a man of considerable education, clever, a well-known con artist," but doubted a petty thief who had served time in New York, Chicago, and Philadelphia prisons would involve himself in such a high-stakes crime.

The public had tired of waiting for an arrest by the time Taggart nabbed Wooster. Inspired by editorials asking the mayor to offer reward money for new information, parents demanded that Stokley protect their children as much as they searched for Charley. They had read the criticism of the investigation in the papers. Speculation over the kid-nappers' motives rattled their nerves even more. They wanted Charley, but they also wanted the kidnappers behind bars before another child went missing.

Two more almost did.

A man in West Philadelphia approached a group of children at play and grabbed a four-year-old named William Painter. A little girl immediately ran to tell an adult, who contacted the police as others chased the man through the neighborhood. Reaching a footbridge, the assailant saw an adult who called William by name. The kidnapper then dropped the boy on the ground and ran away.

Two miles away from the Ross home on East Washington Lane, ten-year-old Elizabeth Coffin played inside her home with her sister May. The family's colonial house sat twenty feet away from Main Street, and maple trees obstructed their view of people walking by their property. One morning, when May left Elizabeth to play alone on the first floor, a man appeared at a window next to her. He told Elizabeth he would give her "candy and other nice things" if she would step through the window and walk with him. Elizabeth called for May. The man told her not to tell anybody he was there. Elizabeth said she needed permission to leave, and she called for May again. The man turned and ran through the yard. Elizabeth's father entered the room in time to see him jump into a buggy and drive off with another man. Germantown's parents, now panic-stricken, told their children to keep away from walking, fishing, and playing in the woods.

Fearing criminal histories would incriminate them, some former convicts offered to help the police search. Others capitalized on the vulnerability of fearful people. A Philadelphia merchant received a letter threatening to ruin his reputation if he did not pay the author a specific sum, and a father from Northeast Philadelphia opened a letter threatening his son. On yellow paper, small letters spelled "Look after that youngster of yours, Harry. He is watched by English snatchers. He's been watched at Norris square. Others had better be careful. ONE OF THE GANG BUT FRIENDLY." Police detectives dismissed both letters as jokes.

A reporter asked Mayor Stokley why he wouldn't offer a reward for Charley and his kidnappers.

"I would be liable to a criminal prosecution if I did that," the mayor said. "I could not offer a reward without the direction of the Common Council. They have had one meeting since the kidnapping, but they took no action concerning it. They will not meet again for some time."

"That is unfortunate, isn't it?" responded the reporter.

"Yes; but then if I had the power, I wouldn't offer a reward for the boy. It is his abductors that we want. When I became mayor of Philadelphia I said to my detectives, 'There is to be no more compounding of felonies. When goods are stolen, I don't wish them returned so much as I wish those who stole them brought to justice. I must have the thieves. If any one on the force turns up stolen goods without bringing the thief to prison, the officer will be discharged from the force.' You see?"

The reporter didn't ask the mayor why he equated a stolen child with other forms of property theft. He did ask if Wooster's arrest encouraged the investigators.

"I don't believe it does," Stokley said. "Many arrests have been made." The mayor then suggested that perhaps Christian Ross knew some things about the kidnapping that he had not yet shared with the authorities.

City Solicitor Charles Collis publicly disagreed with Stokley's thoughts on Wooster. After hearing a rumor that the suspect had an alibi, an *Inquirer* reporter met with Collis during his lunch hour at his office on South Seventh Street.

"Do you think Taggart has the right man?" asked the reporter.

"I have not the slightest doubt of it, and future developments will prove what I say."

"Of course, he must have had accomplices."

"Certainly. A man like Wooster would not act alone in such a matter."

"Why?"

"Because he is too well known to the police, and his haunts, habits and associations are too familiar."

"His reputation is none of the best, then?"

"No; it is very bad, and he has been in prison on several occasions."

"Have you an idea as to who assisted him in the present case?"

"That is a question I would not like to answer at this time. A few days at the furthest will, I think, bring the matter to a close. Things are looking very well, and I have great confidence in the ability of the detectives to bring the perpetrators of this crime to justice."

Unless Collis was quite naïve, he didn't believe one word of this interview that he gave. It is exactly because Wooster was "too well known" that the police should have hesitated to detain him in the first place. Detective Taggart found Wooster on July 17, one day after Christian Ross received the fifth ransom letter and two weeks after the kidnappers abducted Charley and Walter Ross. In spite of his decades-long record of forgery and blackmail, he was also a clown. Prison guards in South Philadelphia enjoyed his tall tales, and the warden wrote that over the course of his stays at the prison, Wooster entertained other inmates and their visitors. He was a rash thief, a sloppy liar, and a likable crook.

But he was exactly the kind of person that the police could pin the crime on. The city leaders' fears were beginning to materialize: citizens were reporting copycat threats, the public was growing more paranoid, and instead of commending authorities for their Centennial preparations, the New York press vilified it for mismanaging the Ross case. Christopher Wooster had no family, a lengthy criminal record, a bad reputation, and an interest in swindling funds through the mail. He was the perfect scapegoat. And then, one day after his arrest, another ransom letter arrived.

PHILADELPHIA, July 18—*Ros:* The blasted editorials have got the city in such a feve bout the child that we can hardly do anything. i tel yu they endanger the child's life at every stroke of the pen. one editor wants to kno why we dont give yu some prof that we ever had the child by sendin some of his close or a lock of hair we have our reason for not sending them. to satisfy yu we have him yu remember his striped stockins are darned in two or three places were they had holes in. ask Walter if we did not put the blanket up in front of him an Charley in behind to hide them. ask Walter if we did not say we wold go down to aunt Susans befor we went out on the mane street to buy torpedos. we wil notice al yu have to say either in *ledger star* or *herald* or *sunday dispatch* anything you wish to communicate to us head it C R R instead of Ros. This man Woster is innocent he has nothing to do with us, do as yu please with him an make the most out of him yu can. the brokers we se have had a metin an think they can restor yu child an bring us to justice—they mean wel to yu but they be actin under a great delusion—if they be friends to yu let them make the mony up which is the only thing can restor the child—if they will not do that yu drop them unless yu want to cut yu child's throat.

The Philadelphia *Public Ledger*. July 21.
"C R R. Mony is ready. How shall I know your agent?"

BURLINGTON, July 21. —*Ros*. we have seen yu own state-ment that yu would not comply with our terms an yet yu say (the money is redy how shal I no yu agent) the fact of us having yu child and you having paid us every dollar we demanded what further use could we have for him? He has answered the end for which we took him; this is one reason why we should give him up. if these terms suit yu answer the followin in the *Ledger* personals.
C R R. i will agree to the terms in every particular.
P. S. —have the money ready as we described we wil send prof with him so yu can no him when he comes.

The Philadelphia *Public Ledger*. July 22.
"C R R. 'I will agree to the terms in every particular.'"

we wil send prof

A<small>N</small> *INQUIRER* <small>REPORTER RETURNED TO</small> C<small>ITY</small> S<small>OLICITOR</small> C<small>OLLIS</small> and asked if he had enough evidence to keep Wooster since ransom notes had arrived after his incarceration.

"Does not the fact that letters have been received by Mr. Ross since Wooster's confinement, evidently penned by the same hand that wrote those in which you believed you detected the chirography of Wooster, weaken your belief that he was the author of the former letters?"

"Not at all," Collis replied. "The class of men to which he belongs are practiced in all kinds of villainy, and it is not at all improbable that they may all have accustomed themselves to write the same handwriting. In this way they may hope to clear their confederate of suspicion."

The *Philadelphia Inquirer* disagreed that men could share "the same handwriting" and continued to question Wooster's authorship in editorials, citing the debate over Wooster as another reason for the police to release the letters.

A police spokesperson again defended the decision to hold them back, saying the letters would "shock and incense the community beyond conception." On July 22, the *Evening Bulletin* stepped back from its public defense of the force and echoed New York's attacks and the *Inquirer*'s questions. The paper blamed the "shameful and unbearable" incompetence of the police for making kidnapping an "easily committed" crime. The same day, the *Inquirer* asked citizens to hire "the whole detective force of the country." It challenged readers to contribute $10,000 within twenty-four hours towards a reward for finding Charley. Prominent bankers and merchants raised funds, and a bank president offered his services as a treasurer. Twenty-four hours later, the paper published the names and donations of contributors. They had raised only $410. However, even though they fell tremendously short of their initial goal, the *Inquirer* had successfully, and somewhat indirectly, encouraged the city to rebel against its leadership. By investing their faith and their finances in a reward fund, Philadelphians were actively challenging the mayor's authority and questioning the ability of the police to maintain public safety.

Stokley watched as his constituents' actions validated New York's verbal assaults on his administration. Less than three weeks before, he had paraded around the city in his carriage on the Fourth of July, preparing himself for the fame that would come with hosting the world at the Centennial celebration. Those who had applauded him on that day now accused him of ineffective leadership. As figurehead of the city, Stokley would receive either blame or accolades for the Centennial preparations and execution. If the mayor wanted to reclaim his public approval and refocus the spotlight on the city's Centennial plans, his only choice was to agree to his voters' demands and convince the city leaders to offer a municipal reward. On July 23, the city papers published the official notice.

MAYOR'S OFFICE, CITY OF PHILADELPHIA, July 22, 1874 – At the instance of the citizens of Philadelphia, I hereby offer a reward of twenty thousand dollars for the arrest and conviction of the abductors of Charles Brewster Ross, son of Christian K Ross, of Philadelphia, and the restoration of that child to his parents."

W. S. STOKLEY
Mayor of Phila.

The statement included descriptions—of Charley, the kidnappers, the horse, and the buggy—as well as a reminder that the kidnappers could have altered Charley's hair and clothing to make him look feminine. Stokley asked for "every newspaper in the United States and Canada" to give his notice "the widest publicity." Clerks in the mayor's office printed large reward posters soliciting the help of detectives nationwide, and Chief Jones wrote a letter asking stationmasters and postmasters to attach the signs to prominent places along their railroad routes. Packages of these posters and letters were then mailed throughout the country.

The municipal reward angered Christian. He insisted that the kidnappers' behavior would become more erratic and violent with a price on their heads. Increasingly longer ransom notes reinforced his concerns: the kidnappers continued to betray their fears by repeating demands, arguing with statements in the press, and explaining new procedures for a ransom exchange. Detectives had continued to try to shift public attention from Charley toward the kidnappers, explaining that regardless of the child's fate, copycat crimes were sure to multiply nationwide, and the only way to forestall future crimes was to arrest the criminals. Although they didn't fully realize it, much of the public agreed with Christian's position. They had asked the mayor to offer money for the child, not the criminals, as the *Inquirer*'s fund stipulated.

The mayor's reward also revealed to the public that his police probably had the wrong man in custody. An *Illustrated New Age* reporter applied and received a permit to speak with Wooster in his cell at Moyamensing Prison. The criminal used the opportunity to identify himself as a pawn in the ongoing tensions between police officers and private investigators.

Wooster greeted the reporter with his trademark good humor.

"You must excuse the looks of this cell. I haven't fixed it up yet."

"I was anxious to see the bad man about whom there has been so much talk," the reporter replied.

"That's right," said Wooster. "That's right, always see all concerned. Don't believe everything you hear on the streets. God knows I'm bad enough, but the police have got me for something now that I don't know anything about."

Wooster said he had "played along" with his arrest, referring to Detective Taggart with his nickname. "Down I went with Josh—and, by the way, he is a pretty good sort of fellow, but he wants badly to do something, he and the Central men being at loggerheads."

In between telling the reporter an exaggerated account of his life history and the circumstances that had led to his life of crime, Wooster acknowledged that his trademark blackmailing jobs were what had him detained after his arrest. Police had confiscated letters that Wooster had written to his wife, compared them with mailings he had sent to his victims, and believed that his handwriting resembled that of the ransom note writer.

"I don't always write the same way," Wooster insisted. "I'm of a very nervous temperament, and you might pick out four of my letters and they might all appear to be written by different persons. They found two letters which they said compared with the handwriting of those sent to Ross. Now that's all bosh. I think they ought to be convinced that I did not write the letters for this reason: a four-page letter was received by Ross since I have been in prison."

When an officer came to say that the district attorney's office had sent someone over and it was time for the reporter to go, Wooster waved him off.

"No, not yet," he said, "give him a little longer. I want to talk to him."

The guard obeyed.

"They may let me out today," Wooster continued. "I think they are satisfied."

Before he was released, Wooster asked to speak with Detective Taggart. He asked why he was locked up for something he didn't do.

Taggart told him sources said he was involved in a kidnapping plot.

Wooster said they were right. But, he told Taggart, he had planned to take a different child before the Ross kidnapping. He said he had abandoned the plan when his accomplices learned that the child was nine, old enough to remember his captors' faces.

Taggart didn't believe in the coincidence of two separate plans to steal two different children at two similar times.

Wooster insisted that he wasn't guilty of taking Charley. "[And] even if I was," he said to Taggart, "you know I wouldn't give anybody away."

The police released Christopher Wooster from custody on July 23, just as he had predicted. The *New Age* reporter who had interviewed him said he celebrated by "getting gloriously drunk." Later, Wooster told the press that he "had no hard feelings against the authorities" and wanted "to lead a different life if the police would let him." He began planning a lecture tour to showcase his story.

Several days later, due to a lack of ticket sales, he postponed his "tour."

PHILADELPHIA, JULY 24—Ros. we have seen yu reply in personal (yu agree to the terms in every particular) we accept yu offer for we consider yu fuly understand the great an momentus obligation yu place youself under when you assented tu this agreement. we be sory that we cannot effect the chang to-day. our creed is such that it forbids us to any bisines of this kind only at a certain quarter of the moon an the phace of the moon has just passed over so we have got tu wate one week befor we can transact any bisines between us. this delay may be a great sorce of torture tu yu but it cannot be avoided.

they are goin to search every
house in the city

SARAH ROSS HAD STOPPED ASKING TO READ THE RANSOM NOTES, but after the arrival of each one, she asked if her little boy was okay. Christian always said yes.

Because the authorities had failed to draw any pertinent information from Christopher Wooster, Detective Joshua Taggart did not receive the Ross family's $300 reward for information leading to Charley. Taggart, though, wasn't hurting financially. For the past two years, he had been accepting "hush" money for protecting the identity of George Leslie, a thirty-four-year-old bank robber and jewel thief.

The *New York Times* and *New York Herald* chastened the police for releasing their one lead, but Wooster soon disappeared from the interests of all parties involved. Within two days of the mayor's July 23 notice, the "one lead" that the police had in Wooster turned into hundreds of false ones. Unemployed workers, indigent street dwellers, tenement families, struggling laborers, police officers, and detectives sought the $20,000 reward by producing "a" Charley who fit the description they had read, heard, and talked about for the past three weeks. Street children of all ages adopted the name "Charley Ross." Poor parents and fortune seekers told their own boys to dirty their hair and assume Charley's identity; the adults then turned their own children in to the police.

Western Union extended a free wire to Christian Ross, and he communicated with police chiefs throughout the country to follow up on promising possibilities. Too often, officers acted on false instincts and took innocent parents into custody. One mother was stopped so often by Philadelphia police officers that Chief Jones gave her a letter stating her child was not Charley. In North Philadelphia, officers arrested a man and a woman because eyewitnesses placed them with Charley. They were quickly released. The child was their own—and a daughter. Authorities also mistakenly arrested a man from Richmond, Virginia, after witnesses insisted they saw him traveling with Charley Ross. The man said his accusers must have been referring to his recently deceased six-month-old infant son, not a four-year-old boy. To verify the story, the Richmond Police had the baby's body disinterred.

A Philadelphia detective traveled to Allentown, Pennsylvania, to investigate a report filed by the Pennsylvania Detective Bureau, an organization that had offered a separate $2,500 reward for information leading to Charley. On the morning of Tuesday, July 7, a carriage carrying two men, a woman, and a little boy parked by a bank. One of the men and the woman escorted the boy into a nearby barbershop and asked the barber, "Fancy Bill," to trim his curls. The child didn't speak. He appeared to be in shock, and the barber heard the woman promise to buy the boy candy and ice cream when they left. The detective listened to the story, but once he learned that the barber shared it only after hearing about the reward, he dismissed the claim. The curious Allentown party then disappeared from the papers.

Neighbors in Germantown remembered two foreign couples who had searched the town for work in a rented buggy during the last week of June. Although wandering laborers passed through the town, rarely did they stay in one specific area without finding consistent work for consecutive days. The police visited area stables, checked rental records, and questioned stable keepers' memories. They traced descriptions to a British foursome living in central Philadelphia and raided their house. The police didn't discover Charley, but they did discover stolen silks and jewelry—evidence of why the group was interested in circling the same households.

Much of Philadelphia believed that Charley had never left the city's boundaries. One letter to the editor suggested the police organize search parties in each ward and investigate "every Philadelphia property for the child." An ex-detective echoed the idea, telling the police to set one day aside to search every house in the city. Editorials disagreed, arguing that eyewitness accounts identified the kidnappers' buggy as an out-of-town rental and the boy was probably miles away. Benjamin Franklin, the Philadelphia superintendent of the Pinkerton Detective Agency, thought so too. He thought the captors had taken Charley to Canada, where they couldn't be extradited for kidnapping.

Hopeful reports and disappointing results devastated Christian Ross, and his doctor confined him temporarily to his bed. The daily stories of false leads and con artists also disturbed the rest of an invalid woman in New York City. Her husband, a gentleman named Mr. Percell, decided to address his own personal to the kidnappers through the *New York Herald*. Without contacting Christian Ross or the Philadelphia police, Percell offered to pay the ransom and act as an agent for the protection of the kidnappers and the safe return of Charley. Percell said he didn't want to "compromise a felony," only to calm his sick wife's worries over Charley Ross.

The kidnappers didn't appreciate his offer.

PHILADA., July 28.— We se in the personals that Mr. Percll a millionaire of New York offers to pay the required amount to redeem yu child an ask no questions, but we have no confidence in him neither would we treat with him if he offered one milion in hand an no questions asked. in the transaction of this bisines we are determined to no no one but yu. if yu have not the mony to redeem him an ask for an extension of time we wil keep him for yu but under no other circum-stances we wil not. No matter how grate the reward is, it signifies nothin with us—they are goin to search every house in the city. we wil give you the satisfaction of knowin that he is within 100 miles of this city an yet we defy al the devels out of hell to find him. we teld yu to put the mony in a box, but we now tel yu to put the mony in a strong, white, leather valise, locked an double straped an be prepared to give it or take it wherever we direct yu. if yu are directed to cary it yuself yu may take al the friends yu pleas with yu—but dont let the cops know yu bisines. if you can have all things ready as we have directed yu by thursday the 30th insert the *folowin in the ledger* personal (John—it shall be as you desire on the 30th.) Ros you may fix any other date that is convenient for you.

ON FRIDAY MORNING, JULY 29, FREDERICK S. SWARTZ, A POSTAL agent on the Reading Railroad, prepared to exchange mail bags in Hamburg, a town in central Pennsylvania. As the train slowed down, Swartz noticed a group of gypsies near the Hamburg station. A tall man held a little boy in their midst. Swartz thought, "My God, that's Charley Ross!" When he arrived at the Pottsville station, about eighteen miles east of Hamburg, Swartz contacted an Officer Kaercher. Kaercher investigated Swartz's story and wired Philadelphia's central station. He was told to arrest the whole band of gypsies.

Philadelphia *Public Ledger*. July 30.
"John, It shall be as you desire on the 30th."

PHILADELPHIA, July 30— Ros. you are to take the 12 P.M. train tonight from West Philadelphia for New York. it arrives at New York 5.05 A. M. take a cab at Cortland or Disbrossers streets, N.Y., an ride directly to the grand central station at 4 avenue and 42d streets. take the 8 A. M. northern express by way of hudson river (take notice) you are to stand on the rear car and the rear platform from the time you leave west phila depot until arrive at jersey city—you are then to stand on the rear platform of hudson river car from the time yu leave the grand central at New York until yu arrive at Albany. if our agent do not meet yu before yu arrive in Albany yu wil find a letter in post office at Albany addressed to C. K. Walter directing yu where yu are then to go. these are the signals: if it be dark the moment the rear car passes him he wil exhibit a bright torch in one hand an a white flag in the other hand but if it be light he wil ring a bell with one hand and a white flag in the other hand. the instant yu see either of these signals yu are to drop it on the track an yu may get out at the next station.

before he intercepts yu

CHRISTIAN RECEIVED THE KIDNAPPERS' INSTRUCTIONS AT 4:00 P.M. on July 30. Earlier that morning, Officer Kaercher of the Pottsville police had sent a telegram to Philadelphia Police headquarters. "I have the child and the parties; what shall I do with them?"

Police Chief Jones and Joseph Lewis made immediate arrangements to travel by train to Hamburg. By 11:45 A.M., the Associated Press received word that Christian Ross was en route to Hamburg to identify Charley. Within hours, thousands of Philadelphians read in the afternoon papers that Charley had been found. The *Inquirer* later reported, "not since the close of the [Civil] war has any piece of news awakened so much interest." Hundreds gathered around the news bulletin boards on Chestnut Street, waiting for confirmation of Charley's homecoming.

Track repairs delayed the train carrying Joseph Lewis and Chief Jones. By the time they arrived in Hamburg at 2:15 P.M., a crowd greeted them. The men pushed their way to the station platform, where police had surrounded the gypsy tribe. Joseph Lewis looked at the child and saw how clearly he resembled the Native American woman who held him. A short dispatch was sent to Philadelphia. "The child is not Charley Ross." The crowds on Chestnut Street turned away.

Meanwhile, police detectives read the kidnappers' latest letter and called an emergency meeting of the advisers. The city leaders approved Christian's departure on the midnight train. He would follow the kidnappers' directions and carry a white valise. Instead of holding $20,000, though, the suitcase would contain a note demanding two conditions:

the kidnappers needed to simultaneously exchange Charley for the money, and they needed to agree on a more intimate method of communication than newspaper personals offered.

At midnight, an undercover officer and Frank Lewis sat in the rear car of a train pulling away from the West Philadelphia depot. Christian stood behind them, outside on the train's rear platform. He held the white valise and grasped the railing. For five hours, Christian scanned the passing landscape. He looked for hiding places and the kidnappers' designated signal: a man waving a white flag and either ringing a bell or holding a torch. Because the trip had been scheduled so quickly, Christian had been unable to change out of his work clothes into more suitable night wear before making his outdoor trek. He shivered as the train moved through New Jersey mists, particularly when it passed through swampland. Underneath the full moon, Christian realized any parties watching could see him as well as he could see them. Later, he would write, "This of course kept up a painful flutter of anxiety over the whole route—for five mortal hours my brain and eyes were in a fixed agony."

He arrived in New York, took a cab to Grand Central Station, and by 11:00 A.M., stood alert once again on the rear platform of a train bound for Albany. The train twisted and turned along the course of the Hudson River. Once again, Christian held his white valise in one hand and gripped the train railing with the other. He squinted through the engine smoke and hot afternoon sun, unable to wipe his face. His mind became so exhausted that he couldn't decipher between railroad flagmen and his potential contact—on more than one occasion, he prepared to throw the valise before recognizing the rail-workers' flags. Christian, his nephew, and the officer arrived at 1:00 P.M., checked into a hotel, and asked at the post office for a letter addressed to C. K. Walter. No such letter had arrived. As tired as he was from the rush of events over the past twenty-four hours, Christian couldn't quiet his mind enough to sleep. He spent the rest of the day wandering around Albany.

The next morning, the men left on a 10:00 A.M. train and returned to Germantown that night.

PHILA 31 July.—*Ros:* Yu seem to have no faith in us whatever. at the time we supposed yu wer gitin redy to effect the change yu were as the *Evening Star* stated on you way to potsvill to see some child there. if yu had done as the last letter instructed you and let the potsvill affair alone yu would now have the plasure of seeing yu child safe at home after we had seen that yu had gone to potsvill we did not instruct our agent to meet yu from the fact we thought it was no use. to save yu al further trouble an vexation in runing around to false reports that yu child is found here, and found there, we tel yu candidly that yu child is not in the possession of any woman or family or that his hair is cut off short.

The Philadelphia *Public Ledger*. August 1.
"John, your directions were followed, you did not keep faith. Point out some sure and less public way of communicating either by letter or person."

PHILA. Aug, 3.—Ros—in not keeping our apointment with yu was entirely a mistake from the fact of havin seen a statement in evening star that yu had gone to potsvill on the day you was to setle this bisines with us. we saw the mistake but not in time to communicate with our agent or to notify yu not to go as we directed yu. Yu say yu want us to point out some sure way by which this money can be transmited to us—of course we can not call on yu personaly neither can we receive it by letter. Ros— We will make the followin proposition to yu and if yu comply with the terms propounded we wil settle this bisines in very quick time satisfactory to both parties concerned so far as the restoration of your child is concerned.

Proposition 1ˢᵗ. Yu wil hand the box with the amount in to our agent when he calls to yu store.

Proposition 2d. Yu wil hand him the box, ask him no questions—not folow him—not put any one to folow him—not tel him what the box contains—not notify the detectives so they can folow him—not do anything that wil interupt its transit to us.

The Philadelphia *Public Ledger*. August 3.
"John. Propositions are impossible. Action must be simultaneous."

PHILADELPHIA, August 4.—*Ros:* do yu supose that we would produce the child and hand him over to you the instant yu paid the money to us. the thing is absurd to think of such a change, we are not redy yet to have chains put on us for life. when yu receive this we shal be at least 200 miles from here we leave the detectives of phila and Mr tagget to work out their clues. we think we have left no clues behind us. Charley wil remain where he was taken the second night after he left home. if Mr tagget can find a clue to that place he wil no doubt get the reward we have no feminies into that place. charley will never come out of there. it shal be his everlasting tomb—unless the ransom brings him out. we are not destitute of a few dollars yet, charley shal never starve to death if death it must be, it shal come upon him as instant as the lightning strock itself. Mr Ros, if you have anything to say to us it must be through the personals of *New York Herald.*

PART TWO:

"the cheapest way"

(AUGUST–NOVEMBER 1874)

we think we have left
no clues behind us

SOUTH OF CANAL STREET IN NEW YORK CITY, A FORMER COW path called Mulberry Street ran through the heart of the city's most infamous slum. Locals knew this area as The Bend. Notorious saloons brewed here, blocks east of Broadway. Women walked through crooked alleys, holding aprons over moldy vegetables, babies to their breasts, and firewood on their heads. Emaciated children with hacking coughs and spotty faces ate stale bread, and grocers paced in front of old, rotten slabs of meat hanging from their store doors.

On summer mornings in 1874, bartenders sidestepped bodies sleeping on lager-drenched wood shavings. The men, remnants of the past night's drinking crowd, had rented a spot on the floor for a nickel. By the time bartenders opened the doors, sunlight had awoken the neighborhood's street children, who yawned and stretched away from those lying next to them. The children stepped over sewage trickling through the streets and foraged for food as they began their morning errands. Some walked west to Newspaper Row, where newsboys collected their daily papers, and others meandered north toward Broadway, where they would look for a spot to polish boots or sell flowers. If the oldest boys made enough money to buy a lager or a whiskey by noon, they could return to the saloons for a free lunch.

Many of the city's saloons were on corners, accessible from several directions. As women sat in front of tenement houses and watched their youngest children play in the streets, husbands and fathers entered the swinging doors of saloons for their afternoon meals. Posters of sports stars, paintings, pictures of nude sirens, and brewery advertisements cluttered the walls. Bartenders pushed tables and chairs, pianos and pool tables to the sides to make room for free lunches of bread, crackers, meat, salad, and soup or stew. Along the bar, men propped tired feet on the brass foot rail and spilled lager onto sawdust scattered over the floor. A mirror behind the bar reflected the back of the saloon keeper's oily head and stiff, white shirt. From the street, hungry children could look through the wrought-iron windows and see men reaching over the bar to pay a nickel for a beer and a dime for a whiskey shot.

Charles Stromberg had owned a nearby saloon on Mott Street for a few months. It wasn't difficult to open a tavern—even a poor man could scrape together $200 and attract a brewer to provide beer, food, and decoration in exchange for a keeper's commitment to sell only his beer and to pay a tax on it. Stromberg, like most bartenders, usually had some time to himself between the free lunch that ended at 3:00 P.M. and the busy evening hours. Occasionally, he paused from his chores in the late afternoon to service a few customers, such as the three men who sometimes met at this time in the back of his saloon.

Stromberg knew one of the men, and he could tell the others were convicts before he met them. The younger of the two was tall, and he had red hair. He usually dressed well, so perhaps he alone could have passed as a working man. The other stranger, though, drew attention to both men. He was older, shorter, and had an odd-looking face. The index finger on his left hand came to a point, and he wore two gold rings on his middle finger. One of them had a red stone set within it. Stromberg knew the third man through Henry Hartman, one of his saloon keepers. His name was William Westervelt, and like Hartman, he was a disgraced New York police officer. The force had dismissed him earlier that year for failing to shut down an illegal lottery office. Westervelt blamed the dismissal on his refusal to contribute to a political fund-raiser. Since then, he, his wife, and his two children had moved into a one-room apartment in a tenement house. To make rent while Westervelt looked for work, his wife had sold some of their furniture.

Westervelt introduced Stromberg to his two friends. He called the redhead Smith, and he introduced the man with the odd face once as Anderson and another time as Henderson. Westervelt said they were business associates of his from Philadelphia. Together, they peddled an insect repellent they called "Mothee" around New York, Philadelphia, and Baltimore. Stromberg didn't trust any of them. After seeing the strangers twice, he began to record their visits. He could never successfully eavesdrop on their conversations, but he noticed that Westervelt usually came in first, followed by the others in fifteen minutes or so. As they talked, Westervelt appeared calm and the others looked frustrated. Smith often seemed nervous, and Anderson/Henderson's voice sounded angry. Each time Stromberg saw them, the strangers left after about fifteen minutes. Westervelt would then wait another fifteen before leaving. Sometimes, Westervelt came to have a drink alone, and when he did, he spoke with his old friend and bartender Henry Hartman. Hartman asked Westervelt one night for his opinion on the Philadelphia kidnapping. He replied that if the authorities arrested the kidnappers, the Ross child would not live for three days.

Stromberg didn't turn to the police with his suspicions or his notes. At night, saloons turned into community centers that represented the ethnicities and political values of the neighborhoods. In the Five Points bars, the patrons shared Irish heritages and lives of poverty and crime. Men turned to them to escape angry wives and hungry children, to talk to friends, to read the paper or play a game of pool. Some who stayed too late bought a box of candy nicknamed "wife pacifiers," and others stumbled outside, joined arms, and sang about lost loves or their dear mothers. The next day, they returned to the brotherhood on the corner, where they looked for work, cashed checks, and left letters for friends, lovers, or associates. So when Westervelt asked Hartman to contact him whenever a chalk mark appeared on a cellar door outside the saloon, he agreed. And when Westervelt once left a letter at the bar for one of his friends, Stromberg kept it despite his discomfort. He returned it three days later, after neither of Westervelt's friends appeared.

Stromberg sometimes met Westervelt for a drink at one of the other bars in Five Points. He asked him some questions about Anderson/Henderson and Smith. Westervelt didn't answer the questions directly, but he did say, "I can tell you confidentially that I can make from ten to fifteen thousand dollars, but by doing so I would have to give somebody away, which would send them to the state prison for ten, or fifteen, or twenty years, or for life." Over another drink on another night, Stromberg asked Westervelt what he thought of the Charley Ross case. Westervelt said he couldn't name any names, but he could bet "two shillings" on the identities of the kidnappers.

Around closing time, stowaways, newsboys, orphans, and beggars walked past the Five Points saloons in search of a space to sleep. Some ducked into one of the lodging houses, originally built as stately homes for the Dutch Knickerbocker settlers. They paid a few cents for a space on the floor and climbed creaky stairs. Kerosene lamps cast small shadows on the walls, wet with moisture, and smells of unclean bodies and boiled cabbage floated through the halls. When a boy found an open spot in a room, he often lay with at least a dozen sleeping men and women, any number of whom were prostitutes, river pirates, and disease sufferers who coughed through the night.

The criminals of Five Points weren't so different at heart from the city leaders who lived blocks away. They just suffered more. In both neighborhoods, swift hands earned money, and money earned power. People expected their leaders to be crooks. The good men cared too much about reputations and business interests to pretend to fight crime.

we know not what to make of that

ON AUGUST 2, THE SUPERINTENDENT OF THE NEW YORK Police Department sent an urgent message to Chief Jones in Philadelphia.

> "Chief of Police of Philadelphia:—Send detective here with original letters of kidnappers of Ross child; think I have information.
>   GEO. W. WALLING,
>   "Superintendent of New York Police."

George W. Walling had joined the force in 1847 at age twenty-four, when a friend retired and offered him his position. From his first post in a small stationhouse, Walling quickly learned that regardless of physical condition or mental acuity, the men who won promotions were those who had the right political opinions. During his years as an officer, he studied feuding in the city and concentrated his efforts on controlling ethnic riots and class tension.

The war years were good for the social lives of the northern upper class. Advertisements and society columns offered distractions from the bloody accounts of war reporters, and perhaps as a way of denying America's suffering, members attended record numbers of social events. Antebellum propriety faded into exhibitionism; workers framed Fifth Avenue mansions with marble and ladies flaunted diamonds and furs on the streets. Amid parties and play, it might have been possible to ignore the war. It was harder to disregard the changes brought by Reconstruction.

When cities rushed to industrialize, the arrival of more than 3 million immigrants doubled the population of urban America. Their work expanded industry, allowing the number of factories and miles of railroad track to double within a decade. Their arrival, however, threatened those capitalists who benefited from their hard labor. As race riots raged in Philadelphia, immigrants in New York protested unsanitary working conditions through strikes, protests, and lockouts at the workplace. Their dissatisfaction revealed something of a contradiction in certain pro-Union ideologies of the northern upper and emerging middle classes: sympathizers wanted a unified country, but they struggled to acknowledge freed slaves and immigrant laborers as their equals. When workers asserted their voices, employers saw danger, not frustration, in arguments over rotting docks and unsafe factories. They knew that a challenge to authority could lead to war. And since they didn't want to negotiate their power, they turned to those men their fathers had hired to watch, target, and punish their competition. Ironically, this fear gave the immigrant and the native a common enemy: the law enforcer.

When Walling gained his first promotion, to the rank of captain in 1853, he organized his men into "strong-arm" police teams that patrolled the streets with clubs carved from locust wood. Soon, every policeman in the city walked with a nightstick, and many held Walling's clubs. Both citizens and the police defined neighborhoods by the class and ethnicity of residents. So when the Panic of 1873 hit, and 25 percent of laborers lost their jobs, the police knew where to go to monitor unrest or search for riot leaders. Tension became so thick around Irish shanties between 91st and 106th Streets in Yorkville and Italian tenements along Third Avenue that officers walked those streets in groups of three or more. Workers with bad tempers and drinking problems knew police clubs could crack human skulls. Fear of the weapons, though, didn't keep many from fighting back, and citizens stood around brutal encounters, yelling "Shame! Shame!" at the police.

During the summer of 1874, officers walked through targeted neighborhoods late at night and demanded that people leave their porches—some of those who refused received a beating. Working women who returned home alone after hours complained that policemen treated them like prostitutes, and they filed assault charges. Politically appointed commissioners and judges protected unethical officers, even after human-rights groups convinced the state to restructure police courts.

After becoming an inspector, Walling was promoted to superintendent. The promotion came just two weeks before he sent the telegram of August 2 to Chief Jones in Philadelphia. Already, he was irritated with changes made to his office. Prior to Walling's nomination, the person named superintendent had had total authority over the force for an unlimited term, and he could expect to communicate directly with any officer, no matter the rank. But Walling's power came with limitations. The Board of the Police reserved the right to remove him whenever they wished, and they implemented a new measure that curbed conversation between the city's thirty-six captains and their superintendent. The captains were told to speak only and directly with one of four inspectors, who then reported directly to the superintendent. Walling had served for twenty-seven years—long enough to watch municipal evolution, understand its politics, and know when, where, and why decisions limiting authorial power were made. It embarrassed him that the board withdrew certain powers as soon as he assumed control.

Immediately upon taking office, Walling learned of a case that revealed a flaw in the new communication system. For a few weeks, an Officer Doyle in the city's thirteenth ward had been communicating with a man who claimed his brother had kidnapped Charley Ross. The police knew the informant. His name was Clinton "Gil" Mosher, and he was a well-known horse thief who had served time in the state prison. Officer Doyle had followed protocol, reporting Mosher's lead only to his superior, Captain Henry Hedden. Hedden's instinct was to dismiss anything to do with Gil Mosher, yet he had mentioned him to his superintendent, Walling's predecessor. That man told Hedden to pursue the lead. But then, internal restructuring in the department had slowed communication. Walling's former boss became police commissioner, Walling was promoted, and by the time he learned Doyle's story, two weeks of conversations had passed.

Walling demanded to see Mosher, Doyle, and Hedden immediately. He knew it would take a few days for the cops to track down

Mosher, especially once the seasoned criminal heard that somebody besides Doyle was looking for him. But he also knew Gil Mosher's type—one that would betray anybody, even a brother, for $20,000. He was right. Gil Mosher soon sat in front of Walling, agreeing to answer his questions.

"What are your reasons for suspecting that your brother William took part in kidnapping Charley Ross?" Walling asked.

"Well, I was approached by Bill, who asked me if I would join him in carrying off some child who had rich parents. The plan was to steal one of Commodore Vanderbilt's grandchildren."

"Which one of the children was to be taken?"

"The youngest one we could get."

"What would you do with it?"

"Hold it for a ransom."

"Where did he propose to conceal the child?"

"In a boat. And, I was to negotiate for the ransom."

"Well, what then?"

"I refused to have anything to do with the business."

"Why?"

"Because I thought there would be too much risk in trying to get money from the Vanderbilts. They are too rich, have too much power and are not the kind of people to be frightened. There would be no trouble in stealing the child, the difficulty would be in negotiating for its ransom."

"So you gave up the plan?"

"Yes; I would not run the risk of being detected. I did not think it was a safe enterprise."

Gil Mosher's story sounded like a criminal's daydream, a child's fantasy, an aging man's attempt at delivering a tale that would earn him some reward money. The plan, as shared with Walling, was too vague to have an implicit connection to the Ross case, and as a seasoned criminal, Gil was hardly one to "[refuse] to have anything to do" with whatever "business" might bring him some extra cash. The Vanderbilts, magnates of the Gilded Age, were untouchable icons—too rich to be within the reach of the working class, and too clever to be outsmarted by petty river pirates. Criminals may have dreamed of taking from them, but the successful ones knew to aim for smaller game. Still, though, Gil Mosher's story had the operative terms "ransom," "negotiate," and "child." If nothing else, Walling could use it as his entrance into the high-profile Charley Ross case and its hefty reward.

After receiving Walling's telegram on August 2, Chief Jones contacted Captain Heins and Joseph Ross, Christian's brother. The next day, the men took the ransom notes to Walling at New York's police headquarters.

"We hope that you at least have some trustworthy information," said Heins.

"I think I have," Walling responded. "Through Captain Henry Hedden, of the Thirteenth Police District, I have heard of a man who professes to know who the abductors are." He called for Hedden to join the meeting.

Joseph Ross asked, "Had you any idea who the abductors were?"

"We suspect two men," replied Walling.

"If we have their names, they can be hunted down," said Joseph.

"Undoubtedly. And that is what we hope to do."

Hedden told Heins and Ross about Gil Mosher and his brother William. "If my suspicions are correct, this William Mosher is the leader of the conspiracy. He arranged the plot and is the writer of the letters sent to Mr. Ross. I am familiar with Mosher's writing, and can tell if I see the letters whether he is the author of them."

"Before we show you the letters," responded Heins, "describe to us the peculiarities of Mosher's handwriting."

William—or "Bill"—Mosher was a career petty thief, but an educated one. Gil told the officers that his brother had gone to school as a child, and that he had always liked to read. Gil also remembered Bill's attempt to write a novel "some ten years before." He said the handwriting was "dirty," hard to read. His brother's signature mark was the way he wrote the letter *Y*—looping the tail so that it spread into the next word.

"He writes very rapidly and is careless," Gil said. "He seldom finishes a page without blotting it. He often writes either above or below the lines. When he folds a letter it is in a peculiar and awkward way."

"At last!" cried Joseph Ross.

After hearing a short description of one man's careless handwriting and paper-folding preference, Joseph Ross returned to Philadelphia believing that the kidnappers had been identified. He didn't, however, share this news with his brother Christian. Walling had advised him not to.

we have heard nothing from yu

ON MONDAY, AUGUST 3, DETECTIVE TAGGART DOUBLED THE reward advertised by the Pennsylvania Bureau of Detectives for anonymous information leading to the kidnappers.

> "$5,000 will be paid by us to any person who will give us a clue which will lead to the detection of the kidnappers of Charley Brewster Ross, and the name of the person giving the information shall be kept secret if desired."
>
> JOSHUA TAGGART
> EDW G. GARLIN
> R. A. LUKENS
> Pennsylvania Detective Bureau
> Southwest corner Fifth and Spruce Streets, Philadelphia

Although Taggart wouldn't pursue a reward that his own agency offered, he could certainly use any information gleaned through it to pursue the city's $20,000 prize.

After a month of searching, amateur detectives across the western hemisphere sent reports of Charley sightings from Cuba, Scotland, Germany. The Ross case offered Americans, no matter how disenfranchised, more than a chance to earn money: it created an opportunity for public attention.

And middle-class America wanted attention. The early successes of industrialization expanded the echelon of business, allowing for the emergence of a more clearly defined middle class in America.

Aside from quality of life, these small-business owners, managers, and "middle men" differed from the upper class in two important ways: they dealt more immediately with the working class, and they were more directly affected by the Civil War, giving them a sympathy that evaded the bourgeoisie. As a result of this Victorian sensibility, the middle class believed in community values, and their convictions resulted in relief efforts for the poor and other disenfranchised peoples. But they also believed that the laboring class was inherently violent, a fault easily overcome through moral education. The prevailing sentiment was that if wage earners insisted on disturbing the peace, thereby disrespecting the social hierarchy and its moral boundaries, then society had no problem judging them as uneducated and unworthy of redemption.

The search for Charley Ross and his captors became a special kind of challenge for the middle class. Saving the child and punishing the criminals appealed to their sense of justice; questioning foreigners and searching through poor neighborhoods appealed to their curiosity, handily disguised as civic responsibility. After the long war years, life moved quickly. More people moved into more concentrated areas at the expense of America's slower-paced, agrarian lifestyle. Another kind of New World evolved within the country's borders—and as survival occupied the minds of workers and family money reassured the upper class, security worried those in the middle.

The *Inquirer* blamed the industrialization for paranoia. "In the good old times, peace, honesty, kindness and obedience to law prevailed throughout the interior of Pennsylvania. Farm houses were without bolts and locks, quarrels never got further than fisticuffs, burglars, thieves, and murderers were rare objects. All this is now changed," it said. "The increase of traveling facilities is the cause. The railroad carries the ruffian and thief from the great cities and sets them down in a few hours in peaceful and unsuspecting neighborhoods where they may commit awful crimes and escape with all the facility and ease which were ready to bring them to the scenes of their outrages."

The kidnappers had, then, a co-conspirator: progress.

The appeal of "the good old times" pushed northern Republicans—Abraham Lincoln's party of progress—further into conservatism.

Railroad tracks may have spread throughout the country, but they facilitated the arrival of the unknown into the familiar, and the departure of
the familiar into the unknown.

If the theft of Charley was an opportunity for the laborer to steal a
piece of middle-class life, then the search for him was a chance for the
middle class to assert their Puritan values. Seeing the kidnapping as
a warning of things to come, they emphasized Christian education
and tightened the protective reins on their households. Communities
detained strangers, removed children from suspicious-looking guardians,
and thought they recognized the kidnappers' features on the faces of
foreigners and outsiders passing through their neighborhoods. Whether
or not those parties fit descriptions of Charley and his captors, they were
often held until a member of the Ross family or the Philadelphia Police
cleared them. Townspeople felt the power of their accusations—
whomever they suspected, the police questioned.

Officers in Denver, Colorado, notified Mayor Stokley of a German
couple who traveled with a small boy. After receiving Charley's picture,
and realizing the boy spoke German, the officers admitted he didn't
resemble Charley at all.

A police chief in St. Paul, Minnesota, noticed a boy with a "bright,
intelligent face" loitering outside of a disreputable bar until a "rough-
looking" man took him away. The chief contacted police headquarters
in Philadelphia, yet had to confess he didn't know where the pair had
gone.

Officers in North Philadelphia asked a four-year-old for his name
and took him to the station when he said "Charley Ross." When his
angry parents came to get him, they told the officers that their child
had a lisp. He had actually identified himself as "Charley Loss."

A man named Murkins in Odell, Illinois, told his creditors that he
"was going to get a fortune from the East" around the same time a couple and two children arrived at his house. One of the children looked
so familiar that a neighbor wrote Christian and asked for Charley's picture, which he then took to the local police. An officer and a state attorney went to Murkins's house and asked to meet the boy. He had brown
hair, brown eyes, and a mark on his left arm identical to a vaccination
scar on Charley. He also wore a dress. The police suspected Murkins of

trying to collect the reward money by disguising an older child as Charley Ross.

Initially, authorities treated every identity question as a lead. Professional and amateur detectives came across the cases of other children who were lost or found. Over the past twenty years, the New York–based Children's Aid Society had sent some twenty thousand boys and girls west on what came to be known as "orphan trains." The idea was to find good homes for those homeless, abandoned, institutionalized, and/or criminal children who wandered the streets. Half of these kids probably were not orphans—indigent parents had the opportunity to ship their kids off to a better life, and some children volunteered to go themselves. Critics, however, pled the causes of parents who said their children were taken without consent, and of children who ran away from abusive placements. The Society denied stealing children and said potential families were screened, but it did not keep consistent, acceptable records. If a foster parent thought he had Charley Ross, chances are he wouldn't have been able to trace the child's true origin.

To the fascination of readers, newspapers published tales of exploited and displaced minors by name.

In New York City, eight-year-old Annie Sebastian left one afternoon to put flowers on her grandmother's grave. When she didn't return after five hours, her father reported the disappearance. Annie's young neighbor said he saw four black men put her in a wagon while Annie screamed, "Wait! Wait!"

Reporters in Albany, New York, reminded citizens of a fourteen-year-old named John Patterson who had been missing for almost a year after failing to return home from his part-time job. His mother and the police had followed rumored sightings of the boy from Yonkers to Kentucky, even asking to see the bones of a buried body at one stop.

Seven-year-old Joe Harlen from South Philadelphia went to the market with his uncle. After making his purchases, Joe's uncle told him to wait by the wagon while he retrieved their horses from the stable. Joe was missing when he returned.

In Newport, Rhode Island, a young girl named Charlotte played with her friends on the beach while her guardians, two Indian women, shopped in town. An eyewitness saw a gentleman walk up to Charlotte and ask her to go with him. "No," the little girl replied. He then offered her candy and guided her into a tent. Charlotte wore different clothes when she left the beach with the man.

Never before had public interest centered so much on the place of children in American society. The public realized that regardless of Charley's fate and their selfish interests in the reward money, children would never be as safe as they were before July 1, 1874. Parents needed the police to find Charley's captors, but even more, they needed them to address unanswered questions—such as, Why Charley? Christian was not a rich man, his business was not going well, and he lived in a neighborhood full of children. Why did the kidnappers select this particular little boy? Why did they risk taking him from his front yard during daylight? Why did they release his older brother? Were they initially hoping to steal two children? Were they looking for another? Were Charley's kidnappers responsible for the disappearances of others? The public needed to believe that the ransom letters contained clues to some of these answers.

The longer the search took, the more people needed somebody to hold responsible. The captors had committed a crime against humanity, but as the *Evening Bulletin* suggested, they weren't the only villains on the scene. The *Bulletin* accused city authorities of using silence to manipulate the public's emotions: "But there has been much that would interest the public which is suppressed, apparently for no better reason than to minister to a sense of self-importance among the few who have made themselves the repositories of this information, and who take a certain satisfaction in looking out from their mysterious retreat upon the common public groping around in the outer darkness."

The Republican advisers continued using the Public *Ledger*, under the authority of William McKean, as their mouthpiece. Ignoring accusations of having withheld information, the *Ledger* placed responsibility on the people. "A search like this can of course only be made by the people: It is beyond the power and the reach of the police, even if there were police in the interior." Ironically, this statement worked against the very authorities it aimed to protect. As agents of the advisers' decisions, police officers represented these city leaders. By diminishing "the power and reach of the police," McKean's paper indirectly told the public that their elected officials were unable to function as leaders. Such reporting overlooked the growing respect for the force. The public's desire to read the ransom letters reflected their interest in police intelligence and their need to feel protected. Had the *Ledger* encouraged faith in the force—for example, by praising its organization of search efforts—the paper would have reinforced citizens' fledgling faith in city authorities and deflected criticism more successfully. Instead, the advisers tried to earn public approval through fear tactics.

In the same article, the *Ledger* wrote, "The stealing of little Charley Ross strikes at every child, every parent and every home in the land, for it is boldly proclaimed by the brigands that it is done solely for the ransom money, and that they intend to make this case a test as to whether they can carry on their brutal traffic with success." The public had feared additional kidnappings, but prior to this article, they hadn't known of the kidnappers' specific references to future crimes. By releasing this information, authorities attempted to scare the city by answering one of its questions: if satisfied with Charley's ransom, the kidnappers would take another child.

In early August, Chief Jones authorized the search of every room on every floor of every building in the city. "Citizens should be careful as to the parties they admit to their houses on the pretence of searching for little Charley Ross," the *Evening Bulletin* cautioned. "Nobody, except a policeman in full uniform, is authorized to make such an examination." The scope of the task generated excitement on the streets, and most suspended complaints to cooperate. While police rummaged through their houses, neighbors more thoroughly explored old coal mines, abandoned buildings, and dark spaces in the corners of ravines, woods, docks, and stables. The citywide hunt failed to produce leads on Charley, but it did uncover contraband and numerous thieves whose illicit activities had gone unnoticed.

ask him no questions

CHRISTIAN ROSS DISAGREED WITH POLICE SUSPICIONS THAT Charley was in Philadelphia or New York. He thought his son had been taken to a place in the Midwest, not a day's journey away as the kidnappers had insisted. Christian did join investigators in sorting through the suspicions and fragmented visions of mediums and con artists who would incorporate published details about the Ross family's life into their stories. He tried to limit the number of false reports by formulating a list of questions for the police to ask Charley look-alikes. It asked the children to state Charley's full name, his hometown, a toy he and Walter played with, and a certain prayer. When potential Charleys passed the interview, inquirers alerted the police, who along with family members decided which possibilities were worthy of a visit. Crowds of hopeful helpers greeted Ross family representatives at railroad stations across the Midwest, down the East Coast, and in Canada and Scotland.

Desiring to help somehow, hundreds of people wrote letters to Christian and Sarah. One came from a former business associate of Christian's in Boston:

MR. C. K. ROSS—Dear Sir:—I believe years ago I did business with you. Since then I have retired from active business life, and you have my heartfelt sympathy in your deep affliction. I think your case the hardest I ever heard of, and if I can be of any help to you, I will be glad to aid in any way in my power. If you should issue an appeal to the press of the United States, I think there would hardly be a newspaper that would refuse to copy your card, and give it a prominent place, without charge. There are hundreds of families that do not know yet, that you have had a boy stolen, and CHARLEY ROSS may be living next door to some of them and they not know it. My wife and I take such an interest in the case that I feel that with as much leisure as I have, that I ought in the cause of humanity spend some of it in helping you. If you have anything in the way of guidance, let me know, and you can have my gratuitous services.

Yours truly,

SAMUEL T. HOLMES

Even though correspondence brought false reports and bizarre advice, it offered Christian his greatest support system. Ten years before, it wouldn't have been as accessible an option.

Up until the middle of the nineteenth century, it cost seventeen times as much to send a letter as it did to mail a newspaper to a friend. People avoided high postage costs by jotting notes between articles, rolling up a paper and mailing it instead of a proper letter. The practice became so popular that the government, wanting the money generated by postage, made communication by "transient newspaper" illegal. It took two other acts for writers to change their habits, however: in 1845, the postal service lowered costs somewhat, and newspapers encouraged readers to pay a small fee to post messages in personal columns. The idea was a success. But people still didn't receive messages at home. They had to either buy a paper on the street or go to the post office to claim messages. Before long, the post office was a community meeting place—and the perfect spot to kindle an affair.

Like so many other institutions, the postal service changed dramatically during the Civil War. Officials thought it more appropriate for women to learn of family deaths in the privacy of their homes rather than the public sphere of the post office. In 1864, sixty-six American cities instituted home delivery. For the first time, it was possible to anonymously place a letter in a container at a post office, hotel, bar, or letter box, and know it would reach a designated person exactly where he or she lived.

It made sense then, that people scanned the personals so often that they could find and keep track of the Ross camp's answers to the kidnappers. It also made sense that the kidnappers chose the mail to communicate an anonymous ransom. And as their threats intensified, they knew the words would terrorize the Ross family alone in their home before the authorities could read anything.

if death it must be

ON SATURDAY, AUGUST 10, CHRISTIAN AND WALTER RODE THE train to New York City. Christian knew they would be meeting with Superintendent Walling, but he didn't know why. Even though Christian's brother Joseph had heard about the Mosher brothers more than a week before, Christian had not been told about them. Walling greeted Christian at his hotel and introduced him to Captain Hedden, who made plans to meet with the Rosses in the morning.

That night, tragedy struck Germantown. In spite of earlier summer rains, a drought had depressed Philadelphia's rivers, leaving the Wingohocking Creek so parched that it revealed the sharp rocks usually hidden underwater. Staggered storms arrived on Friday, August 9, and when they turned into a steady downpour lasting more than twenty-four hours, the basins overflowed.

Germantown's home owners had changed the patterns of the town's streams by digging outlets around their properties, creating man-made angles that trapped branches and dirt during storms. North of the Ross home on Washington Lane, a little bridge crossed a stream called Honey Run. Throughout the storm, gas and water-main pipes trapped driftwood, sand, and trash underneath the bridge piers, and the force of the water unsettled the bridge's foundation. On Saturday night, a concerned neighbor stood with a lantern near Honey Run. No gas lamps were lit along the route, but the watchman managed to warn an oncoming wagon or two to turn away from the unstable bridge. There was one he couldn't save: eighty-five-year-old James Sherrard and the fifteen-year-old son of his employer, a boy named Henry Steel, were headed for the train depot. They traveled too quickly to see the lantern or heed the warning; before morning, police joined neighbors in a search for the bodies.

Somebody found the corpse of the drowned horse first. It had been trapped, attached to the buggy, underneath pieces of the bridge. About 250 feet away from the horse, Sherrard's body had settled against the riverbank. Just before noon, somebody spotted the boy. His hand appeared to be reaching above the water's surface further downstream, held in place by the ruins of another broken bridge.

Superintendent Walling became so determined to track Charley himself that he tightened the flow of information in his investigation, even instructing Captain Hedden not to tell Christian about the Mosher brothers. Walling wanted to do it himself, but only after Hedden asked Walter to identify a possible prime suspect. The following morning, the Captain took Walter and Christian on a walk outside their hotel. Pointing out a man who stood a short distance away, Hedden asked if Walter had ever seen him before, perhaps in the buggy that carried Charley away.

"No, sir, never," Walter answered.

Hedden turned to Christian. "I did not think he was one of the persons who took the children, but I wanted to be certain he was not; yet I believe he is connected with the matter, and is in communication with the abductors." Hedden took Christian and Walter back to police headquarters, where Walling told Christian about Clinton "Gil" Mosher and his brother Bill. Walling also identified the man Captain Hedden had asked Walter about earlier in the day. His name was William Westervelt, and he was Bill Mosher's brother-in-law.

now we demand yu anser

W ALLING KNEW IT WOULDN'T BE EASY TO FIND BILL MOSHER. The man knew how to hide: he had been a criminal for more than half his life.

Mosher had grown up on a section of Brooklyn called Green Point. His father had been a somewhat successful ship captain, and when Mosher was a child, his older brother Gil taught him the family's boat-building trade. In between jobs, both brothers worked with river-pirate gangs. During one robbery, a cask fell on Mosher's left hand, an injury that caused the flesh around the nail of his index finger to wither into a sharp point.

At the time of the Ross kidnapping, the brothers weren't speaking. Their parents had died, as had twelve of their thirteen siblings. In his younger years, Gil's crime of choice had been stealing horses. He had served time in prison for his burglaries but maintained his naval trade and a relationship with his family. The Mosher parents hadn't been so forgiving with Gil's younger brother Bill. They had disowned him years before they died because of his criminal associations.

In his twenties, Bill Mosher joined a successful gang called the Daybreak Boys. He and his partners Nicholas Saul, William Howlet, Slobbery Jim, Patsy "the Barber" Conroy, Cowlegged Sam McCarthy, and Saul Madden spent time at James and Water streets in Manhattan, an intersection the police nicknamed Slaughter House Point. The Daybreak Boys, one of the first river-pirate gangs to organize themselves as a private crime enterprise, attacked ships in the East River, the Hudson, and the Hudson's harbors at dawn. Between 1850 and 1852, the gang stole more than $100,000 in merchandise and murdered at least twenty men. Police often found victims floating around docks with their pockets turned out. In 1853, a ship watchman surprised the heads of the gang, Nicholas Saul and William Howlet, when they climbed aboard his boat. Witnesses watched as Saul and Howlet shot him in the heart. Police arrested the two when their rowboat came back to shore, and the judge sentenced the men, aged nineteen and twenty, to death. They were hanged inside a prison nicknamed "the Tombs" on the outskirts of the Five Points. After the execution, the Daybreak Boys broke up. Mosher kept his hand in river piracy, appearing before the police chief as a suspect for one particularly gruesome robbery four years later. The police couldn't hold him long. Unfortunately, someone had beaten the ship's captain with a handspike during the incident, and the wounded man couldn't identify or remember his assailants.

Over the next twenty years, Bill Mosher married a much younger woman, took on woodworking jobs, and dabbled in failed business ventures. Once, he secured a financier to set him up in a fish business on Ridge Street in Manhattan. Six months later, the business failed. Mosher then opened a saloon, where he lived with his wife and their baby. Within a short time, the little boy died. Having no money for a funeral, they buried his bones in the wall. They left them there when the bar closed for good.

Mosher also worked for "fencers" who received and repackaged stolen goods, and he helped train younger burglars. In his hometown of Green Point, Mosher recruited a young teenage thief named Joseph Douglas. Mosher introduced Douglas to a tenement house in Manhattan where older thieves taught younger ones how to better burglarize, blow safes, blackmail, and pickpocket. Superintendent Walling first knew Joseph Douglas when his name came up in the Ross investigation as Joseph Smith.

Mosher and Douglas developed a part-time piracy practice along the shores of Baltimore, Philadelphia, New Jersey, and New York. The two men built a shack on Berrian's Island in Long Island Sound, where they hid their bounty until they were ready to sell it at fencing operations doubling as haberdasheries, tailors' shops, and furniture houses in and around the Five Points. From there, they set out on a trip by boat that took them to Red Bank, New Jersey, robbing country stores along the shore as they proceeded. On another night, after filling their boat with fancy clothes on a Red Bank run, they passed some fishermen. Later that night, police raided their island shack and found them sleeping inside of it. Three river police officers named Doyle, Silleck, and Moran made the arrest. The thieves were tied by their necks and taken to the Monmouth County Jail. Their stay was brief. Cutting through a wall, Mosher found a way to escape. Later, he learned that it was not the fishermen but his brother Gil who had informed the police about his Red Bank robbery.

With his partner in hiding, Douglas moved to Brooklyn, changed his last name to Clark, and found a job as a streetcar driver. The police next heard about the two men six years later, when Gil Mosher brought their names to Officer Doyle's attention in July of 1874.

If he wanted to bring Bill Mosher in for questioning, Walling knew he had to rely on Gil: the man's greed for the reward money, combined with his criminal connections, would lead him to Bill before Walling's men could track him. What Walling wanted most from Gil was a sample of his brother's handwriting so police could connect Bill Mosher directly to the ransom letters. Since his visit to Walling's office at the beginning of August, Gil had traveled with New York officer Doyle to Camden, New Jersey, Philadelphia, and Baltimore. Gil had also made numerous stops to the New York apartment of William Westervelt in search of his brother. After Westervelt and his wife, Mary, repeatedly told him that they had not seen Bill, Gil's wife, Liz, began visiting the Westervelts and asking for Bill Mosher's family. Westervelt questioned her motives, and Liz said detectives wanted to ask about some stolen silks. Westervelt assumed she was lying and that she and Gil were trying to collect the $20,000 reward.

On August 10, the same day that Christian and Walter went to New York, Westervelt wrote to Bill Mosher. The letter informed Bill of his brother's repeated visits to Westervelt's apartment and was sent to Monroe Street in Philadelphia. Two days later, Gil returned to Westervelt's door and gave him a letter for Bill. He said it requested a meeting. Westervelt forwarded the note to Philadelphia the next day.

Bill Mosher and his accomplice Joseph Douglas showed up at Westervelt's apartment on Wednesday, August 14. Mosher had received Westervelt's warning in the mail. Westervelt asked if he had received the letter from Gil he had mailed the day before. He had not.

"What does he want?" Mosher asked.

"Don't know," Westervelt replied.

"Where does he work?"

"Moss's shop on Mangin Street," Westervelt answered.

"Let's go down and see what he wants," Mosher said.

Three blocks away from the store, Mosher told Douglas and Westervelt to find Gil without him. He said he would wait inside a saloon on the corner, and when the others found his brother, he wanted them to take Gil on a walk past the saloon so he could see how he looked.

Douglas accompanied Westervelt to Moss's shop.

"Is Gil Mosher here?" Westervelt asked the storekeeper.

"I don't know that name," the man answered.

Westervelt described him.

"A man named Ryan fits the description," the storekeeper replied. "He's not here."

Westervelt and Douglas walked to the corner of Allen and Houston Streets, where Mosher waited inside the saloon. Westervelt went inside, and Douglas went across the street to visit a fortune-teller named Madame Morrow. Madame Morrow also had a home in Philadelphia, where she went by her married name, Morris. Her sons Ed and Ike were longtime acquaintances and sometime colleagues of the Mosher brothers.

When Douglas returned to the saloon, he told Mosher that Gil had also been looking for him at Madame Morrow's. Mosher stood up and then rushed across the street to ask Madame Morrow more questions about his brother. Fifteen minutes later, he returned, crying and cursing. Westervelt tried to calm him down, but Mosher demanded that Westervelt go to Gil's house with a letter. He asked the bartender for paper, pen, and ink, gave them to Westervelt, and asked him to write as he dictated:

"Tell Gil I do not see what he can want of me. I have no time to meet him or money to spend. Tell him to explain more fully what he wants."

Westervelt agreed to take the letter to Gil. He arranged to meet Bill Mosher and Douglas at Stromberg's saloon on Mott Street later in the day, then went to Gil's house.

Liz Mosher answered the door. She asked again for Bill Mosher, repeating her concern that police wanted to arrest him for stolen silks.

Westervelt read the letter out loud to her.

"Can I trust you with the truth?" she asked Westervelt.

"Yes," he replied.

"The police suspect Bill of taking Charley Ross," she said. "Gil needs to talk to him."

Westervelt went to Stromberg's and found Bill Mosher and Douglas at a table in the back, far enough away that the bartender could hear only mumbles. By now, Stromberg had noticed that while Westervelt remained calm when he talked to his two friends, the one he called Henderson (Bill Mosher) became upset and fidgety. Before the men left Stromberg's that afternoon, Bill Mosher asked Westervelt to go to Philadelphia and convince his wife, Martha, Westervelt's sister, to leave the city with their children. Bill asked Westervelt to let him know if his family was safe from Gil by posting an ad in the New York Herald.

"If she is fine, and nobody is looking," Bill said, write "Napoleon— I have seen them and they are well."

"But if they are in danger," Bill continued, write, "Napoleon—I have seen them and they are not well."

Westervelt went home, changed his shirt, and left on the 7:00 P.M. train for Philadelphia.

Kate Morgan settled into her rented room at the Henderson home in South Philadelphia. It was a fine enough place for a single woman to live. People minded their own business there, so she could come and go as she pleased. Her landlord didn't appear very often. When he did, he usually arrived with his younger red-headed friend. In mid-August, a neighbor named Mrs. Mary O'Leary noticed a former male tenant visiting the Hendersons. The man was big and burly, with whiskers, a moustache, and dark hair. He, his wife, and their two children had lived with the Hendersons earlier that year. Mrs. O'Leary knew the landlady, Martha Henderson. She saw her boys playing around the house, and she knew the woman had stayed inside her home most of July, especially the week of the 13th, when she gave birth to a girl.

Kate Morgan noticed the visitor, but had never seen him before. William Westervelt had moved out of the house by the time Kate arrived. Over the past month, she had, however, become familiar with Willie, Charley, and Georgie—Mrs. Henderson's three boys. Kate noticed that the boy Charley was called "Lovie" most of the time.

Martha Mosher told her brother that she couldn't immediately move her children and their belongings to New York. She said she needed time. Westervelt left his sister's home on Saturday, August 14. Before taking the train back to New York, he traveled up Germantown's Main Street and entered a store. He asked the keeper, a Mr. McDowell, for some water. McDowell obliged, pausing to talk with his visitor about the day's warm temperature. Westervelt asked him if this was the town where the child Charley Ross had been kidnapped.

"Yes," McDowell said. He mentioned the parents' grief and his own sadness for them.

"Do you know Christian Ross?" Westervelt asked.

"Yes," responded McDowell. "He goes to my church."

Westervelt asked if he knew whether Christian's business was failing.

"I know nothing about it," said McDowell, "but I think that's true."

"Is his brother-in-law a rich man?" continued Westervelt.

"I believe he is," McDowell answered.

Westervelt thanked McDowell and left the store. The shopkeeper would remember this conversation, but he didn't share it at the time.

After returning to New York, Westervelt chose not to post the "Napoleon" ad in the Herald as Mosher had asked. Three days later, one of Martha's tenants took her, the three boys, and her newborn daughter to the train station.

The same day his sister arrived in New York, Westervelt met a former police colleague at another saloon on Grand Street in Five Points.

The acquaintance told him that Superintendent Walling wanted to speak with him. Westervelt trusted his companion enough to walk with him to the Thirteenth Precinct.

The Thirteenth Precinct was located inside police headquarters, a four-story building with a white stone exterior at 300 Mulberry Street. Two doors led visitors and prisoners inside—the front on Mulberry Street, the back on Mott Street. Marble framed the front entrance on Mulberry, and when Westervelt walked under the words, "Central Bureau of Metropolitan Police," he was only blocks away from Stromberg's bar, his point of rendezvous with Mosher and Douglas.

As soon as Westervelt entered the building, Captain Hedden met him and took him upstairs to the second floor. Hedden escorted Westervelt into a suite reserved for the commissioners, and then into a smaller room, where he asked him to submit to a search for pawn tickets that matched some stolen silks. Westervelt resisted. Hedden forced him to empty his pockets and left the suite with the contents.

Hedden didn't return for two hours. During that time, Westervelt waited alone. Most of the office spaces at headquarters had white walls and plain carpets. The furniture matched in the different rooms—a few chairs in each faced a desk carved from black walnut wood. White linen shades hung from the windows. On the street below, the Five Points scene contrasted sharply with the minimalist police building. Bars attracted their typical clientele through this night's hours. Drunks, workers, and criminals moved past headquarters just like they staggered by any other building on Mott and Mulberry Streets. Two floors above them, Westervelt wondered what Captain Hedden would try to make him do when he returned.

Another officer accompanied Hedden's arrival. Both demanded that Westervelt undergo a strip search. When he refused, they arrested him. Hedden walked Westervelt back downstairs, past the Superintendent's rooms on the first floor. But instead of leading him down another set of stairs to the basement cells, he took Westervelt to Walling's private residence on Nineteenth Street.

Hedden and the other officer stood watch at the superintendent's front door, as if waiting for thugs to spring from the dark and try to rescue Westervelt. Inside, Walling talked to the disgraced ex-cop. He asked if Westervelt knew that his brother-in-law was suspected of kidnapping Charley Ross.

Before arriving at Walling's home, Westervelt had plenty of time to think about why Hedden was bullying him. Surely he knew that the police would ask for Bill Mosher, and by the time Walling got to the point, Westervelt had studied his answer options.

"Bill Mosher wouldn't have taken a child," he said. He told Walling that Gil Mosher and his wife Liz were framing Bill in order to claim the reward money.

"That money can be yours," Walling replied, "if you locate Mosher for us."

Westervelt called him a liar.

Walling repeated that Westervelt could have the reward money. He asked him to put himself in Christian Ross's shoes, to imagine what he would do if he knew that somebody could lead the police to the kidnapper of his child. Westervelt didn't empathize very easily. He talked to Walling for two more hours before admitting that he had been in recent contact with Bill Mosher and Joseph Douglas. The offer of a reward no doubt engaged his interest in continuing, perhaps conducting, parts of the conversation.

Walling asked if Mosher had responded to his brother Gil's letter.

"Yes," Westervelt answered. He said he himself had written the reply. He told Walling that he would consider cooperating if his conditions were met: he didn't want Mosher and Douglas to know about his betrayal, and he didn't want Walling's officers to know whatever information he gave the superintendent. Walling accepted the terms and released Westervelt from custody. He then directed Westervelt to communicate only with him.

As Westervelt left Walling's home, he assumed control of the next part of the investigation. Walling may have thought that the disgraced policeman would do what he could to claim the reward money and rebuild his reputation with the force, but Westervelt had spent enough time on the streets—as a cop and as a criminal—to know that Walling's motivation was selfish. Why else would the superintendent have had Hedden bring him to his home, instead of instructing the captain to lock him up in a cell, where Walling could easily question him whenever he wanted? Westervelt knew that Walling could claim something from the reward just as much as he could—but he could only do so with Westervelt's participation. As soon as he got the information he wanted, Walling could arrest Westervelt along with Mosher and Douglas and reconstruct—maybe even completely deny, with Hedden's help—the late-night conversation. Westervelt, though, would have the superintendent's complete attention as long as he provided enough information to keep him interested. And while he played the role of informant on his own terms, he could figure out how to best use his newfound power to his advantage.

Soon after the meeting at Walling's home, Westervelt contacted Walling with a lead. He told him that Mosher and Douglas were bound for Astoria on the ferry, and if they stationed officers on the East River at Ninety-second Street, they could catch the thieves, who would be dressed as fishermen and carrying a slate-colored bag. Walling immediately contacted the Thirteenth Precinct and sent Westervelt's message to an Officer Moran.

Moran had grown up in Douglas's neighborhood. He had also been an arresting officer in the burglary that sent Mosher and Douglas, tied by the neck, to jail. Years before this arrest, Mosher and Douglas had briefly found positions as deputy marshals in Moran's police district. After the criminals shot a man unlawfully, Moran arrested them for "felonious assault." Mosher and Douglas were soon released.

The day of Westervelt's tip, the police had a hard time locating Officer Moran. By the time he got the message and arrived at the ferry, Moran found out that men fitting the description of Mosher and Douglas had passed through minutes before. The officer had either unfortunately been detained in other business or had not wanted to arrive on the scene in time to trap the thieves.

NEW YORK, August 21.—Mr. Ros: we have heard nothing from yu since we wrote yu about 3 weeks ago. we have therefor come to the conclusion that yu don't mean to redeem yu child on the conditions which we proposed. yu must bear in mind we would never agree to any other terms. the fact of yu saying the action must be symultainous is absolutely imposible. we would require at least a few ours to examine the mony and see if it were spurious or all marked up and then but a few ours more would be necessary to place yu child in yu possession for he is not so far off as yu may imagin. now we demand yu anser yes or now as we are going to urope the 24 Sept and he has got to be disposed of one way or the other by that time. if you say redeem him it has got to be on our terms alone if yu do not answer we shall take it as granted that yu dont mean to pay yu money. we shall act accordingly. address (John New *Herald* personals.) you are listing to old womans visions and dreams which wil never find yu child. we could have told yu it was useless to go to illinoise to look for charly but yu would not have believed us.

New York Herald. August 23.
"John. Did not answer, because your proposition led my friends to doubt whether you ever had it. Write, giving better proof, and name an attorney, or other person, through whom arrangements can be made."

ALBANY, August 26.— *Mr. Ros*—ask Walter if one of the men did not hold him between his legs an partly on his knee with the cloth in front of him while Charley set behind us both entirely out of sight—ask him if he did not want to go up on main road to git fireworks and we told him would first go to ant Susy's that she kep a shop we could get them cheaper. ask him if we did not keep givin him pieces of candy as we rode along. ask him if we did not go from your house west to Morton street and then south instead of going towards the depot on Washington lane as it has been stated in the papers these remarks we think are suficient to prove to yu that we are the men who took him if yu have received any other letters headed other than Ros or Mr. Ros they are forgeries, we have sent you 8 or 10 letters in all, if you had accepted the proposition we made yu some four weeks ago yu would now without doubt have yu child safe in yu own house but yu rejected the offer and left us without the means to negotiate with yu. do you want to daly along and keep your child month after month living in a place where the strongest Could not live over one year. we would not let him unnecessarily sufer but this exteriordary search has made it necessary to keep him where the light of the sun has never shown upon him since the 2d day of July. we have seen Charley about 4 days ago his whole cry is he wants Walter to come see him and he is afraid he wil not go to Atlantic City with his mother.

WALLING INTERPRETED THE KIDNAPPERS' REPETITIVE INSTRUC-
tions, pleading threats, and increasingly desperate tone as proof that
the police were closing in on an arrest. He wrote to Captain Heins on
August 24.

> I am more confident than ever that the parties, Clark and Mosher,
> alias Johnson, are the parties we want. I knew before receiving your
> letter that they were somewhere in this vicinity. Some one has let
> them know that they are being looked after, and that is the reason for
> their change of tone. They are frightened, and would, I believe, make
> terms very moderate, provided they could be assured of safety. There
> is no danger of their going to Europe; they have no money, and
> Mosher's wife and children would keep him here. Of this you can
> assure Mr. Ross, providing I am right as to the parties, and I have no
> doubt of it. I think it would be well for Mr. Ross to keep in commu-
> nication—if possible—with them.
>
> Yours, in haste,
>
> GEO. W. WALLING

Summoning Walter once again, the authorities asked him the questions listed in the latest ransom letter. He agreed with all of the kidnappers' answers except one: Walter insisted that the wagon did drive up
Washington Lane toward Germantown Avenue.

The press informed the public of telegrams sent, almost daily,
between Philadelphia and New York. They asked why the authorities

withheld correspondence from a city that responded emotionally to every false report of Charley's recovery. They also wondered why Mayor Stokley had been on vacation at the beach. The *Evening Bulletin* said the "management" needed to account for those decisions that disappointed the public.

> We refer to the absurd and reprehensible excess to which the attempt at secrecy has been carried, not so much, perhaps, by the police authorities, whose professional training has taught them when to be silent and when to speak, but by a little coterie of non-professionals who, for their own gratification or from an idea of, their superior sagacity, have injected themselves so skillfully into the management of this case as to have made the police of an almost secondary importance and authority.

The *Inquirer* agreed. The paper continued asking readers to place faith and money in private detectives. "County district attorneys cannot, unaided, contend with this demoralization. They need assistance from shrewd and experienced men above the class of township constables, men who know the ways of professional criminals, and know how to circumvent them." A private group of citizens heeded this advice when they obtained Christian's blessing and hired the Pinkerton Detective Agency. Immediately, the Philadelphia Pinkerton office offered a more specific reward than that of Stokley, Taggart, or the Pennsylvania Detective Bureau.

Abduction of Charlie Brewster Ross— ### $1,000 Reward

The above reward will be paid to the person who shall first discover and give information of the owner of the horse and buggy used in the abduction of Charlie Brewster Ross, and for information of the house where the abductors were stopping at the time of and previous to the abduction; or $500 will be paid for either of said specific information.

This approach made sense. After almost eight weeks, no detective, officer, or neighbor had traced the horse and buggy used for the kidnapping. Daily, Pinkerton would report its progress to a group selected by those who hired them.

The *Inquirer* applauded the decision to hire Pinkerton. It wrote that while "the wisest and most eminent of our citizens" had failed the investigation, Pinkerton had a reputation for solving crimes. Benjamin Franklin, a former chief of the Philadelphia detective corps and head of the Philadelphia office, printed more circulars with more detailed descriptions of Charley, the kidnappers, and the horse and buggy. Pinkerton sent the flyers to police stations, train stations, and public offices throughout the country in early September. They also sent a private memo to the nation's police officers and detectives; it listed confidential questions, answers, and identifying information to help investigators distinguish the real Charley from the field of lost children and con artists.

Who is your uncle on Washington Lane?—Uncle Joe.

What is your cousin's name?—Cousin Joe or Cousin George or Cousin Frank.

Who lives next door to pap?—Marcellus McDowell or Jennie McDowell.

What horse does mam drive?—Polly.

He can recite Jesus loves me, this I know, for the Bible tells me so.

He knows only "O" and "S" of the alphabet.

He will state his name as Charley Ross, but asked if he has another name, will say "Charles Brewster Ross."

He can give the names of his brothers Stoughton, Harry, Walter, his sisters Sophie and Mary, of Dr. Dunton, the family physician, and the name of his Sunday school teacher, Miss Mary Cope.

Privately, Christian asked his own set of questions.

"With whom is he?

"Are they kind to him?

"Do his childish eyes which knew nothing but home and home kindness see sights revolting?

"Is he closely confined, or has he been carried far away to avoid pursuit?

"Does he hear brutal language?

"Are the scenes about him so strange that his memory of us gradually fails, and his recollections of love, home and friends will all be swept away?"

Until this point, Christian had refused to release a photograph of Charley because he feared the kidnappers: their letters continued to warn him about cooperating with detectives, and if Pinkerton reprinted a photograph of Charley, they would know Christian had provided it. But perhaps the news about the Mosher brothers made Christian feel stronger, because he agreed to pass a picture of Charley along to Benjamin Franklin. The only one available had been taken when Charley was two, so an artist interviewed Sarah about her son's features and augmented the photo appropriately. This photo, along with pictures of Christian and Sarah, was mailed with the private memos.

The *Inquirer* asked its readers to contribute to the fund for Pinkerton's expenses. "Those who desire to aid in these renewed and promising efforts to recover the child of Mr. Ross through Pinkerton's Agency can do so by sending contributions to GEORGE PHILLER, Esq., President of the First National Bank, Philadelphia, by whom it will be acknowledged and judiciously applied." The request received immediate feedback. Judges, lawyers, and businessmen contributed along with those from humbler means. One response came from schoolchildren.

> ED. PHILADA. INQUIRER:—Papa has been telling us what you say in your paper about wanting money to pay detectives to find CHARLEY ROSS, and he says little boys who have got money should give some. We want CHARLEY ROSS brought home to his papa and mamma, and give these six dollars to help find him.
>
> Frank, Harry, John and Dana Chesterman.

The *Public Ledger* warned readers against wasting their money on private investigators who would most likely attempt negotiating with the kidnappers and asked why the criminals would endanger themselves by communicating with a third party. Privately, the advisers feared Pinkerton's involvement. As a chapter of Pinkerton's national bureau, Benjamin Franklin's office might expose the political motives behind their strategy, so instead of soliciting Franklin as a consultant, the paper compared all private detectives to the thief catchers of the past. In a way, they were.

While many law-enforcement officials continued to contract themselves out as thief catchers, the job had been most popular prior to the establishment of the organized police force in the 1840s. Even so, in the 1870s, only a few private detective agencies tried to protect their reputations by publicly distancing themselves from criminal association. Pinkerton was one of these agencies. The public assumed most other detectives—private and police—compromised their official work for their own financial gain. With the Centennial on the horizon, Mayor Stokley knew that in order to attract tourists to the city, its citizens needed to feel safer. And that wouldn't happen as long as editorials reminded them of police corruption and incompetence. Even if the Ross investigation lingered, he needed to find a way to promote a more positive civic image. In an effort to build the integrity of the force, Stokley authorized Chief Jones to release a statement to the press.

"I, Kennard H. Jones, Chief of Police, do hereby notify all citizens that the officers of this department forego any part or portion of said reward in favor of the person or persons who will communicate with me secretly or otherwise such information as will lead to the arrest and conviction of the abductors and restoration of the child."

KENNARD H. JONES, Chief of Police.

The papers acknowledged that the announcement represented an intention to follow Pinkerton's stance against criminal association. It didn't, however, stop the pens of writers who continued to accuse the mayor and Chief Jones of abdicating their authority to the Republican counselors. The *Evening Bulletin* challenged Mayor Stokley to free himself from the advisers' instructions: "The time has fully come for the Mayor and the police authorities to take such action as will make them the sole judges in this matter of public information." Even if this charge had pressured Stokley into asserting his voice, his police didn't have the time to engage in a power struggle with "the mysterious directorate." Correspondence piled onto the stacks of potential leads: across the country, con artists continued to lay claims to the reward, and even though out-of-state authorities conducted their own investigations, they often asked Philadelphia's force to come and confirm their suspicions. So many police detectives paid their own travel expenses that the *Evening Bulletin* suggested the mayor develop an expense account.

Although the paper was generally critical of police behavior, the *Bulletin* spoke highly at times of Captain Heins, a man they identified as "running after any and every shadow that gives the faintest trace of hope, seemingly never tiring, yet always returning with downcast countenance." One reporter obtained an interview with him at a train station in mid-August.

"Do you want to talk?" the reporter asked.

"No; what can I say? I've got nothing to talk about," Heins replied with a smile.

"Is there anything to look forward to?"

"Well, you know I am a very hopeful man. I can't give you anything definite, but I don't give the case up. I hope we will get down to something. I hope in God we will."

"Why cannot we publish the letters that have been received?"

"They are withheld because their publication would be of no avail."

"Are they in the possession of the police authorities?"

"No; Mr. Ross has possession of them."

"And he refused to allow of their publication?"

"Yes—at the advice of others."

"Is he advised by the police?"

"No. He is so advised by his own counselors."

The public could not condemn these "counselors" as much as the *Bulletin* and *Inquirer* demanded because they did not fully understand Christian's role in the investigation. They assumed he and the advisers were members of the same group, and therefore their attitude toward Christian affected their perception of the advisers. Initially, people's empathy for the Ross family excused reportorial anger aimed at the advisers because Christian was the figurehead of the search. Editorials criticizing the faceless advisers conjured images of the distraught parents, and readers could easily dismiss writers' civic frustrations as political statements. Yet as Pinkerton's search provided no real leads, this dynamic began to change. When readers began agreeing with criticism written about the advisers, Christian Ross, the public image at the forefront of the investigation, became a suspect. New York millionaire Arthur Purcell, the man who publicly offered to pay the ransom and negotiate the return of Charley, was one of the first to question Christian's integrity in the *New York Herald*.

> I advertised more than one month ago (July 26) for the immediate return to me of the boy Charley Ross, on certain conditions and for a stated reason. This I did in good faith. I did not, nor do not, propose to deal with second parties, police, detectives or the Ross family. I so stated, clearly. A full month has passed and I am not in receipt of any direct information. As I now have good grounds for doubting that any crime has been committed, and for believing that this affair will be officially compounded, I hereby withdraw the reward. I will not be duped by any official combination. As only detectives and confidence men have replied, I have no one to thank.
>
> ARTHUR PURCELL

On the one hand, Purcell's bitterness speaks from a wounded ego. He had said in July that his motive was to relieve the worry of his invalid wife. Had the kidnappers accepted his terms, they would have been $20,000 richer and Charley would be home. The public would have exalted Purcell as a model husband and an American idol. But the kidnappers didn't take his money. Purcell failed in his efforts to be a hero. His language, full of "I did," "I will not," "I have," asserted his control over the situation he created; faulting other parties for his botched efforts, Purcell channeled any criticism aimed at his withdrawal to speculation over Christian's honor. Instead of saving the day, he made it worse.

Still, his words reminded the public of one important question: Why hadn't the kidnappers taken Purcell's money? The millionaire had offered exactly what the kidnappers wanted, yet they refused it. Their rejection meant one of three things: the kidnapping was about more than money; Charley was dead; or the involved parties couldn't agree on how to proceed anymore. From what Walling and the police could determine from Gil Mosher, it didn't seem as though the suspects had a personal vendetta against Christian Ross; based on conversations they had with William Westervelt, they knew that Bill Mosher and Joseph Douglas were on the run from something. Whoever the kidnappers were, their ransom notes revealed various truths about Charley's language and health that they could know only with the passing of time. Investigators' instincts suspected he was still alive. So why did the kidnappers refuse Purcell's money? The only remaining logical answer was that they couldn't agree on how to end their crime.

Like Purcell, members of the public and the press turned on Christian because they felt like pawns. Somebody was manipulating their emotions by changing the rules of the game. When it began, the finish line was the ransom payment and the prize was Charley. Now, reward after reward later, this wasn't the case. The kidnappers weren't playing by the rules. The masters of the game had either lied or been replaced—regardless, people had a new unknown to process. Christian was the only player whose face they knew, so he became the target of blame.

Prior to Purcell's public withdrawal, the advisers had resumed their conversation with the kidnappers.

The *New York Herald*. August 26.
"John. He [Walter] denies the direction you give. I require conclusive proof. Send clothing to any point that you please, and advise."

NEW YORK. Sept 6—Your friends yu say ask for more proof that we ever had him they are as foolish as percell for he says you never lost him. your detectives have never had the slightest clue or trace of him since the our he was taken but in order to convince these sceptical friends that we had him and have him we will now give the detectives a small clue to work upon but it will serve no other end only to convince these sceptical friends or yours that we have him. on the night of 2d July at 11 o'clock we passed through Trenton, N.J. Charley lay in my arms asleep. after we had passed about 2 squares up bridge st Charley's hat drop off and we did not notice it until he woke up and asked for his hat we would not go back for it. you can get this hat by advertising for it there if it is not worn out. if it should be worn out you can find out who found one that night or the next morning.

this thing is drawing
to a final crises

PHILADELPHIA ENTERED THE FIFTH WEEK OF A DROUGHT IN September. Police forbade citizens from washing the streets or using fountains for anything but fire prevention. Dust followed customers into shops, and many storekeepers circled display tables, brushing dirt off of merchandise. In the country, twenty-four-hour watch patrols kept daily fires from ravaging the land, but many fences burned to the ground. Grain stalks withered, fruit ripened early, and brown grass aged the fields by two months. Farmers worried about a winter feed shortage and rising hay prices.

Neither the dry fall nor the Ross investigation postponed preparations. "The change from week to week at the Centennial grounds is almost magical," wrote the *Evening Bulletin*. "Every portion of the work is pushed forward with a celerity that will be apt to infuse confidence into the most timid and doubting in regard to the completion of the work long within the time specified."

Although Philadelphia was attracting more eyes than Stokley dreamed it would at the beginning of July, it was not all the kind of attention that the mayor desired. Crowds gathered behind a large fence on the exhibition grounds. Unlike the inaugural world's fair at London's Crystal Palace, Philadelphia's event would have more than one main building. It would have six. It would also be the first world's fair to dedicate an entire exhibition hall to the arts; Memorial Hall would hold only paintings and sculptures. Around the construction sites, people watched engineers and masons step around carpenter shacks and stacks of bricks, stones, and lumber. The artisans worked rapidly to build railroads so they could distribute the one hundred carloads of stone arriving daily from the Conshohocken quarries. Some of the sightseers, though, were there to find places where Charley Ross might be hidden. These Fairmount Park grounds caused Stokley enough trouble without his having to worry that they concealed a child.

Workmen were operating on schedule, but funds were not arriving as anticipated. The government's check, approved by Congress to cover 50 percent of the project cost, was delayed for unknown reasons. The Centennial Commission had planned on using the federal money to finance the first phase of construction; the absence of these funds threatened to delay these plans. Stokley did not want the Commission to postpone anything. Instead, the City Council agreed to advance a loan from the city budget provided that, when it arrived, the government check would immediately repay these funds. Stokley knew that this decision was a risky one. For Congress to approve its share of Centennial monies, Philadelphia had already needed to assume financial responsibility for the remaining 50 percent of costs. Whatever amount, then, the Centennial Commission could not raise by soliciting local donors and selling exhibit space, the city would have to cover. So far, hardly any of this money had been raised. The Commission needed to attract interest, and Mayor Stokley needed to find investors that would take a risk on the Centennial and pledge money to Philadelphia— where children disappeared, strangers were interrogated, and citizens invaded private space.

September's papers brought more stories of the missing. Readers speculated about connections between Charley's disappearance and the details in these reports.

A three-month-old baby disappeared from his home on Long Island after his former nurse failed to bring him home from an outing. After lingering around the family's property, the nurse, who had recently been fired, had obtained permission to take the infant on a two-hour sailing trip. She returned alone the next day, her arms covered in blood. The nurse said two men had blindfolded her, cut her arms, and taken the child before she could escape. The police did not believe her but could find no leads to disprove her story.

Police could also not find a three-year-old boy, son of a poor mountaineer, who had wandered away from his family's log cabin in western Pennsylvania. His mother had left the boy in a room when she took some of her six children to pick blackberries, and when she returned four hours later, he was gone. Her niece found a piece of the boy's clothes on the windowsill, underneath a window too heavy for him to lift on his own. Investigators thought he had walked outside and lost his way in the forest.

Near Washington, D.C., neighbors observed a British couple leaving a small boy with a family that lived in a remote cabin. Philadelphia sent two detectives to investigate. They thought the child's clothes resembled descriptions of Charley's and took the boy to a local police station. The boy further excited the police by telling them he had brothers and several sisters at his real home. Detectives traced his biological parents, who told them they were too poor to keep him and had asked friends to help take care of him. The *Evening Bulletin* said, "And if the fact that the boy has brothers and sisters is to be accepted as evidence that he is the lost child, the situation of vast numbers of small boys will become exceedingly solemn. The development of a detective with some other kind of a head than a wooden one would be a grateful occurrence at this juncture."

Townspeople in Orange County, New York, notified the local sheriff with suspicions that the esteemed David Henry Haight family hid a strange child inside their mansion. Because the town respected the family, and Mr. Haight was frequently out of town, officers ignored concerns. Further gossip prompted the sheriff to contact the Philadelphia police, who told him to visit Mrs. Haight. She introduced him to the boy, pointed to a gash on his head, and said a priest had taken him from an abusive Cuban home, where he had been tied to a bed and whipped with a buckle strap. The sheriff asked to speak with the boy privately.

"Where did you go from when you went away?" he asked.

"From Philadelphia," the boy replied.

"How did you go?"

"They took me in a wagon."

The boy stopped talking when Mrs. Haight reentered the room. The sheriff said he would return in the morning with a picture of Charley Ross, but by the next day, Mrs. Haight had decided not to cooperate. She ordered the officers to leave when they arrived at her door. Legal counsel for the police told them to leave the child alone until the priest returned. When he did, Father Kenney proved the boy was older than Charley. He also admitted to taking the child from an abusive home. The *Bulletin* complimented Philadelphia's force for finally identifying a lost boy. "Success in this inquiry may atone somewhat for the failures thus far chargeable upon the proceedings and search in the case of the Ross child."

Police also located Charlotte Wyeth, the little girl who was taken from the Newport, Rhode Island, beach in August. Passengers on a steamer to Providence recognized her and asked her female escort where she had met the child. The woman said she transported Charlotte by "order" of a man she called "Pa." "Pa" told police he had taken Charlotte because she was a little white girl in the company of Indian women. He said onlookers at the beach wished him "Godspeed" as he walked away with her.

The *New York Times* questioned why Philadelphia's force could uncover numerous leads in the cases of other lost children but failed to find an actual clue to Charley's disappearance in Germantown, a town about two and a half miles long, a mile and a half wide, and six miles away from central police headquarters. "The chief mystery in regard to the difficulty of discovering a clue in the case relates to the horse and buggy. Who owned them? Where did they come from?" While the *Evening Bulletin* was happy to criticize its own city's force, it again bristled at New York's condemnation. "If the New York detectives are so superior to our own, how comes it that they do not find Charley Ross, and pocket this handsome reward?"

Ninety miles north of Philadelphia, Superintendent Walling was trying to do just that. Unlike Philadelphia's police department, the NYPD released no statement disavowing their interest in individually collecting reward monies.

Walling bribed Westervelt's cooperation by promising him the reward money and police reinstatement. He also began regularly inviting Christian Ross to visit the Mulberry Street headquarters. Walling encouraged Christian with summaries of his conversations with Westervelt, telling him that the informant believed Charley was hidden somewhere along the train rails between New York and Philadelphia. Meanwhile, Walling's men followed Westervelt to Stromberg's bar and others in the Five Points. Their reconnaissance convinced them that they could trace and arrest Joseph Douglas more easily than Mosher. Walling told Christian that within forty-eight hours of an authorization from Philadelphia, Douglas could be in custody.

Christian didn't want this. He feared Mosher would hurt Charley and continue to hold him as a bargaining chip if Douglas was taken in. "In view of the threats contained in the letters of the abductors, that the life of the child would be taken in case one of their party was arrested, I [fear] to run the risk of having Douglas taken without Mosher being arrested at the same time."

"We will have them both," Walling replied. "We know them and will pursue them until we find them."

Captain Heins must have wondered why Walling had not been able to gather more information from his informant in a month's time and questioned Westervelt's involvement in the particulars of the case. Walling found himself defending the integrity of his spy, a man released from his own force earlier that year. He wrote Heins on September 11, finally sharing a lead from Westervelt.

DEAR SIR.—Since writing you this A.M., I have seen Westervelt; he says he knows nothing of the whereabouts of Mosher. He says Mosher lived in your city, about four months ago, on Monroe street, near 3d street, and that he had a stable between 3d and 4th streets, in some street name not known, but the third or fourth street from Monroe towards Washington avenue. The stable was an old wooden building with very large doors, and near 3d street; that a wagon answering to the description you gave me was in said stable at that time, and may be there yet, but probably not; that they kept in said stable a dark bay horse; but he is confident the horse has been sold, but does not know to whom. I showed him the drawing of the wagon you gave to me, and he says he could not make a better one had he it before him, except that he thinks his would not be quite so much rounded at the top.

Yours, etc., GEO. W. WALLING, *Supt.*

Heins pursued the lead on the stable. It was on Marriott Lane—right where Westervelt's directions had placed it—just before it was torn down. After a little probing, police learned that a man by the name of Henderson had rented a stall for a horse fitting eyewitnesses' descriptions of the kidnappers' horse. They had been unable to obtain this information when the stable was still standing because it had switched owners on July 1, the day Charley was kidnapped. During initial searches for the horse and wagon in early July, the new owner had claimed to have no information on the horse or men fitting the kidnappers' descriptions.

New York Herald. September 14.
"John—Hat not found. Am ready to pay sum demanded, but only through an attorney. He dare not betray you. Name one anywhere."

NEW HAVEN, Sept. 23—*Mr. Ros.*—we did not see yu last answer til to day. we was in new brunswic british province and cold not see the New York *herald* we went there to se if the law would permit us to make a symultaneous change with yu but we find no such change can be efected with safety to our selves. Mr. Ros we cannot show the child to yu and we cannot give you any more proof than we have; yu must expect this as the only alternitive left you to ransom him or murder him, for one or the other wil and shal take place before many days. Yu as his father have been mor cruel to him than we have. We told yu that his place of cencealment was such that no living being could find it and that it was not a fit place for any one to be in the length of time he has been there. We do not keep him there to punish him; your detectives have made it much worse for him than he would be had they not such a close search for him; he has kept his health wonderful considering his close confinement. We do not see him often or even hear from him. The last time we se him he had been ailing with pain from stoppage of urin he would go 24 and 30 ours without making water and then he would cry with pane when he would urinate, but his custodian got him som medicine which helped him. we tel yu positively Mr. Ros his hiding place must be his tomb unless you bring him out.

New York Herald. September 29.

"John, your terms are accepted. Name time between payment and delivery."

NEW BRUNSWICK. September 30. *Mr. Ros:* this is the way we propose to do, we will take him to some ministers house at night put a label on him stating this is Charley Ros take him immediately to 304 Market st phil or washington lane germantown yu will find a sufficient sum in his pocket to pay yu for yu trouble no reward will be paid. we have sent word to his parents stating where he is. Mr. Ros it is true yu have got tu rely entirely on our honor for the fulfilment of this part of the contract but you can rely with implicit confidence. bad as we are and capable of the blackest deeds yet we have some honer left. your large rewards have in a measure proved this there are 4 of us to divide the $20,000 among and either one of the 4 could went and got the whole amount to himself if he had been without principal.

others will rely on our word

THE LETTER OF SEPTEMBER 23 VERIFIED THAT THE KIDNAPPERS still had or had recently seen Charley. The authorities told Sarah that it mentioned Charley's difficulty urinating. Sarah said Charley had suffered from this problem for a while. When it occurred, she went to the pharmacist to get nitre (potassium nitrate), which alleviated the problem. Christian knew this meant Charley was in pain.

His desperation deepened. As the days lapsed, the newspapers indirectly attacked his manhood with their theories on why he wouldn't or couldn't pay the ransom. The war years strengthened women; society acknowledged this by recognizing their emotional tenacity while allowing them to mourn. Men were not afforded this balance. Society expected them to respect the 620,000 lives lost in the Civil War by asserting their masculinity. The taking of a child demanded universal shock and sadness, and the public responded with deep sympathy for the Ross family. Christian could of course mourn the loss of his son, but he knew that he was not alone in suffering loss.

Increasingly, reporters included Christian's failing health and worn nerves in their case updates. These descriptions, combined with accusations against the authorities and reports of the Lewis brothers' wealth, emasculated Christian Ross. The press was right—he didn't have a voice in his son's case. What they didn't know was that he was losing a voice in his household. Against Christian's wishes, one of his wife's brothers showed Sarah a ransom letter. And while Christian emphatically denied rumors claiming the Lewis brothers offered $10,000 to the kidnappers, they could afford to do so. He could not. Sleepless nights and anxious thoughts plagued Christian, and as he felt weaker, Sarah Ross became stronger.

Christian watched leads fade and claims turn to contradictions. Unclear on what path to follow next, he sought the advice of a German psychic in New York. Sarah had consistently consulted spiritualists throughout the case, and both Christian and the police had taken some of the psychic advice offered to her seriously. Until receiving an intriguing letter from this specific medium, however, Christian hadn't visited one himself. Such a trip may seem like a hypocritical one for a Methodist Sunday-school teacher to take, but the practice was popular in the Victorian era.

Spiritualism offered a literal "medium" between religion and science. The eighteenth-century Swedish mystic Swedenborg believed that God offered spirits as a vessel for communication between things mortal and immortal. His spiritual descendents applied their understanding of human physiology and natural philosophy to access the immortal world, using scientific inquiry to better understand, and not defy, religion. Spiritualists were fascinated with electricity, particularly with its effects on both the telegraph and the human nervous system. To thousands of Americans, it made sense that a human conduit could transport communication from the dead just like the telegraph could transport messages from one geographical area to another. Before the Civil War, groups of men and women met in circles around "planchettes," forebearers of the Ouija board, to converse with the dead. During the war years, the massive death toll led to the popularity of daguerrotypes, photographs of the dead believed to capture and preserve the spirits of the deceased. Survivors took comfort in these meetings, séances, games, and photos, believing that spiritualism, directed by God, engaged scientific principles to transmit important information between worlds.

Christian and a detective traveled to the neighborhood of the New York psychic. They knocked on her front door. Nobody answered. They then walked inside her entryway and knocked on another door. Nobody answered. The police officer entered the woman's residence and Christian heard a woman's voice.

"Get out of this, go into the next room, I'll soon be there," she said.

The men obeyed.

An old woman entered and sat across from Christian at a table. She spoke with a heavy German accent.

"You must believe there is a sympathy exists between you and your child. I propose to use that to bring him back," she said. "Do you believe I can do what I say?"

"No, but I would like to ask you some questions," Christian replied.

They talked until Christian was satisfied that she couldn't offer any new information. When he went home, he wrote a note thanking her for her concern.

Of the letters from spiritualists, Christian and Sarah separated the serious from the bizarre, one of which offered a German witchcraft recipe for finding Charley. Christian decided against killing a chicken, piercing it in several places while chanting, and burning it in the name of God. He also realized that most writers who alleged to offer "new information" had simply restated theories offered in newspapers.

What he couldn't understand was why public opinion began to turn against his wife and his son Walter.

Christian had tried to shield five-year-old Walter from reporters, gossip, and nosy inquisitors, but throughout the summer, he allowed private detectives and police investigators to continue probing his son's memory of July 1. Gradually, their suggestive questions confused details in the boy's mind, and his answers began to conflict. The *New York Herald* suggested Walter had been repeating versions of a story he was told to memorize and turned its suspicions more fully on to the activities and relationship of Christian and Sarah Ross.

The paper wondered whether Christian kept the ransom letters from Sarah because they accused her of immoral behavior or because they revealed a detail incriminating Christian as an accomplice—his business could, after all, certainly benefit from a $20,000 ransom payment. So could the Ross family. Had the press or the kidnappers spent time researching Christian's family finances, they could have easily learned that the net worth of Catherine Ross, Christian's mother, was only half of the ransom fee.

The *New York Herald* attacked Sarah more directly. "The parties

who actually made away with the infant have written long and vituper-
ative letters to the parent, abusing the mother to such a shameful extent
that the father is unwilling that the abuse should appear in print," the
reporter alleged. "To my mind," he continued, "this fact conclusively
proves that the parties who stole the child have a personal enmity
towards Mrs. Ross, and that they effected their diabolical purpose solely
to gratify a personal revenge against her."

Philadelphia's *Evening Bulletin* continued to rebut the theories
offered in New York newspapers. "We have not heard of anything being
accomplished by the Vidocqs of Gotham. The truth is that the criti-
cisms of the New York papers on the management of this distressing
case are mere idle and spiteful words, fed by correspondents either sent
or hired here to feed the New York gossip market with anything and
everything." For the most part, Philadelphia papers withheld attacks
on Christian's personal integrity yet blamed him for setting the pace of
a slow investigation. Had Christian immediately released his son's
name, the *Bulletin* said, he would have expedited reconnaissance
efforts. What it failed to realize, though, was that the police were at
fault for the slow initial progress. For the first twenty-four hours after
Charley's disappearance, they had dismissed Christian's fears; it was he
who had convinced them that a search was necessary.

Libel laws did govern newspapers: publishers averted them by having reporters insert phrases like "it is said" or "some believe" when
writing stories that read as editorials. Writers at the time did not have
bylines, so it wasn't possible for readers to know who wrote what; readers knew the names of publishers, and newspapers were defined by
political affiliation. It was not difficult, then, for writers to insert their
opinions within their prose. In 1874, new Pennsylvania legislature
redefined libel law, giving reporters even more room to stretch the
truth. Papers were allowed to publish any information designated "matter proper for public information, provided that the article, if libelous,
was not maliciously or negligently published." The Ross case tested
the apparent contradiction within this statute: how could "libelous"
information not be "maliciously" or "negligently" printed?

The challenge to this law appeared to come from one of Germantown's own. In September, a man identifying himself as "G" and a

neighbor of Christian's, published a letter entitled "Ross Case A Humbug" through the *Reading Eagle*, a paper located west of Philadelphia, closer to Christian's hometown of Harrisburg.

> The following is the theory of those who knew the family, and who are acquainted with Ross personally: Some months before the kidnapping Mr. Ross received letters from his first and only wife, asking and demanding the children. It will be recollected that even up to this time he has refused to show any of the letters he received, with the exception of the blackmailing note, and it will also be borne in mind the attempt was made to steal both children. It was not until three days after kidnapping that the fact was made public, and until that time the child was safely in the hands of its mother or her friends in the West. We think Mr. Ross knows now and always did know, where his child is, but refrained from making it public, for family matters. As regards the advertisements, the blackmailing note, &c, we think they are all forgeries, written either by Ross himself or his friends, intended to divert public attention from the facts."
> Signed G.

The following day, the *Inquirer* and the *Evening Bulletin* reprinted the letter, and by the end of the week, newspapers across the nation carried it.

Christian called these allegations "of a character to injure me in my said business and to blacken my reputation."

James V. Lambert, Christian's colleague and a well-known lawyer, came to his defense. "Were [the kidnapping] a humbug, would the Commercial Exchange of this city at one of its largest meetings have unanimously requested the Mayor to offer a large reward, which, however, under present laws could not be done?" He encouraged Christian to bring libel charges against the publisher of the *Reading Eagle*.

When he did, he learned that the article had not been generated from a neighbor, or one familiar with his family, or even from Germantown. The writer "G" was really named Milford N. Ritter. His father, William, one of the publishers of the *Eagle*, would be one of the two defendants on trial. According to Milford, he had learned about the

Rosses' marital problems from his mother, who had heard them from a neighbor at a tea party, who had said the story was "the common talk of Mr. Ross's neighbors" and told "in a store on Columbia Avenue, where women were passing in and out all the time." After writing down the gossip, Ritter gave it to an editor authorized to publish the paper's articles. Had the editor insisted Ritter change the format, and publish the tale as speculation, there wouldn't have been a problem; but by publishing it as a letter written by a Ross neighbor, an authority on the matter, the paper had incriminated itself.

All parties involved testified at the fall hearings. Except for Christian. From the witness stand, his doctor explained the absence. "He is in a very prostrate condition. He is unable to leave his bed. He has been in this condition since Sunday; the prostration is such that he is unable to concentrate his thoughts or express himself; his brain is affected to that extent. He has no recognized disease. He is very thin. He doesn't sleep naturally."

John C. Bullitt, a member of the city advisers, represented the Ross family. He questioned the neighbor who had spread the gossip at a tea party. She said she had only given her opinion of the Ross case when asked by a friend.

"I said I hardly knew what to say about it," the woman continued, "and then I said that it was reported in the city here that the present wife of C. K. Ross was his second wife, and that they had supposed here that the friends of the first wife had taken the child and sent it out to his wife and friends out West."

The bailiff swore in Sarah Ross.

"We have had seven children," Sarah said, noting the appearance of all but Charley in the courtroom. "I have no knowledge of any relation my husband could have with any other female which could account for the abduction of my child; he has been a very domestic man."

One of Sarah's brothers spoke as a character witness on Christian's behalf. "I have known Mr. Ross for thirty years or more," Henry Lewis said. "He was never married until he married my sister." Henry attributed only one flaw to Christian's character. "He is poor."

Milford N. Ritter admitted to authoring the slanderous letter and signing it anonymously as "G." The publishers of the *Reading Eagle* said that they had not known the article was untrue prior to publication. The prosecutor disagreed. In his closing testimony, he argued that the defense had failed to absolve their clients of "malicious intent," the only grounds on which they could be acquitted under Pennsylvania's state constitution.

The judge charged the jury to base its decision on the answer to one question: "Can an article containing the foulest aspersion upon the character of a citizen be considered proper for public information?" After deliberating for only a few minutes, the jury found the defendants guilty. The defense filed an appeal, but when the matter was closed, the publishers paid a $1,000 fine.

A guilty verdict did not keep America's newspapers from reprinting the slanderous letter. Papers did carry small summaries of the libel trial, but even the writer's confession failed to efface Ritter's salacious story from their minds. Americans joined the *New York Herald* in questioning why the kidnappers, whose actions were obviously premeditated, had selected this particular family. New rumors attempting to connect the kidnapping with Christian's failing business surfaced.

A guilty verdict also did not help Christian's mental health. The doctor told Sarah to keep him confined to bed until his condition improved. Sarah's brothers tried to calm Christian's anxiety over his reputation, but the daily interviews, vigorous denials, and constant disappointments had sapped him of his physical and mental energies. Powerless and feeble, he retreated to his mother's house. Christian would remain bedridden in central Pennsylvania for the next two months.

Sarah believed her husband would not fully regain his sanity until Charley returned to them. She asked her brothers to pay the full ransom amount.

New York Herald. October 7.
"John, the money is ready; state clearly and fully mode of payment and manner of delivery."

NEWBURG, N.Y. October 11.— Mr. Ros: You say the money is ready how is it then we can't come to a speedy compromise if yu was anxious to get yu child and wiling to pay yu money then there is no troble about it we are anxious to give him up but only on the conditions we have before told yu you ask again how we are to deliver him to yu we told yu in our last letter plainly how we would return him to yu is not that way satisfactory yu don't want us surely to turn him loose on the road at the ded our of night we wil never bring him to you personaly nor wil we ever take him to any one you appoint but we will take him to a strange family where it is least expected and where you will be sure to get him if the way of delivering him is not satisfactory to yu then we cannot come to terms for we are determined in delivering him to yu that no person shal see our face.

keep faith with us

SARAH ROSS'S ANXIETY, COMBINED WITH CHRISTIAN'S RAPIDLY declining health, worried Captain Heins. The kidnappers were closing in on a $20,000 deal, and if he didn't make an arrest soon, he probably never would. Although he didn't completely trust Walling, Heins's working relationship with the superintendent had strengthened throughout the fall months; Walling respected the captain's discretion in keeping the believed kidnappers' names from the press, and he regarded him as the head of Philadelphia's search efforts. Heins's quiet demeanor allowed him to communicate directly with Walling without updating the city leaders, but their determination to micromanage the case had temporarily weakened anyway.

Slow progress in the investigation had turned the advisers' attention back to Centennial preparations. To the dismay of the city council, local merchants appeared uninterested in financing the exposition. The national government had not yet released a promised check to help cover construction expenses, and the planning commission needed investors to help defray the hundreds of thousands of dollars in costs. The *New-York Advertiser* gave one explanation for the lack of support: "profound and prevailing apathy has discouraged all attempts to procure money or sympathy here." So far, Philadelphia had diagnosed New York's "apathy" as jealousy, an opinion which had certainly not helped them solicit funds. The western states had pledged quick support through exhibitions, but if the city was going to keep from going into greater debt, then it needed to stop worrying about its pride and humbly ask other eastern cities for money. New York papers said the burden was on New England to show more Centennial support. "What is most desirable now is that Massachusetts and her sister States should enter into the spirit of the enterprise, and help, as they can without hardship, to make it creditable in the eyes of the world." Like New York City, Boston had felt the sting of the honor bestowed upon Philadelphia. "It is time now that the doubt will be settled," the *New-York Advertiser* wrote. "We earnestly hope it will be settled as Massachusetts would have wished to have it if Boston had been selected instead of Philadelphia for the grand commemoration."

Trying to handle the problem internally, the Centennial Commission targeted local business support through regional celebrations, including one for the fiftieth anniversary of the Franklin Institute. Fifty years after two mechanics proposed the idea at a town meeting, the "Institute" had presented twenty-six showcases of the mechanical arts, but it had no building of its own. The anniversary event, lasting six weeks from mid-October through mid-November, featured displays of light fixtures, textile fabrics, cabinetry, tools, instruments, and the soda fountain of Robert M. Green, the man who presented America with its first ice-cream soda on one particularly busy day. The exhibition earned the Franklin Institute almost $60,000, enough for a committee to begin scouting properties for a year-round exhibition building in Center City.

The press praised the police for maintaining peace during the showcase. They had patrolled corridors, watched out for pickpockets, accommodated weary visitors by setting up benches, and established order in the lines of those waiting outside to purchase tickets. In fact, the authorities were so busy keeping the peace that they may not have been as vigilant in criminal profiling as they had been over the past few months. Bill Mosher was a criminal, but he was also a professional artisan. He and Joseph Douglas could have very well been two of the thousands who had strolled through the main hall, perusing displays, tools, and inventions that celebrated craftsmanship. If Westervelt was to be believed, and William Mosher had successfully traveled back and forth to Philadelphia unrecognized in the aftermath of Charley's kidnapping, a popular festival commemorating the mechanical trades would have been hard for him to ignore.

* * *

As Heins continued pursuing the clues offered by William Wester-velt and Superintendent Walling, the advisers turned their attention to transforming Philadelphia's image from a violent, industrial metropolis into a clean, cultural haven. The *Evening Bulletin* wrote, "The condition of the streets will be marked by everyone, and comparisons will be made with other cities in this country and abroad. Nothing will tend more to make the city inviting and create a favorable impression among visitors than a neat and tidy condition of the public highways." The city planners authorized funds for street cleaning machines, solicited bids for repairing roads and installing streetlamps, and encouraged cit-izens to remove garbage from the streets. Police spread circulars with "No Refuse Allowed" throughout town and worked to contain street violence.

Nevertheless, throughout the fall months, brawls spilled from saloons onto sidewalks. A group of men in one corner bar beat a bar-tender when he ordered them to stop smashing full-pint glasses with empty bottles. Street thugs fought one another with blackjacks and brass knuckles. They beat a seventy-five-year-old man to death, nearly kicked a "feminine-looking" man to death, attacked women, shot one man in the eye, another in the throat, and assaulted officers for arresting their friends for rape. Police locked up twelve-year-olds who threw stones at windows, a fireman who threw a cat into a furnace, an angry drunk who stabbed a fellow drinker in the head, and the proprietresses of three brothels, their female employees, and their gentlemen guests.

As updates on Charley Ross's disappearance slipped from the papers, the story of Mary Elizabeth Carton, another abandoned child, enraged the public. In Kensington, the neighborhood where Walter had been abandoned by the kidnappers, Mary's father, Francis Carton, had stumbled home drunk one night and beat his wife to death in front of two of their six children—ten-year-old Mary and a ten-month-old infant. By the time Mary was called to testify at the murder trial, her father's family and two of her own brothers claimed that neighbors and police had misinterpreted the crime scene. Police had, in fact, kept Mary under close supervision at a neighbor's house, fearing that her family members would kidnap her before her testimony. While Mary waited for the trial, her father sent Mary and the neighbors threatening letters.

The district attorney angered the public when he charged Francis Carton with second-degree murder. He said the state could not ask for more because Carton did not use a weapon. The *Evening Bulletin* said, "It is true that the use of a deadly weapon presumes the deliberate intent to commit murder. But is it equally true that the absence of a deadly weapon presumes that there was no such intent?" It warned of the consequences should the judge agree with the prosecutor's decision. "If so, it will be quite an inducement to murderers to practice the art of manual and pedal murder, and so keep themselves safe from the gallows." The judge supported the district attorney's decision; he attributed the charge not to the absence of a weapon, though, but to Carton's intoxicated state at the time of the murder. After Mary's testimony, the jury found Francis Carton guilty and the judge sentenced him to eleven years and six months in prison.

Reporters reminded the City Council that they had less than two years to transform Philadelphia's reputation for ineffective policing. "Foreigners will judge the nation by what they see in Philadelphia." But instead of giving stronger punishments to violent offenders, the city fathers ignored the papers' warnings and focused their efforts on patching the town's aesthetic flaws. As workers built and street cleaners tidied, foreign ministers across the globe received invitations beckoning them to visit Philadelphia and reminding them to reserve exhibition space for their own countries. When potential investors continued to withhold pledges, the city planners decided to recruit more aggressively and widely. A fund-raising delegation traveled to Massachusetts hoping to capture Boston's interest with the council's grand plans. If successful, they could count on the rest of New England and a jaded New York City to follow Boston's lead.

your substitute

MARY WESTERVELT, WILLIAM'S WIFE, WAS GROWING INCREASingly frustrated with her husband's unemployment. Not only were she, her husband, and their two children renting two rooms in a tenement, but throughout the fall, her husband's sister Martha Mosher and her four children had been sharing the space. Mary Westervelt had not realized her sister-in-law's family would be moving into her home until they showed up at her doorstep before 7:00 A.M. on August 20, two days after they had left Philadelphia. Mary resented their presence. Although the Moshers had accommodated her own family earlier in the year when her husband had lost his job, their home had been larger, and Mary and her children had had their own room.

Two months after her in-laws moved in, Mary and her family had to leave their two-room apartment and move into a cheaper tenement where they could afford an extra bedroom. Mary grumbled about the location. To help make rent, which was one dollar more a week, she worked as a seamstress.

Meanwhile, Westervelt indirectly directed the NYPD force of 2,500 men where to look for Mosher and Douglas. Westervelt advised Walling to keep an eye on Smith and McNeal's, a restaurant the kidnappers frequented. He directed him to investigate the Astoria ferry, where the men could fish for food. He told him about a boating trip he had recently taken with the kidnappers; after they had traveled upriver to a venue called Rondout, Westervelt said, Mosher had asked him to accompany them on future burglaries. He described the kidnappers' clothes, their fishing poles, and the type of bag they carried. Following

Westervelt's directions, one officer replicated the journey to Rondout in search of the kidnappers.

Westervelt also accompanied his sister Martha Mosher on trips to Five Points. There, she often visited Madame Morrow on Houston Street, where her husband sometimes met her. Sometimes Westervelt and/or Joseph Douglas joined their brief meetings. Westervelt continued to frequent the usual haunts, neighborhoods, and shops he had come to know well as a police officer. One day in late October, Joseph Douglas entered a store on Broome Street and asked for Westervelt. A young man in the building mistook Douglas for an plainclothes police officer.

"What does Walling want with him?" he asked.

The question startled Douglas. He ran out of the store and told Westervelt about the encounter.

For the first time, William Westervelt realized the police were following him. He threatened to cease contact with Walling and blamed the superintendent for his financial frustrations. He reminded Walling that he was betraying his own sister's husband and his own sense of loyalty, and that despite several weeks of working as an informant, he had received neither Mayor Stokley's reward nor his job back on the force. Walling told him that despite his best efforts, he didn't think the police commissioners would let him back on the force. Privately, the superintendent feared losing his contact. Police officers, detectives, and neighbors across America and Europe had failed to find Charley Ross, and he, George W. Walling, had contact with the only lead in the investigation. He tried to assuage Westervelt by finding him a temporary job as a streetcar conductor.

Walling placed great hope in the specific details Westervelt offered. He was confident that any day, his officers would, through these leads, find and arrest the kidnappers and deliver Charley Ross in heroic fashion to his grieving parents in Germantown. If this were to happen, Walling would have begun his career as superintendent by cracking one of the nation's toughest cases. Unless Sarah Ross's brothers were to pay the ransom. Then, the child would be returned on the kidnappers' terms, and he would have no glory. On October 22, Walling warned Heins against negotiating.

Dear Sir:—I saw my informant last night he says that we are surely on
the right track, but they [the kidnappers] have hopes of getting the
child redeemed, and he has not been able to find where it is. I think
any arrangements made with the kidnappers for the restoration of the
child would be a public calamity; no child would be safe hereafter if
it had parents or friends who could raise money. I am confident that
I shall get the guilty parties and the child at some time not far distant,
provided no compromise is made with them.

    Very respectfully yours, etc

        GEO. W. WALLING, Superintendent

Again, Heins cooperated with Walling while suspecting Westervelt's intentions. Through Walling, Heins learned that the kidnappers
had resumed their criminal habits in order to support their lives on
the run. He knew they were steering a green skiff around New York's
harbor at night, sometimes mere feet from police boats searching for
them.

The deep, sheltered New York Harbor provided numerous hiding
places. Fishermen and traders navigated hundreds of miles of inlets,
streams, and channels near the city by day; burglars such as Mosher
knew how to steer the maze of waterways in the dark. Using a small
boat, thieves would sneak onto the shores of communities in New
Jersey, Long Island, or Westchester, rob stores or homes, put their
goods in the boat, and take off. If they couldn't reach their "fencing"
destinations by daybreak, they would hide the stolen property somewhere along the water until they could return for it another night.
That way, if eyewitnesses had spied their boat at the scene of the
crime, the police would find nothing when they later searched it.
Mosher had grown up playing hide-and-seek with the police. It would
make sense for him to move Charley, one more stolen good, among his
best hideaways.

Walling rented a steam tug, and Heins sent Detective Wood
from Philadelphia to join New York's Detective Silleck, Gil Mosher,
and another officer on a twelve-day reconnaissance of this territory.
Detective Silleck was known among his peers as a former "sea-
faring man" who "knew all about coasting." The group deferred to

his judgment as a navigator. The foursome traveled up the Hudson River to Poughkeepsie, moving ashore to interview squatters and to scout islands, woods, small towns, and little houses. They looked around Newburg, where the last letter had been posted. They poked around the East River, observing the wharves near the entrance to Long Island Sound. In a report he gave at the end of the trip, Detective Wood said they had "searched thirty or forty islands in the Sound, containing from four to five acres to a hundred acres each." He also said that Gil Mosher had uncovered many potential hiding places.

Heins continued to wonder why William Westervelt, a man who made no pretense of hiding his grudge against the police, would cooperate in an investigation against his own brother-in-law. Westervelt's details were entertaining, but they had not yet been instrumental in providing the police with any concrete evidence—certainly no more than Walling's men had learned through their undercover work in Five Points. Heins agreed to keep contributing time, money, and resources to Walling's theories, but he didn't trust Westervelt enough to fully interfere with the Ross family's decisions.

Walling recognized Heins's hesitation, and as he had done before, shared enough information about Westervelt's statements to keep the captain involved in his plans. He sent a telegram to Philadelphia on October 28.

> —Yours of yesterday received. On Monday night Clark alias Douglas went to where they used to meet, but found the lager beer saloon closed. He inquired for Westervelt. I heard it yesterday morning, and about an hour afterwards Westervelt came and told me Clark had been inquiring for him. Of course I did not tell him I knew it; so I think Westervelt has kept faith with me.
>
> Yours, etc.

Heins agreed with Christian Ross's earlier position on Douglas. The kidnappers' letters revealed insecurities that could trigger their threats against Charley's life at any moment, so in Charley's best interest, Douglas should be left free until the police could arrest Mosher as well.

Walling's continued confidence, however, made enough of an impression on Heins for him to encourage the Ross/Lewis family to postpone negotiations. He told them that he believed the New York Police would soon catch the kidnappers.

The family disagreed. Dismissing the better judgment of the authorities, the Ross camp decided to make the exchange as quickly as possible, regardless of the kidnappers' refusal to simultaneously trade Charley for the money. Only there was another problem. The kidnappers had said they would only deal with Christian, and he could not get out of bed.

New York Herald. Oct. 28.
"John, too sick to take journey. Will relative answer?"

PHILA Oct 31 Mr Ros if you have any relation or friend that you can delegate to this important bisines then we are ready to deal with him we care not who he may be if it be mr hines or the states attorney—we are willing to negociate with him but mr Ros we want you not to deceive yourself in this bisines for we tell you plainly his acts will involve the life or death of your child we shall regard him as your substitute in every particular and hold the life of your child responsible for his actions. send your substitute to New York tuesday 3rd november with the means to settle this bisines. your substitute on arriving in new York must put a personal in *herald*. say. John i am stoping at ____ hotel with his name in full.

New York Herald. November 3.
"John, change address of personals. Relative will not sign his name in full."

NEW BRUNSWICK, November 3—*Mr. Ros*. it looks very strange to us that you should quible about the name to address us. is your object to keep the detectives informed of our whereabouts by having us writing you so often. by the by we could tell you much about them but our place is to keep mum and yours to investigate before you give more money out. it makes us jealous to see you pay out your mony foolishly when they can give you nothing in return but a parcel of fabricated lies. —and if you want your child safe and sound this is the final day of salvation. this address will do (John Johnathan is stopping at so and so. Johnathan or who he may be must not leave the hotel till he hears from us. if you mean square bisiness have your personal in Friday's *Herald* (N.Y.) and be in New York on Saturday morning.

a parcel of fabricated lies

WILLIAM STOKLEY ANTICIPATED A WIN ON ELECTION DAY, Tuesday, November 3, 1874. The mayor's run for a second term didn't get much press, even though victory would mean a raise for him when many of his constituents were out of work. In spite of recent articles reminding the public that the Republican advisers kept Stokley on a tight leash, the mayor had remained popular enough to keep his reelection bid from becoming a contest. This didn't mean that he or the machine had nothing to worry about.

The Republican party was changing. Under Grant's watch, Lincoln's messages of liberty were overshadowed by motives of industry. The Democrats, while still unfriendly to freed slaves, identified themselves more with the working man. During the next two decades, both parties become allied with those interests that would define them for generations.

In 1874, America was entering the sixth year of Grant's presidency, and while ambitious supporters predicted a third term, others were not so sure. People weren't happy. The Civil War death toll hung over the middle and lower classes. Unemployment numbers were high. Racial and ethnic tensions ignited riots. Critics spoke of the president's inability to reunite the country.

Of Philadelphia's Republican ticket running that fall, only the district attorney faced early, strong opposition from the Democrats. Stokley and his advisers knew the people would speak through this high-profile contest. By overthrowing the incumbent, voters could more immediately show their frustration with city government and threaten tighter municipal competitions for the spring. Throughout the country, the machine anticipated the results of races like that of Philadelphia's district attorney, aware the verdicts would be harbingers of things to come.

Pennsylvania Republicans pushed every member to vote for every party candidate, regardless of one's personal frustration with any incumbent. Capitalizing on unemployment fears and industry investments, they emphasized the Democrats as "a movement against American industry" that did not acknowledge "the doctrine of protection." If Democrats had their way, the Republican papers said, they would repeal tariff laws, allowing foreign products to enter the country—just as easily as feared foreigners. "If the wall is broken down so that British goods can enter free, the industries of this State will be paralyzed, the mills will be closed, hundreds of thousands of workmen will be permanently unemployed, the merchants among whom these men spend their earnings will be ruined, the capital which gives them work will be locked up and made unprofitable, and incalculable injury will be done to business in all its departments."

Philadelphia Police expected political tensions to escalate into fights at voting locations, just as they had on election days past. Chief Jones prepared two omnibuses full of officers ready to respond to any distress signals.

No such messages arrived. In addition to cracking down on fraudulent votes, the election reform of 1874 had led to more voting locations—which meant less people at each station—and to different tallying procedures, which meant delayed results and the potential for fewer angry mobs.

By 7:00 P.M., bonfires flickered into the darkening sky. Hundreds gathered in the news district, waiting around Independence Hall for the returns. Telegraph lines communicated results between state offices in Harrisburg, the Mayor's office, and the Union League. Hours passed, and when people walked home around 11:00 P.M., at least one Democratic parade partied through the streets. Paperboys grabbed their stacks later than usual the next day and began reciting the headlines. The district attorney had lost.

Nationally, Democrats had gained control of the House of Representatives, denying Republicans their long-held Congressional rule. The *New York Herald* attributed all blame to the President and his failed

Reconstruction plans. "General Grant . . . has surrendered a precious political inheritance."

The *New York Evening Post* refused to acknowledge the results as a Democratic victory. "The Democrats, as a national party, offered the people only one thing. They had no policy to submit. They had no record on which they could ask the people to trust them. They had no carefully matured or coherent measures for the future better than or materially different from Republican measurers. They did offer one thing—a change. The people took the change; they did not take the Democrats. Whether they will take them remains an open question."

Back in Philadelphia, Mayor Stokley read the signs of the changing political tide. They wouldn't affect his promised raise, but they did threaten his political advancement beyond a second term as mayor. Stokley needed to assure the machine of his political capital; at the same time, he needed to convince the press and the voters that he wasn't a pawn. If he was not savvy enough, these goals would contradict each other, and he would look weaker.

What the mayor needed was to become a character in a high-profile story. Something that he could control—better yet, save from possible disaster. Something that would accent his strengths and ensure his legacy.

The year 1874 gave Stokley two such stories: the Charley Ross case and the rapid approach of the Centennial. Both had given him some merit of success, but his police had botched the search for Charley. As a result, they had defaulted the now-famous investigation to the New York Police, rendering themselves impotent in the press. The mayor had earned some praise for offering a reward, but that was only after public pressure—and it too had led to nothing; if anything, it would probably end up in the hands of the New York authorities. Stokley needed to do what he could to maintain a professional presence in the case, yet simultaneously distance himself from it. Otherwise, any blame for its eventual failure—especially if it rendered a dead child—could very well fall on him. The Centennial offered him the perfect distraction.

The celebration's finances were in trouble, but the engineers were good and the grounds had been attracting positive attention. In their coverage of early July events, the press had portrayed Stokley as the overseer of Centennial plans, allying his image with the upcoming party. By throwing himself into preparations, the mayor could work the machine's political connections and fight for the financial recognition of New York and New England. He could stake his reputation on this. For such an image campaign to work, however, the press needed to concentrate more on the successful Centennial plans than on the flawed Charley Ross investigation.

Luckily, the mayor had the connections to make this happen.

New York Herald. November 6.

"John, you must change the name of John for personals. It has become too well known."

PHILA., Nov. 6.—*Mr. Ros:* we told you in the last positively we would not write you any more. this dozing about puts us to no small amount of trouble we had left phila for New York thinking you were ready to close up the business. we told you positively procrastination is dangerous. had we accomplished what we have been fishing for the last three months your child would now have been dead but we have not yet caught the fish we wanted. yours is but a small item compared with something else. Walter said you owned the two new houses right opposite you or we should never troubled you. Mr. Ros you have asked to keep this negotiation a secret between ourselves it is a wise policy in your doings not that we fear being traped in our own game. This is positively the last from us. if you are sincere you would be anxious to settle this business if you regard the life of your child. we mean to fulfil every promise we made you in good faith. the result depends entirely with yourself whom you appoint to transact this business for yu we want at least two days notice before you come to New York for we may be 500 miles off and we ask for time to get there yu can say tuesday no 10. Saul of Tarsus. (choose your own name say i will be stoping so and so all day. do not leave the hotel wherever you may be stoping for one minute during the day). this thing must come and shall come to a close in a few days.

we ask for time

THREE MONTHS AFTER THEY WERE HIRED, PINKERTON HADN'T produced any substantial leads on the case. The private detectives had frequently been meeting with the men who had hired them, but they weren't frequently communicating with the police. Instead of working together to find Charley, the two groups were competing against each other for recognition and reward monies.

At home on Washington Lane, Sarah Ross did what she could to run her household and keep the press from her five children without the help of her husband. In mid-November, the number of visitors had subsided. Letters still arrived daily, but the family didn't come into contact with as many strangers or gawkers on the property as they had in the early weeks of the investigation. Still, the police continued to patrol the street regularly.

Sarah's neighbors did notice one particular man lurking on Washington Lane. Privately, they wondered what he was doing there. He didn't seem to speak with anybody. They thought he could be either stalking the Ross house, or connected with yet another string of robberies in the area, or both. Sarah noticed him also. She waited until she saw him more than once before contacting Officer Frank Eldridge. Eldridge spoke with Sarah's neighbors and developed a clearer picture of the man and his haunts. Before long, he made an arrest. When Eldridge took the suspect to the Germantown station house, he learned that the man's name was R. W. Petty. Petty identified himself as a Pinkerton detective.

The Lewis brothers, meanwhile, wanted to protect their sister and her family from further harassment and fear. In Christian's absence, they attempted to turn the case back into a private family affair, just as the kidnappers had intended. They informed Sarah and the authorities in New York and Philadelphia that whether or not the advisory committee approved, they would be contacting the kidnappers according to the instructions in the latest letter.

But the kidnappers did not see a message addressed to them in the paper on Tuesday, November 10, as they had asked. Because both parties involved could not agree on exchange details, Walling and Heins had more time to convince the family not to make a trade. Walling especially welcomed yet another delay, confident that the kidnappers were running out of options and would soon get caught. He told Captain Heins that he hoped Douglas would betray Mosher in exchange for leniency.

> November 12, 1874
> The parties are hard up and have come to the end of their tether.
> We are pushing them so hard that they dare not get out to do anything.
> I don't think Douglas will squeal unless we can get hold of him.
> > Yours, etc.,
> > GEO. W. WALLING, Superintendent

Walling refused to believe that he had spent his contacts, time, and funds in vain. He summoned Westervelt and questioned him once again, this time mentioning the kidnappers' latest contact name—Saul of Tarsus.

If Mosher and Douglas show up on the day the family names, Walling told him, they will receive their money.

Walling then tried postponing this "day" by encouraging Heins to intimidate the family.

> DEAR SIR.—Please see Mr. Lewis and say to him that I think it dangerous for parties to meet relative to any negotiations for the child, with a large amount of money, unless they have some officers within call, as the parties might be disguised, and in case the villains were to fail in making terms, they might take desperate chances to obtain the money.
> > GEO. W. WALLING, Superintendent

The Lewis brothers waited a few more days for the police to make an arrest. On Monday, November 16, they placed an advertisement in the Herald.

Saul of Tarsus. Fifth Avenue Hotel, Wednesday, the 18th inst. All day.

F.W. LINCOLN

Henry Lewis and his son Frank took the train to New York on November 17. They arrived at the Fifth Avenue Hotel in the afternoon and registered under the name F. W. Lincoln. They held a satchel carrying $20,000, divided into one- and ten-dollar bills. Neither man left the room that day or the next. The night of the eighteenth, they walked another personal advertisement to the *Herald* office.

New York Herald. November 19.
"Saul of Tarsus. We have performed our part to the letter, you have broken faith; we will have no more trifling; action must now be simultaneous."

Walling sent an officer to arrest Westervelt on Thursday, November 19. He confronted him in a private room at police headquarters on Mulberry Street, reminding him that he had staked his reputation on his faith in Westervelt's cooperation. Walling accused Westervelt of double-crossing him by using police intelligence to warn the kidnappers of a possible ambush at the Fifth Avenue Hotel.

Westervelt maintained his innocence.

Walling demanded to see a memo pad that Westervelt kept on his person. Previously, he had seen the name "Saul of Tarsus" written on one of its pages.

Westervelt handed it over.

Walling flipped through the little book. He found no incriminating evidence. Instead of releasing Westervelt, he stalled by inviting him to dinner. As he ate, Westervelt complained that he was going to be fired from his job as a driver on the Eighth Avenue line because he had been arrested at work. Walling agreed to write to his employer and ask for leniency on Westervelt's behalf.

PART THREE:

"dead men tell no tales"

(DECEMBER 1874)

dead men tell no tales

ON THE EVENING OF DECEMBER 13, JOSEPH DOUGLAS WALKED toward a cemetery on Second Street, blocks away from the Bowery in Manhattan. For nearly four months, the police forces of two cities, the Pinkerton Agency, and hundreds of amateur detectives had attempted to track his movements through these misty streets. Plainclothes officers drank in Douglas's favorite saloons, ate at his favorite restaurants, and watched the lodging places of his rumored associates. They often saw him. Several men could have apprehended him several times but for Superintendent Walling's orders. Again and again, Walling had repeated instructions to inspectors, who carried them to captains, who told sergeants, who informed their men roving the area around the Five Points in groups. *Douglas must not be touched. Douglas must be left alone until he takes us directly to Bill Mosher. The location of the child is secondary to the arrest of Mosher.*

For nearly a decade, Douglas had accompanied Mosher on enterprises both criminal and legitimate. They had even gone to prison together for the botched burglary in Red Bank, New Jersey. The arrest scared Douglas, so after Mosher cut through a prison wall and escaped, he had separated himself from his mentor, finding a respectable job as a streetcar driver in Brooklyn. Two and a half years later, two years before the kidnapping, he had learned that a man with a funny nose had been asking for him at his workplace.

Mosher began coming around so often that Douglas's colleagues nicknamed him "Nosey." The boss noticed Nosey and Douglas whispering when they were together, and soon, Douglas, one of his finest workers, quit. Douglas moved to South Philadelphia, where Bill and Martha Mosher had rented a home under the name "Henderson" on Monroe Street. Mosher took odd jobs and handled the room rentals, and Martha took care of the children. Once Douglas came to live on Monroe Street, the men spent days driving around the suburbs and the Pennsylvania countryside in a wagon painted red. It was full of Bibles, moth preventative, roach poison, secondhand furniture, bedbug poison, picture frames, and a stove polish that Mosher had concocted. One June day, they visited the oak-lined streets of Germantown to peddle their products. A few weeks later, they returned to steal Walter and Charley Ross from their father's front lawn.

Douglas arrived at the cemetery before 9:00 P.M. on December 13. He stepped into the shadows. Another cold winter had hit New York, and Philadelphia still held a $20,000 bounty over the kidnappers' heads. So far, hatred of the police had kept the lips of bartenders and rival criminals shut, but Douglas knew somebody would talk soon, and he was far from his promised ransom cut. After thirteen ransom letters and two botched meetings, Mosher hadn't made the exchange with Christian Ross's family. He had almost made the exchange nearly a month before, at the Fifth Avenue Hotel on November 18, but Westervelt had warned him away. Walling had told Westervelt the kidnappers would get what they wanted if they made the exchange on the day appointed by the Ross family; reading between the lines, Westervelt thought he recognized a police trap and warned Mosher to abandon the meeting. Since then, neither party had scheduled another meeting, and now Walling suspected Westervelt.

On the one hand, Douglas could cut his losses and flee the country, but on the other, if he wanted to maintain his reputation in the criminal community—the only community that would give him work once this was finished—he couldn't sell Mosher out. Douglas waited in the shadows of the cemetery. Even if he had wanted to turn himself in, it was too late to strike a financial deal. Gil Mosher had snitched on his own brother back in July, and he still hadn't received any of the reward money. Douglas knew he had to continue following Mosher's advice, roam the streets alone, and steal to pay for food and lodging until he could figure out his own escape route. He could potentially convince the police to offer him immunity in exchange for Mosher, but Douglas couldn't openly ask for favors. He needed a broker: somebody the police already trusted, somebody he could maybe blackmail into protecting him. At 9:00 P.M., he saw a figure coming toward him. Douglas stepped from the shadows and joined William Westervelt for a walk along the Bowery.

The men stopped at a saloon for oysters. Then they walked a few blocks west to Broadway, and Douglas reminisced about his childhood days in the neighborhood. They passed rows of tall, boldly colored mansions on either side of the street. Five- and six-year-old beggar children tried to sell flowers for pennies. Young girls—many of whom were already prostitutes and blackmailers—wore old shawls and sold fruit, candies, and peanuts from oversized baskets. Douglas and Westervelt walked north on Broadway toward Bleecker Street and stopped at Hunt's saloon for coffee. It was almost midnight. The men turned off of Bleecker Street and walked back toward the dirty, drab tenements along the Bowery. But instead of turning south toward Five Points, they continued east toward the bay. Lights vanished and shadows disappeared. Prostitutes lured customers down the dark alleys. Many mornings, the harbor police pulled floating, mangled corpses from the river. Westervelt turned to go home, but Douglas feared continuing alone. "Come down as far as the ferry," he asked.

Newsboys tried to pass off their last papers and walked through trash-filled yards, headed to gambling games in saloons or lodging houses, brothels riddled with venereal disease, a night's sleep on top of steam gratings. When Douglas reached the corner of South and Catherine Streets, Westervelt mentioned that he often visited this block on Sunday mornings to buy fish. Douglas told him he could do so the next day, which was a Sunday, if he stayed with him overnight at Vandyke's, a nearby hotel. Westervelt agreed.

Douglas awoke at 6:00 A.M. He and Westervelt made plans to meet again in a few days, and Douglas walked down Catherine Street alone. He and Mosher had a plan to burglarize summer homes along the Long Island Sound, and later that day, they had gone over their plans. They would use a black cat-rigged sailboat that Mosher had built for a man from Bridgeport, Connecticut, when he was in prison. The man had paid the authorities $150 for it, and Mosher was so proud of his work that he tracked the boat down and stole it after he was released. The police found it in Boston Harbor and returned it to its owner, who made sure his last name, "Wilmot," was branded in several places on the boat. Two months after the Ross abduction, Mosher stole it again. Although most river pirates would have carved off the brandings and disguised the vessel as another craft, Mosher did not. Instead, he spread newspapers over the markings.

Douglas joined him by 9:30 P.M. The water was choppy as they steered for a half hour to Bay Ridge, a bluff covered by woods along the Long Island shore. Strong winds blew through the trees and the fields. A storm was coming. The men easily hid the black boat in one of the coves along the shore. Then they went to Winant's, a hotel on a pier. The bartender noticed the men and their whispering. From the tavern, they walked about a mile to a group of villas next to the bay. Each man possessed a gun and a knife. They stopped at a widow's home and jacked open a window. One man slipped through it and opened the door for the other, just before they heard voices and steps. The break-in had awakened the owner, who in turn awoke her servant and charged through the house, asking who meant to rob her. Douglas and Mosher ran through the door before she saw them.

They quietly passed the country home of a Mr. Holmes Van Brunt. A light was on in one of the windows upstairs. The men moved across the lawn to a smaller, pretty cottage a short distance away. Around 2:00 A.M., they broke in and turned on a light. Covered furniture filled the rooms. It was, evidently, a summer residence. As Douglas searched for something worth stealing in the pantry and the dining room, he heard a key turn in the lock of the back door. The men turned out the light and ran downstairs into the cellar, pulling a trapdoor closed behind them. Douglas heard gunshots. He and Mosher pulled out pistols and waited. Somebody opened the trap door. They heard voices coming from four men on the floor above them. Gunshots rang out. Mosher ran upstairs first.

"There they come!" one man screamed. "Give it to him!"

Douglas heard another shot, followed by, "Give it to him!"

"I'll give it to him," another responded. More shots.

Douglas climbed upstairs and held his gun in his right hand. Mosher lay facedown on top of his gun. He had uttered, "I give up," before falling to the ground. A man knocked Douglas's right arm with a weapon. Douglas swore. As he took his gun with his left hand, he was shot in the chest and in the head before more bullets hit him. Douglas stumbled outside and walked along a fence. A man screamed, "Look out for that man, he has got a pistol!" Another warned that he wasn't really hurt, just playing possum. Douglas fell to the ground. The four gunmen gathered around him. Neighbors ran outside. Blood poured from Douglas's head and chest. Organs spilled from a wound in his stomach.

He asked a woman for a glass of whiskey.

"Whiskey for him!" she exclaimed. "For the man who tries to kill my husband? Oh, no! I don't want him to live—let him die! At all events he gets no whiskey from me!"

"It serves you right," said a servant girl to Douglas. "It's just good for you."

Douglas looked up at her. "Oh, madam, I've been a very wicked fellow, I know."

The girl smirked. People began asking Douglas questions.

He told them he was single and without a home. He mentioned two siblings he hadn't spoken with in years. He said Mosher was married and lived "in the city" with his five or six children. He didn't give Mosher's address, but asked for the boat to be given to Mosher's wife.

A sailor named Herkey, a neighbor of Van Brunt's, overheard Douglas talking. He saw the bullet wounds in Mosher's corpse, which had been pulled outside. After hearing Douglas ask again for whiskey, he brought some to his lips. Douglas couldn't drink it. He asked for water. The sailor again helped, getting some for Douglas and pouring sips into his mouth.

"It's no use lying now," Douglas said. "I helped to steal Charley Ross."

Herkey stared and called others to hear the confession. Someone held a lantern over Douglas's body.

They asked where Charley was hidden.

"Mosher knows all about it," Douglas responded. Herkey told him Mosher was dead. Douglas didn't believe him. Men lifted his shoulders off the ground so he could see his dead mentor lying in the grass.

"God help his poor wife and family!" he cried.

Herkey again asked about Charley.

"Inspector Walling knows, and the boy will get home all right," Douglas answered. He asked for a minister. He asked God for forgiveness. Douglas told Herkey he had forty dollars in his pocket. "All I ask of you is that you give me a decent burial. Give me a decent burial, that's all I ask."

Joseph Douglas died at 5:00 A.M., two hours after he fell to the ground. Men dragged his and Mosher's bodies behind the house and covered them.

Constable Holland of the New York Police Department arrived in the early morning and sent a dispatch to Central police headquarters informing Walling of Douglas's confession. He had made a formal arrest of the four shooters until the coroner could make a proper investigation. Walling sent Detective Silleck of the New York force to identify the bodies. By the time he arrived at noon, the police had found sets of burglars' tools on Mosher and Douglas, and a third set in the boat moored in the cove. Once Silleck stood over the bodies on the grass, an officer uncovered them.

Silleck identified Douglas as "Joe" and pointed to Mosher's body. "Take the glove off that left hand," he said, "and you'll find a withered finger."

tell C.K.R. quietly

WINDOW-SHOPPERS STROLLED BETWEEN CHRISTMAS DISPLAYS on either side of police headquarters on Chestnut Street in Philadelphia. They gazed past their reflections, scanning the candies, toys, jewelry, and carpets behind the glass. Farmers from New Jersey sold vegetables, fruits, and chickens on the pavement in front of long wagon lines and sidewalk booths stocked with holly wreaths and candles, decorations for the cedar and pine trees sold on the corner. At night, when women stepped into streetcars that whisked them to holiday parties, the silver sheen on their pastel dresses sparkled under the streetlights.

When he awoke on December 14, Captain Heins had two new leads on Charley Ross's kidnappers. The previous Thursday, a buggy had pulled alongside two boys playing in Hoboken, New Jersey. A man inside of it asked eight-year-old John Neville and his friend if they wanted to take a ride with him. The friend declined, but John stepped into the wagon. His family hadn't heard from him since. Heins also waited on news from a member of the Ross family who had traveled to Chester, Illinois, to investigate a Charley look-alike named Levi Scott, a child who had arrived in town with two poorly dressed, bearded men. The boy gave vague answers to the prepared Pinkerton questions but did tell police that his name was Charles Brewster. Heins did not brief Philadelphia's force on all of the communications that he received from Superintendent Walling. Mayor Stokley knew of the captain's quiet demeanor, but if he questioned Heins's loyalties or protested the withholding of information from his office—which Stokley would share with the advisers—Heins's methods did not change.

And then, he received another telegram from Walling at 10:00 A.M. on December 14.

> "Mosher and Clark were both killed last night while committing a burglary. Clark, when dying, said Mosher knew where Charley Ross was."

Heins immediately contacted his superiors. He also told Joseph Ross to ready Walter and Peter Callahan (the Rosses' gardener) for a possible trip to identify the bodies in New York; he said he would send a telegram with further information, but Walter was not to know the purpose of the trip. Joseph immediately telegraphed Middletown, Pennsylvania, where Walter and Sarah Ross were visiting Christian at his mother's house.

> "Tell C. K. R. quietly that Mosher and Douglas were killed last night, while committing a burglary, near New York. Douglas confessed that they stole Charley."

Within two hours of receiving Walling's telegram, Heins and William McKean, city adviser and editor of the *Ledger*, left to meet Walling at the Metropolitan Hotel in New York.

As soon as the Ledger posted a dispatch on its press board at Sixth and Chestnut Streets, news of the kidnappers' confession and deaths spread among Christmas shoppers and storekeepers. Once again, crowds gathered at the news boards. The *Inquirer* asked Detective Charles Wood, a Philadelphia officer who had been a member of the search party in Long Island Sound, about his role in the investigation. Wood's testimonial offered the public their first look at police intelligence since they had learned of the kidnapping and the kidnappers' descriptions five months before.

"For a long time," Wood relayed, "we knew that the men who committed this act were in and about New York, and during that time, together with the officers of New York who gallantly entered into the work, we have together been hunting down these men. We were cruising about Long Island for a long time."

When Wood was asked how the deaths would affect the search for Charley, his answers reflected information given in the ransom notes.

Christian Ross

Washington Lane, 1876

July 3

Mr. Ros— be not uneasy
you son churly bruster
he al writ we is
got him and no powers
on earth can deliver
out of our hand— you
wil hav two pay us
befor you git him from
us— an pay us a big
cent. to— if yu put
the cops hunting for him
yu is only defeeting
yu own end— we is
got him fitt so no living
power can gits him
from us a live— if
any aprock is maid
to his hidin place
that is the synil
for his instunt
anihulution— if yu
regard his lif puts no

The first ransom letter

one to search for him
you mony can fech
him out alive an
no other existin powers
dont deceve yuself an
think the detectives
can git him from us
for that is one imposebel
you here from us
in few day

The first ransom letter, continued

Mr. Ros
304 Market st.
phila.

penn.

The first ransom envelope

ABDUCTION OF CHARLIE BREWSTER ROSS.

On July 1st, 1874, at about four o'clock, P. M., Charlie Brewster, and Walter, the latter about six years old, sons of Christian K. Ross, were taken from the side-walk in front of their father's residence, on Washington Lane, Germantown, Pa., by two men in a buggy. Walter was carried about five miles, and there left upon the street; but of Charlie no subsequent clue has been obtained; it is earnestly solicited that every one, who shall receive this circular, make diligent inquiry, and promptly furnish any information obtained, and if the child be found, cause the detention of the parties having him in custody.

This circular must not be posted up, and care must be exercised, that suspicious persons do not obtain access to it.

Members of the press are specially requested to refrain from publishing the interrogatories hereafter given, so that the parties having the child in custody may not obtain the means of training him regarding his answers thereto.

On the discovery of any child, who shall be suspected of being the lost one, a photograph should be immediately obtained, if possible, and forwarded; and photographs of the parents will be sent for identification by the child.

$20,000 REWARD has been offered for the recovery of the child, and conviction of the kidnappers; all claims to which, however, will be relinquished in favor of the parties giving the information which shall lead to this result.

First page of Pinkerton pamphlet sent to police across America

Right: Pinkerton pamphlet, continued

DESCRIPTION OF THE CHILD.

The accompanying photograph is a correct likeness of the child when stolen. He was four years old on May 4th, 1874; his body and limbs are straight and well formed; he has round, full face; small chin, with noticeable dimple; very regular, and pretty dimpled hands; small, well-formed neck; full, broad forehead; bright, dark brown eyes, with considerable fullness over them; clear, white skin; healthy complexion; light flaxen hair of silky texture, easily curled in ringlets, when it extends to the neck; hair darker at the roots, slight cowlick on left side where parted; very light eye-brows. He had no blemish, mark or scar, on any part of his person, except from vaccination on one arm, but on which arm it is uncertain. He wore an unbleached Panama hat, with broad brim and black ribbon (brown) new kilt-plaited suit, skirt and pants of same length; striped blue and white stockings, and black laced balmoral shoes, No. 7 size; he talks plainly, but is reffing, and has a habit of putting his arm up to his eyes, when approached by strangers. His skin now may be stained and hair dyed, or he may be dressed as a girl, with hair parted in the center.

QUESTIONS FOR IDENTIFICATION.

Tests may be made upon his memory. He can recite, "Jesus loves me, this I know," for the Bible tells me so." Knows "O" and "S" of the alphabet, but no other letters. Will state his name to be Charlie Ross, but when asked if he has any other name will say, "Charlie Brewster Ross."

To the following questions he should answer, to-wit:—

Question.—Who is your uncle on Washington Lane?

Answer.—Uncle Joe.

Question.—What is your cousin's name?

Answer.—Cousin Joe or Cousin George or Cousin Frank.

Question.—Who lives next door to papa?

Answer.—Marcellus McDowell or Jennie McDowell.

Question.—What horse does mama drive?

Answer.—Polly.

In like manner, he can give the names of his brothers, Stoughton, Harry and Walter, and sister, Sophie and Marry (for Marion,) and of Doctor Dunton, the family physician; also the name of his Sunday-school teacher, Miss Mary Cope.

DESCRIPTION OF THE KIDNAPPERS.

No. 1, is about thirty-five years old; five feet, nine inches high; medium build, weighing about one hundred and fifty pounds; rather full, round face, florid across the nose and cheek bones; giving him the appearance of a hard drinker; he had sandy moustache, but was otherwise clean shaved; wore eye glasses, and had an open-faced gold watch, and gold vest chain; also, green sleeve buttons.

No. 2, is older, probably about forty years of age, and a little shorter and stouter than his companion; he wore chin whiskers, about three inches long, of a reddish sandy color; and had a pug nose, or a nose in some way deformed. He wore gold bowed spectacles, and had two gold rings on one of his middle fingers, one plain and one set with red stone.

Both men wore brown straw hats, one high and one low crowned; one wore a linen duster; and, it is thought, one had a duster of grey alpaca, or mohair.

All communications by letter, or telegraph if necessary, in reply to this circular, will be directed to either of the following officers of

PINKERTON'S NATIONAL DETECTIVE AGENCY,

Viz: BENJ. FRANKLIN, Sup't, 45 South Third St., Philadelphia, Pa.

R. A. PINKERTON, Sup't, 66 Exchange Place. New York.

F. WARNER, Sup't, 191 & 193 Fifth Avenue, Chicago, Ill.

GEO. H. BANGS, Gen'l Sup't.

ALLAN PINKERTON.

Philadelphia, August 22d, 1874.

Wm. F. Murphy's Sons, Printers, Stationers, 509 Chestnut St., Philada.

$20,000 REWARD

Has been offered for the recovery of CHARLIE BREWSTER ROSS, and for the arrest and conviction of his abductors. He was stolen from his parents in Germantown, Pa., on July 1st, 1874, by two unknown men.

DESCRIPTION OF THE CHILD.

The accompanying portrait resembles the child, but is not a correct likeness. He is about four years old; his body and limbs are straight and well formed; he has a round, full face; small chin, with noticeable dimple; very regular and pretty dimpled hands; small, well-formed neck; full, broad forehead; bright dark-brown eyes, with considerable fullness over them; clear white skin; healthy complexion; light flaxen hair, of silky texture, easily curled in ringlets when it extends to the neck; hair darker at the roots,—slight cowlick on left side where parted; very light eyebrows. He talks plainly, but is retiring, and has a habit of putting his arm up to his eyes when approached by strangers. His skin may now be stained, and hair dyed,—or he may be dressed as a girl, with hair parted in the centre.

DESCRIPTION OF THE KIDNAPPERS.

No. 1 is about thirty-five years old; five feet nine inches high; medium build, weighing about one hundred and fifty pounds; rather full, round face, florid across the nose and cheek-bones, giving him the appearance of a hard drinker; he had sandy moustache, but was otherwise clean shaved; wore eye-glasses, and had an open-faced gold watch and gold vest-chain; also, green sleeve-buttons.

No. 2 is older, probably about forty years of age, and a little shorter and stouter than his companion; he wore chin whiskers about three inches long, of a reddish-sandy color; and had a pug-nose, or a nose in some way deformed. He wore gold bowed spectacles, and had two gold rings on one of his middle fingers, one plain and one set with red stone.

Both men wore brown straw hats, one high and one low-crowned; one wore a linen duster; and, it is thought, one had a duster of gray alpaca, or mohair.

Any person who shall discover or know of any child, which there is reason to believe may be the one abducted, will at once communicate with their Chief of Police or Sheriff, who has been furnished with means for the identification of the stolen child.

Otherwise, communications by letter or telegraph, if necessary, will be directed to either of the following officers of

PINKERTON'S NATIONAL DETECTIVE AGENCY,

Viz:
BENJ. FRANKLIN, Sup't, 45 S. Third St., Philadelphia, Pa.
R. A. PINKERTON, Sup't, 66 Exchange Place, New York.
F. WARNER, Sup't, 191 and 193 Fifth Avenue, Chicago, Ill.
GEO. H. BANGS, Gen'l Sup't.

ALLAN PINKERTON.

PHILADELPHIA, September 1st, 1874.

(POST THIS UP IN A CONSPICUOUS PLACE.)

Left: Pinkerton flyer, as posted in public places

Superintendent George
W. Walling

Main Street
(Germantown Avenue)
at Rittenhouse

Main Street at Manheim

Main Street life

"Are you nearer the child now than before?'

"I don't think they can keep it out of the way. Either the 'two other men' have got it or Mosher's wife has it. I don't think she can keep it out of the road. She has no means—neither have the other two men—for we know that the whole gang were reduced so low that they had to make forays into the town and commit house robberies. It was while upon such an errand that last night Mosher and Clark were killed. They had to steal to live, and to steal to be able to hide the child."

"Is there any likelihood that they will kill the child?"

"No, no; I don't think that. They may 'drop it.'"

"By that do you mean set it down in some place where it may be picked up?"

"Yes, something of that kind."

The kidnappers had mentioned that they were four in number in earlier ransom notes. The police never were sure what to think of this statement. Only two kidnappers were described by Walter and eyewitnesses, and once Gil Mosher identified his brother and Joseph Douglas as suspects, the police operated on the theory that the duo—longtime partners in crime—were the only ones responsible. Certainly Mosher and Douglas had been connected to a larger criminal community, so they could have enlisted the help of others to watch Charley or protect their identities, or they could have brought their own family members into the operation . . . or they could have been lying. If there were two others involved, the police assumed they would have been two people that worked well with Mosher and Douglas.

Douglas was subservient to Mosher, and from what he said in his final breaths, he wasn't in touch with his family. Mosher had two brothers living, but according to Gil, they weren't close and often quarreled. Mosher was, however, on good terms with his wife Martha, William Westervelt's sister. Although Detective Wood and others speculated over Martha's involvement in hiding Charley, Walling defended her from the moment her husband was killed.

Two of Walter's uncles took the boy and Peter Callahan, the gardener who saw Mosher and Douglas kidnap the Ross children, to police headquarters in New York the next day. Walling had emphasized to Heins and his own men that Walter was neither to learn about the Bay Ridge shootings nor speak to anybody before he identified the bodies. Walling himself met with Walter in his office before a detective took him and his uncles to the Brooklyn morgue.

Detective Dusenbury escorted Callahan, the uncles, and Walter inside. The night before, the bodies of both men had been lifted from Van Brunt's lawn into rough boxes and then taken to the coroner, who placed them in a vault. The coroner walked Walter to Mosher's body first. He uncovered the entire corpse. The little boy looked at the body, riddled with bullets. He became too upset to immediately identify Mosher.

"That's the man," he eventually said, "who gave me candy in the buggy."

"I remember him by his nose," Walter continued. "I never saw a nose like that before."

Callahan also recognized Mosher. "I am certain that he was one of the men from his general appearance; but whenever I attempted to look at him when I met him last July he put a handkerchief up to his face. This partly hid it."

The coroner walked Walter over to Douglas's corpse. He uncovered only Douglas's face, protecting Walter from this shattered torso.

"Oh, that's awful like him; he's the driver." Walter remembered Douglas as the one who gave him money to buy firecrackers at the Kensington store. He pointed to Mosher.

"He sometimes had candy too."

After Walter and his uncles left, a large crowd gathered around the entrance to the morgue. At 2:30 P.M., a police officer entered with two women. Patrick McGuire, the morgue keeper, met them. They asked to see the bodies.

One woman wore a green dress and a dark felt hat with a blue velvet tip. Her dark eyes looked around the room, and she pulled a red shawl around her shoulders. The older woman next to her was identified as Gil Mosher's wife, Liz. She wore a black dress. McGuire led the women into the back room, where Mosher's open coffin lay in an icebox. The younger woman shook and turned toward Liz, who held her composure. They whispered together and asked to see Douglas. McGuire walked to a vault in the ground, accessible by a fifteen-foot stepladder. Liz refused to climb down the ladder, but a police officer accompanied the younger woman underground. Five minutes later, she ascended, shaking from the cold and visibly angry. McGuire took the ladies into his office and sat them by a stove. They removed their gloves, warming their hands. Both left without talking to reporters.

A half hour later, a woman in her late twenties entered. She asked McGuire, who stood next to his ten-year-old son, if any women had arrived that day.

He said no.

"Yes, Father, there were two ladies here a little while ago," McGuire's boy said. "Don't you recollect them?"

"Oh, yes. I do; but those women wanted to see someone in the hospital," McGuire lied.

The woman asked to see the bodies. By the mid-afternoon, a small crowd stood around the icebox holding Mosher. She worked her way to the front and said, "That's the oldest one." A reporter from the *New York Herald* heard her and followed the woman into McGuire's office, where she sat by the stove. She agreed to an interview.

"I am a sister-in-law of William Mosher," the woman said. She identified herself as the wife of Alfred, one of three Mosher brothers still living, and the mother of five children. She said twelve of Mosher's other brothers were deceased, and that her husband, Alfred, had not allowed William in their home for the past several years.

The reporter asked why she wanted to know about the two women who entered earlier.

"I was afraid I might meet anybody belonging to Will Mosher. I don't mean his wife. I am waiting to see her, but any of his companions, women, or any of his brother's connections. I do not want to see any of them. When I read all about this thing in the evening papers last night I resolved to come to see poor Will, but that's all. I don't want to know the others. I went down to Bay Ridge this morning, and there heard that two other women were looking after the bodies, and that was why I hesitated to come in here, for fear I should meet them. So, it seems, they weren't here after all."

The reporter asked Mrs. Mosher to describe the women she feared. He then told her that McGuire's boy was right: two women fitting her description had been there earlier.

"Yes, I know them," she continued. She referred first to Liz Mosher and her husband Gil. "She and he and all their connections are bad, and I don't want to know them. The other is the one that calls herself Douglas's sister. Her name is Mary, but that is all anybody knows about her. She is not his sister, and she is not his wife—that's all I need say. [Gil] lives in Delancey Street, New York, with his wife, and is fifty-seven years of age. Douglas used to live with Mary, who calls herself his sister, in Columbia Street."

"William was married, was he not?" the reporter asked.

"Oh, yes. I am only surprised his wife has not come here yet. They have four children living and two they buried. The two eldest of the living ones are William and Georgie; Willie only four years old. She is a tall woman like me but stout."

"What does your husband think about William's abduction of Charley Ross?"

"Oh, he doesn't believe a word of it, nor neither do I. William was always too fond of his own children, and of everybody else's. He wouldn't harm a child, though he might kill a man. The life of thieving was his only vice. He never drank a drop of liquor in his life, never took a chew of tobacco, and never smoked a cigar nor a pipe. I never heard him use even a foul word. He never had a fault but the one of wishing to acquire sudden riches and he had a beautiful education." Mrs. Mosher said she had known William Mosher prior to his arrest six years before. "He was just making his living the best he could, until just after that time when he lost his child and fell into bad company with thieves and detectives."

"Did you see what Detective Silleck said: 'That Mosher was always a river thief'?"

"Yes, I know those Sillecks."

"Oh, you do? You know Detective Silleck?"

"Yes. I know him once, and if he and the other Sillecks put their hands over their mouths they might find more at home than they would want everybody to know. Oh, I know him. Oh dear! How many people hold office to take care of others that ought to be watched themselves."

the resemblance is most striking

CHRISTIAN'S BROTHER JAMES ARRIVED IN CHESTER, ILLINOIS, during the week of the shootings. The family had sent him to identify a little boy whose presence made the town uncomfortable. Recently, a heavyset man with a lame leg named Thomas Scott had arrived in Chester with the child and another male companion. The second man's name was Henry Ship. Ship wore a thin black suit and had gray spots in his black whiskers. The townspeople noticed that both men looked about fifty years old, and they both had very soft hands. The men said the child's name was Levi Scott, but the town thought the nervous little boy resembled the picture of Charley Ross on the Pinkerton flyers. The police arrested the men and took the boy to a safe house.

James Ross's train arrived in stormy weather. At 1:30 P.M., police met him at the station. As soon as the child's caregivers introduced James to "Levi Scott," he saw that while the boy was not Charley, his natural appearance had been changed. Somebody had thrown acid in the child's face, and his hair had obviously been dyed. When those in the room heard Levi was not Charley, they begged James to reconsider. They blamed the child's posture for confusing James. His back had been whipped so many times, they told him, ripples of scars now marred its curvature.

The boy's scars make him unrecognizable, they said.

Please, Mr. Ross, they pleaded. Wait until tomorrow to make your decision.

In spite of the weather, townspeople gathered in the rain outside the house where James and Levi talked through the evening. James telegraphed Philadelphia with word that the child could very well be Charley, although he hadn't recognized his Uncle James. The child gave some incorrect answers to the questions, James telegraphed, but the men who accompanied him agreed to travel to Philadelphia to provide more information. Sarah Ross and her brothers told James to bring the men and the boy immediately. Knowing of the town's distress, and concerned for the boy, James agreed to talk to Levi again in the morning. By the end of their second conversation, Levi shared what he could remember of his story. James sent another telegram to Philadelphia before noon. "I do not think it is Charley, although the resemblance is most striking."

Levi didn't remember who he really was or where exactly he had originally come from. He just knew the men were not family members. Levi had forgotten that his real name was Henry Lachmueller. Two years before Charley was kidnapped, "Thomas Scott" and "Henry Ship" had taken five-year-old Henry from his home in St. Louis. Henry's father, also named Henry, had worked at a stone quarry. Every day, his children brought dinner to the workers. One evening, the children stopped at a store on their way back home, and little Henry ran barefoot into the store's backyard. When he did not reappear, the children told their mother. That night, a search party ran into two men who said they watched the boy fall into the river and drown. Authorities searched the river.

Hours after they had grabbed Henry, his captors walked him to the river and rowed him to the opposite shore. They forced him to walk through the woods and lashed his back with tree branches when he fell down. They stopped at a small cabin and a woman joined their party. Over the next two years, the three adult drifters traveled the Midwest with Henry. They forced him to beg for money, and if he received less than one dollar a day, they beat him. Right before the party arrived in Chester, the woman had died.

When James Ross's decision spread through Chester, townspeople demanded that the police refuse to return the boy to Thomas Scott and Henry Ship. One man applied for a restraining order to keep the men from the boy and to place him in the custody of a guardian. Citizens began writing letters to other towns and cities with a description of Levi.

In St. Louis, Henry Lachmueller Sr. read about the unfortunate child in Illinois. He asked the police to obtain a better description. The morning after his son's disappearance in 1872, while workmen dragged the river, an eyewitness had told him that two men had crossed the river the night before with a child resembling Henry. Over the past two and a half years, he had purchased "LOST" advertisements in European and North American newspapers, and he had traveled through both continents following false leads. During this time, his little boy had been panhandling through the Midwest, but nobody had recognized the child scarred with acid until the Charley Ross case created a national hysteria, sharpening Americans' observations and paranoia.

Henry Lachmueller Sr. and his wife traveled to Chester. As soon as young Henry saw his father, he remembered his family.

At his mother's home in Pennsylvania, Christian Ross received word of his brother James's latest telegram.

"It is not him."

Detective Silleck knew that

Superintendent Walling's first statements to the public attempted to clarify the role his name played in Douglas's dying confession. In response to a question about Charley's location, the kidnapper had said, "Inspector Walling knows, and the boy will get home all right."

Walling addressed neither Douglas's specific words nor his reference to the rank "Inspector." Instead, he emphasized the obvious, ethical distance between his position and the kidnappers' criminal intent.

"I knew of these two men only as two thieves," he told the press. "I cannot refer you to any conviction of either of them, but they are well-known characters among the police force of this city."

The new headlines revived interest in Charley's disappearance. Writers repeated the circumstances of the botched burglary and speculations over Charley's hiding place. Readers consumed story after story, seeking further clues. The unexpected identification of the kidnappers reminded them of their initial fears over copycat crimes, their empathy for Christian and Sarah Ross, and their anger with the police for refusing to release details. The sensational deaths of Mosher and Douglas reinforced their instinct for retributive justice, allowing them to feel more reassured about their own children's safety.

Walling claimed responsibility for the relief spreading across America. The more he talked about the case, the more he turned himself into a hero by emphasizing his role in the investigation. The *Evening Bulletin* wrote, "To Captain Walling belongs the credit of originating the theory that these were the guilty parties." Walling did not publicly recognize Detective Silleck and Captain Hedden, the officers who first told him about Gil Mosher and facilitated the meeting between the criminal and the superintendent. He also did not acknowledge his predecessor, Superintendent George Matsell, who had first heard of Hedden's connection with Gil Mosher and encouraged the officer to take the career criminal's story seriously.

Instead, George W. Walling stood like a general in his uniform and took credit for catching the kidnappers of Charley Ross. "Soon after I received the description as given by the boy Walter and others who had seen the two men in the buggy who took little Charley away, after a conference with Captain Hedden, and the obtaining of other information, I knew my men," he said in a statement to reporters. "You will remember that that description said one of the men wore goggles and had a 'monkey nose,' as the children called it. Despite the goggles, the detailed description of the man's deformity of nose and the description given of the other man told us who the men were. Let me show you how quickly Mosher was recognized. I called in Detective Silleck one day, and after describing Mosher and the peculiarity of his nose, mentioning him by his alias of Henderson, I told him I wanted to get hold of him, but did not tell him for what. Silleck at once exclaimed, 'Why, I know him; that's Bill Mosher.'"

A reporter for the *New York Herald* asked Walling how he had led the investigation.

"We arranged our plans very secretly, and no one knew anything about them, with the exception of the officers engaged in the hunt and some of the members of the Ross family, with whom I have been in communication about the men for four or five months by mail and telegraph."

"Was the search made in this city?"

"'In this city?' I should say it was. There was never made in my experience so thorough a search for anything as has been made by us in this case. Officers have been secretly detailed everywhere—at the ferries, at the depots, wherever, in fact, we had an idea we could get a clue to the men."

Within forty-eight hours of Mosher and Douglas's deaths, Walling had so manipulated the sequence of events over the past six months that it seemed as if the police, under his leadership, had planned and orchestrated the murders at Bay Ridge. Many newspapers, including the *Bulletin*, accepted Walling's statements as justification for controversial police secrecy early in the case. "One satisfactory result comes from this sudden turn of affairs. It gives the police an opportunity to vindicate themselves from the unjust aspersions under which they have been placed by the necessary ignorance of the public regarding these operations."

The *Philadelphia Inquirer*, however, used Walling's words to criticize the police. "That they did not find them at all until they were shot down in the commission of [a] crime by a private citizen, does not greatly indicate their skill or earnestness in the pursuit. There was awful bungling somewhere."

Walling blamed his men for the length of the chase. "Every officer in the city was on the lookout for them," he told the *Herald*. "We would have had them a month ago but for the stupidity of one man whom I put on the track. I sent him to see if they were in a certain place which I thought they frequented. An officer was sent with him, and wafted outside some distance from the place. The men were not there, and my man foolishly asked for them. The result was that he was followed from the place and seen meeting the officer. Of course Mosher and Douglas were notified, and they haven't been near the place since. We sent an expedition on a steam launch to try and find them on the water. Every bay and inlet of the Sound, the bay and the rivers, were explored, but we failed to find our men. The expedition was searching for ten days."

"Mr. Walling," the reporter asked, "what effect will the death of Mosher and Douglas have on the Ross case? If the boy was in their care may he not have been concealed in some place unknown to any other persons, and thus starve?"

"It is a rather hard question to answer, whether the death of these men will have a good or a bad effect upon the case; whether it will facilitate Charley Ross's discovery if in the hands of other persons or not. My opinion is that it will be all right now."

He spoke much too soon, of course. The truth was, he and the police needed the public to believe everything would be "all right."

The new superintendent was a gifted speaker. He knew how to spin information. In the days following the kidnapping, Walling had reviewed the facts in such a way that it appeared he had anticipated the murder of the kidnappers, therefore creating the illusion that the police had been in control. Some journalists saw through his rhetoric. Others did not. Instead of seeing the murders as further evidence of incompetent forces hesitating to act for personal and political reasons, they believed Walling's delusion. He convinced the public to take comfort in the death of the kidnappers, not to worry about the lost child. Deftly, Walling had changed the story. It was now primarily about Mosher and Douglas, and finding the people who had helped them— not saving Charley Ross, whose case was subject to whether the kidnappers' deaths had "a good or a bad effect upon it."

The change was significant. Of course journalists would continue to mention the Ross family and people would keep looking for Charley, if for no other reason than somebody could still earn Mayor Stokley's $20,000 reward should another abductor be tried and found. By acting like everything was "all right" now that the kidnappers were dead, Walling concentrated the public's interest on the power the thieves had possessed. In so doing, he allowed Mosher and Douglas to have something they had predicted all along: future notoriety. The kidnappers lost their lives, but they did get away with the abduction on their terms: the Rosses had refused to give them money, so they had refused to return Charley. They had outwitted the police and avoided prison.

Others would study and emulate their kidnapping model.

On December 15, Mayor Stokley, Police Chief Jones, police captains, and two of Christian Ross's brothers met at police headquarters on Chestnut Street to discuss whether they could continue offering $20,000 for Charley's return.

That night, New York's Detective Doyle and two officers prepared to raid a small, deserted island off of Westport, Connecticut, in Long Island Sound. Doyle had learned about an elderly couple who sold provisions to fishermen and wanderers from their home on the island. Assuming that Mosher and Douglas had stopped there more than once, Doyle thought the pair could very well be hiding Charley Ross. Doyle assembled a team, secured a search warrant, and landed on the island at 3:00 A.M. on December 16.

Domesticated animals and birds roamed the grounds outside of several shacks. When officers knocked on the main cabin, nobody answered. They pounded harder. An elderly man cracked open the door. Behind him, an old woman stood holding a candle. In a shaky voice, the man asked why they were bothering him so late at night. Doyle's men pushed the door open, entered the cabin, and said they were there to take Charley Ross back home to his family. As the couple watched the officers search their home and the surrounding shacks, they insisted that they never let anybody stay with them, not even a child. Officers asked about Mosher and Douglas. Boatmen came to visit them often, the couple said, but only to buy provisions. Doyle left without making an arrest.

Later that morning, the *Philadelphia Inquirer* questioned the logic of praising police efforts now that Mosher and Douglas were dead. "Neither the police authorities of New York or Philadelphia accomplished any discovery which has led to one appreciable result; and, if the child should be restored through the terrible infliction upon the abductors, while perpetrating another crime, it cannot, in any wise, be credited to the vigilance or sagacity or efficiency of either of these police authorities or of any one who has aided them."

The Baltimore *News* also chastised Walling and his men for their blatant self-promotion. "The New York police, for the sake of their own credit, had better keep quiet about their knowledge of these men for had they done their duty Charley Ross would not have been stolen." Questioning why the police hadn't arrested the former convicts earlier, the paper realized members of the department had hoped to profit from the ransom. "These things look very suspicious, and if they were not in league with the police, then the police were certainly very indifferent to their duty."

For Walling to retain the spotlight, he needed to find Charley fast. Doyle's mission to the Connecticut island had failed, and any associate of Bill Mosher's who had information on the child wasn't coming forward. Douglas had said that Mosher didn't trust him with details on the boy, and if he were to be believed, then perhaps Mosher didn't trust anybody.

The integrity of one of Walling's top investigators, Detective Silleck, had also been compromised. In her interview at the Brooklyn morgue, Mrs. Albert Mosher had directed allegations at the detective, implying that the Silleck and Mosher families had shared the same ignoble acquaintances. They had. Like Officer Moran, Detective Silleck had not only grown up around Bill Mosher, but he had also arrested him. Silleck had revealed his familiarity with Mosher when he publicly identified the body at Bay Ridge, and Walling knew he had been the officer to bring Gil Mosher to the attention of Captain Hedden back in July, the single action ultimately responsible for Walling's current high profile in the press. It was Silleck whose knowledge of the harbor led a search by the joint Philadelphia and New York forces, and it was he who had told the authorities that Bill Mosher's deformed nose was due to either cancer or a disease, like syphilis.

Two officers and two criminals—Moran and Silleck, Mosher and Douglas—had grown up along those same Long Island shores so favored by river pirates. Ever since they were children, thieves had gravitated to their East River world, targeting shipments headed to isolated piers along the bay. The authorities tried not to interfere much. The force allotted such a small number of men to the harbor police that only hideous robberies—such as ones where captains were beaten with handpicks—were investigated. Pirates knew the odds were in their favor, and so they thrived—until the very end of the nineteenth century, when a fearless police commissioner named Theodore Roosevelt overthrew their stronghold. Until then, it was hard to tell between the law enforcer and the criminal. Their worlds overlapped too frequently. It was too easy to become a police officer: all one had to do was find a veteran officer who would either sell his position or nominate the newcomer for one. And once an officer, it was too easy to operate as a criminal: all one needed was to maintain enough underworld connections to collect a decent paycheck as a thief catcher or as a thief protector.

Walling and Silleck knew that more of the Moshers could begin talking soon, and the police had no control over what they would say, contradict, or allege. Based on Mrs. Albert Mosher's interview at the morgue, reporters were certain to ask more about the family's past associations with Silleck. In the meantime, the detective continued working closely with Walling.

The day after the shooting, Walling learned about a Mrs. Russell—a junk dealer and landlady on Ridge Street who had funded Mosher's failed business attempts as a fishmonger and saloon keeper. He decided to go undercover as a sanitary inspector to investigate her. Walling went to Russell's broken-down lodging house, and after introducing himself to one of the tenants as a member of the Board of Health, declared the house a target for diphtheria and unacceptable for children. He asked to speak with the proprietor about the flooded cellars.

The tenant said Mrs. Russell had left for her country home an hour before.

Walling asked to go upstairs.

The tenant said she would be gone for at least one night.

Walling pushed past him, walked upstairs, and knocked at a bed-room door. Another man answered. Identifying himself as Russell's son, he told Walling to take his complaints to the neighboring stable responsible for the flooding.

Walling asked where Mrs. Russell could be found in the country.

Both men said they didn't know the address.

Before leaving, Walling perused the halls and the rooms. He then walked to the stable, and while he pretended to examine the alleyway between the buildings, Detective Silleck watched the front door.

A few minutes later, Silleck saw Mrs. Russell and her son exit the lodging house. He followed them and stopped when he could to tele-graph Walling.

"Got the woman in Twenty-fourth Street. What shall I do?"

"Follow—to Canada if necessary" Walling replied.

Silleck telegraphed next from Grand Central Station. "Just bought tickets for New Britain, Connecticut."

Walling now had a more concrete answer for those who asked why Douglas's dying confession had connected his name to Charley's hiding place: he and his men were watching the criminals' former accomplices. "I do not think the boy is concealed in this city," Walling told a New York reporter. "To be frank with you, I never believed that he was con-cealed in this city. It is not for me to tell you all I know about the case in its present aspects, but I am of the opinion that we are still on the right track."

Another reporter asked whether Mosher's wife, Martha, now known to be living in New York City, ever had the child. Walling dismissed the idea. He said he would have noticed if Mosher had communicated with his wife through the papers.

"My idea is that the boy may be picked up now," he continued, confident Silleck would soon wire him from Connecticut with good news. "You see, there is no hope of reward any more than there is for fear of a conviction of the parties who may now have the child—and I think I know what I'm talking about—and he will be a burden to his keepers; of no use to them, in fact. How easy will it be for them to 'set him afloat,' put him out in the streets, with the knowledge that he would soon be taken up by the police as a 'lost child'?"

Silleck telegraphed the next morning. "Nothing here; coming back."

Back in New York, Silleck told Walling that Mrs. Russell went to visit her nephew and niece in New Britain. While in Connecticut, Silleck had traced rumors of a little boy in their company to a child who had died a month before.

"Did she say anything to you about Mosher?" Walling asked.

"No, but she said, 'I know what you are looking after; you are looking after that boy.'"

Walling disagreed with Silleck's summary of "Nothing here." He and Charley's uncle, Henry Lewis, traveled to New Britain the next day. Mrs. Russell's son answered the door.

"You're a queer young man not to know where your mother lived," said Walling, referring to their earlier encounter at the lodging house. Mrs. Russell appeared once Walling demanded to speak with her. Although she refused to give straight answers about her sudden departure from New York, she identified the dead child as a relative. If the police didn't believe her, she said, they could talk to the boy's doctor, who also happened to be the town mayor.

Walling turned to questions about Mosher. Mrs. Russell said she might have seen his wife recently, but she didn't remember when.

"Was it two years ago?"

"It might be."

"Was it eight weeks ago?"

"Perhaps it was; yes, it was about that time."

Walling asked about Mosher.

He owed me money, Mrs. Russell said.

Why would you deal with a criminal?

It is nobody's business, she replied, if I choose to help somebody earn an honest living.

Walling found the town mayor. After confirming Russell's story about the dead child, he and Lewis returned to New York.

Either Joseph Douglas, riddled with bullets and gasping for breath, lied about Walling's knowledge on his deathbed, or the superintendent was only acting like a man who had no idea of Charley's location.

Henry Lewis was a successful and shrewd businessman. Chances are, he wouldn't be easily conned into following Walling on a wild goose chase to Connecticut. However, by calling him a kidnapper of Charley Ross, he had the country believing Douglas's dying confession—a confession that also stated, "Walling knows, and the boy will get home all right." Eyewitnesses believed Douglas to be of sound mind at the time of his death. Walling insisted that Douglas was mistaken. If both men were being honest, then either Douglas had underestimated Walling's knowledge or somebody had moved Charley without telling the superintendent.

If Walling was lying, then he was protecting somebody.

we'll defend ourselves

Such a large crowd arrived at the coroner's inquest in Brooklyn on December 17, 1874, that the coroner delayed the morning proceedings by half an hour.

At 11:30 A.M., he charged the jury overseeing the inquest to deduce how Mosher and Douglas had died. Four men remained under police supervision: Mr. J. Holmes Van Brunt, the brother and next door neighbor of the burglarized home owner; Albert Van Brunt, Holmes Van Brunt's son; William Scott, their gardener; and Herman Frank, a hired man.

Due to an illness, Mr. Holmes Van Brunt had been allowed to go home and await the inquest's verdict from his bed. The other three men remained in police custody until the trial, that Thursday morning. The *Herald* defined them as honest men who did what the police could not—confront Mosher and Douglas without waiting for the opportune time. "And scarcely have we time to wonder over this chance before the inevitable policeman pops a stupid visage out of nothing, like a clown in a pantomime, and says, 'We were just going to do it, Sir.'"

Albert Van Brunt testified that his neighbor and uncle, Judge Van Brunt of the New York Supreme Court, had installed a telegraph burglar system in his summer cottage. Should an element trigger the alarm, it would sound in the bedroom of his brother Holmes next door. At 2:00 A.M. on Monday, December 14, J. Holmes Van Brunt heard the alarm from his bedroom. Albert's mother and sister were awake, aiding an ill child in a separate room, while Albert slept upstairs. Albert recalled his father summoning him to his bedroom and saying, "Albert, go over and see what has sounded that alarm. I guess the wind has blown open one of those blinds again."

Albert said he left with a pistol, saw a light in his uncle's window, and awoke his father's gardener, William Scott, who lived in an adjoining cottage. Both men saw shadows against the window curtain. Soon after, Albert alerted his father and their hired man, Herman Frank; the four men held guns and hid behind trees between the properties. According to Albert, his father directed the men to "capture" the thieves without killing them unless they needed to defend themselves. He said his father had divided them into groups of two, sending one pair to the front door and one to the back. "Whichever way they come," he remembered hearing, "let the two who meet them take care of them as best they can. If they come out and scatter both ways, then we'll all have a chance to work."

Herman Frank said that he and the elder Van Brunt had walked through the rear door and lifted the trapdoor into the pantry. Holmes Van Brunt claimed in an earlier police report that he could have shot both men early in the discovery, but he restrained himself until he was sure that violence was needed. Both he and Herman Frank swore that the burglars shot several times before they defended themselves with their pistols. Albert Van Brunt said Joseph Douglas shot so close to his face that powder blew against his cheeks.

No bullet from either kidnapper's gun harmed any of the men. However, at the end of the shooting, two bullets had pierced Mosher's back and so many had entered Douglas that the morgue keeper refused to let females and Walter Ross view his body below his face.

The coroner's jury agreed with the men's interpretation of events. "We, the jury, find that the killing of the deceased in the manner set forth was perfectly justifiable, and we commend the act of their defending their lives and property in such a courageous manner under such trying circumstances." The coroner agreed. New York's *Evening Telegram* joined the *Herald* in complimenting the Van Brunts on succeeding where Walling had failed. It also blamed police negligence for allowing the criminals to be shot before they were interrogated.

Martha Mosher arrived at the Brooklyn morgue on the day of the inquest. A male companion walked to her husband's coffin. Martha knelt down, held her husband's neck, and kissed his face until Patrick McGuire, the morgue keeper, pulled her up.

"I am his wife," Martha cried to McGuire. "I have come to him, and will go wherever he is, no matter what the consequences to me." McGuire began asking her questions about her husband's body, but the male companion interrupted him.

"Look here, look here, you can't find out anything from her. You must ask her through me."

"I want to ask her a question you can't answer," McGuire retorted. "I want to know if she is going to bury her husband or leave him here?"

"Yes, I will bury him," Martha replied through her tears. "He shall have a decent burial. I will take him away." Ignoring reporters' questions, Martha asked McGuire if she could visit her husband's body again. He said she could return as many times as she wanted.

Martha had written the coroner, asking him to release Mosher's body into her care, and a young woman identifying herself as Mary Douglas wrote for permission to bury her "husband," Joseph. The coroner approved both requests. A man named Munn, an undertaker and friend of the Mosher and Douglas families, washed the bodies and dressed them for burial. He knew them so well, he said later, that he didn't charge them for his services. Munn told McGuire that he would bury them in Cypress Hills cemetery, a place where several of their friends rested. He also told McGuire that a source had told him "that boy Charley will be found before sundown today."

"How do you know?" McGuire asked.

"Well, that is my business; but I will tell you this, that I'll stake my honor on this, that Charley Ross, if he isn't found tonight, will be on his way to Philadelphia tomorrow."

I thought the boy was dead, McGuire told Munn.

"Not a bit of it," retorted Munn, "or I wouldn't say what I do. I know better."

When Munn finished dressing the bodies, he placed them in imitation rosewood coffins with silver clasps.

Martha Mosher agreed to an interview after her husband's funeral. On Monday, December 21, her story appeared in the *Philadelphia*

Inquirer. The writer described Martha as "good-looking and genteel in appearance."

Throughout her adolescence, Martha said, her family had known the Moshers very well—at one point, the two families even shared a house. When she was fifteen, Martha married Bill, who was forty. "No girl could get a kinder husband than I did," she told the reporter, "and from the day he married me up to the one when I saw him last he never changed to me."

Initially, Bill had supported her by building boats and shaping wire into objects like birdcages. "I have seen few men in my life that were more industrious or attentive when everything went well with him, but sometimes bad luck would come, and then he was subject to fits of melancholy. They would not last long, because he was a good-natured, easy-dispositioned man naturally, and his dullness soon wore off." Despite her husband's mood swings, Martha said, he "would be the last man I should expect to hear of interfering with another man's child."

A reporter asked if Martha remembered the first time she had heard of the Ross kidnapping.

"I first heard of the Ross case from outside parties," she answered. "But from what I learned since and what I know now, I am sorry to be obliged to confess I think he was one of the men who took that child. Where the boy is, I don't know; I wish I did. His mother should soon have him. If I lost one of my own little ones I could not suffer more than I have since I believed my husband took that one. I would willingly give one of mine to restore Mrs. Ross her child, if that would do it. I never knew anything about it, until some suspicions of late, and what I heard since I have communicated to Superintendent Walling. He knows all I ever heard or suspected, and I only hope any information I can get for him will enable him to find the child."

By the time Martha's interview appeared in the papers, the press learned that she had fled Philadelphia months before the "suspicions of late," which she said had informed her of Mosher's complicity. Even though Walling had repeatedly defended Martha against charges of complicity throughout the fall, he did bring her to headquarters for questioning one week after the shootings. Afterward, he again defended her innocence.

The day after Martha's interview appeared in the *Inquirer*, the *New York Herald* asked Gil Mosher about his sister-in-law. "If Martha Mosher don't know where Charley Ross is, she knows those who do know," alleged Gil. "I guess Superintendent Walling knows all about them. There's been somebody behind them all along. That child will be found one of these days, and then it will all come out."

Did Bill know that the police suspected him of the kidnapping? The reporter asked.

"What! Know what the police were doing? Yes. Every move," Gil answered. "They did not stir but he knew it. Why, of course they were after him. I can't tell you what started them now, but you come to me when the boy is discovered, and I'll tell you such a history as never was written. Take you a week to write it." Gil returned to his thoughts about Martha. "She is a good woman, no better, a kind mother and as true a wife as ever a man had, but she's not so innocent of Bill Mosher's doings as she pretends. Time will prove that. Let Superintendent Walling alone: he'll bring all of that out. That woman would do anything Bill Mosher told her; yes, and lots of things he didn't tell her, to please him. She was all bound up in him, from first to last, and she thought of nothing else in the world but him."

When asked about the coroner's inquest, Gil scoffed. He accused the authorities of dismissing the fact that the victims had been needlessly shot. If the shooters were honestly defending themselves, Gil asked, then why did Mosher and Douglas have bullet holes in their backs? "Now, there's that coroner," Gil continued. "He didn't see the bodies? No. Well, you might have read how [Van Brunt and his men] told [Mosher and Douglas] to surrender, and then how the shooting began. Now, will you tell me, or can anyone explain, how, if he was fighting them, he came to have a shot in the back of his head and another in his back? Why wasn't that brought out at the inquest?"

Gil was right about the shooters. According to forensic evidence, the men were trigger-happy. The authorities should have questioned their behavior more thoroughly. But they didn't—and not because the Van Brunts were rich and powerful; status hadn't kept the shooters from testifying at the inquest. Their actions were excused because less than thirty years before, the "neighborhood watch" had preceded the police department. Citizens were allowed—encouraged, even—to treat their neighborhoods as jurisdictions that they supervised. Even if Van Brunt and his men hadn't justified their actions as self-defense, the implicit laws of the old guard probably would have protected them.

Still, Gil Mosher's criticism showed sufficient sibling loyalty. When Gil had put the police on his brother's path back in July, he had his eyes on the reward money, not another death in his family.

The Moshers' rivalries had led to bad feelings and at least one prison sentence. At the same time, they weren't so hardened that they rejected their sibling bond. Both brothers had lived through the deaths of their parents and twelve of their siblings. Gil Mosher had mentored his younger brother into thieving and a shipbuilding career, and Gil had tracked him down to let him know when their estranged mother died. When Westervelt told Bill Mosher that his older brother was acting as a police informant, the kidnapper's intense emotional response revealed the sting of betrayal, among other things. The men may not have liked each other, but they were emotionally connected. Had one wanted the other dead, there would have been plenty of opportunities earlier in their lives to make that happen.

Any allegiance Gil felt for his dead brother didn't cover his brother's widow. Martha Mosher now retracted earlier statements defending her husband against kidnapping charges. She still claimed she was ignorant of the crime, and although Gil called her "a good woman," he had also said she was "not so innocent" of her husband's activities. Believing Martha could lead to Charley, Gil implied that Walling shared whatever knowledge she had. Like Joseph Douglas, he used the words "Superintendent Walling knows."

The person most familiar with Walling's knowledge was somebody connected to both Douglas and Gil Mosher: William Westervelt. Walling had insisted that Westervelt communicate only with him, and at times, only in private. Any information that Walling told his fellow officers could have put them in closer contact with the reward, so he wouldn't have shared everything. Westervelt would have been the only person who knew what he told Walling.

Westervelt had spent the evening before Douglas's death with the kidnapper. He had been in touch with Gil Mosher early in the investigation, and later, as the two men were related by marriage, they remained in close physical proximity to Martha in the days surrounding her husband's funeral.

Whatever Westervelt had told Walling, he could have easily told Joseph Douglas, and Gil Mosher, and Martha Mosher.

By calling and relying upon Westervelt, Walling had given third parties an opportunity to incriminate him. As much as Mayor Stokley needed to distance himself from the case to ensure his political future, Walling needed to claim leadership of it to protect his reputation.

serve the public

THE *NEW YORK HERALD* WAS THE FIRST NEWSPAPER TO RAISE suspicions of Christian's involvement in Charley's kidnapping during the summer of 1874. Since then, Sarah Ross and her brothers had blamed the flurry of sensational journalism and the libel trial for Christian's deteriorating health. In late December, the *Herald* issued an apology.

"While [the Herald's] investigations of the matter carried on at a distance were meant simply to serve the public, they were in certain particulars erroneous in theory and facts. Our correspondent, acting upon false information, believed by him to be true, did the character of Mr. Ross a gross injustice."

Christian remained at his mother's home in central Pennsylvania through the holidays. Daily, he waited for a telegram saying the police had found Charley, or that a stranger had led him home to Germantown just as the Kensington man had aided Walter five months before.

On December 20, Sarah's brothers met again to discuss their frustration with slow police progress. Recent interviews with Mosher family members and friends contradicted initial police intelligence. Although Walling had repeated to the press that he could prove the kidnappers sold their horse and buggy en route to New York from Germantown on July 2, friends and members of the Mosher family placed the men in Philadelphia on July 3, and a Philadelphia bartender remembered talking to Mosher on the 4th. On that day, he told the *Inquirer*, he had allowed Mosher to pay his bar tab with small wooden carvings of miniature schooners.

The police also wasted time and resources allowing average citizens to contribute to the investigation. Along with one of Christian's nephews, Detective Heins agreed to meet a spiritualist who claimed she had seen Charley's spirit since September. Her latest trance, she said, revealed Charley sitting in bed while reading a book. And on December 17, Walling spent a large part of his day inside of his office, receiving any New Yorker who had a suggestion about how to proceed with the search. It was a smart public-relations move. Walling appeared to be exhausting every opportunity to learn more information. That day, one reporter counted sixteen "drop-in" advisers, most of whom were "gentlemen" of the town. When one of these men asked Walling why the police couldn't offer immunity to whoever returned the boy, the superintendent praised the idea but said he couldn't make such a promise if Charley were held across state lines. Walling did not, however, pursue this "good idea" in New York.

According to the *Evening Bulletin*, investors in Mayor Stokley's initial reward encouraged the idea of immunity. "It is stated that the contributors to the fund for the reward of $20,000 for the arrest and conviction of the abductors and the return of the child, are now considering the propriety of setting aside a portion of the amount for the recovery of the child, with 'no questions asked.'"

The Lewis brothers were the first to step forward with such an unconditional offer. Although Christian had no knowledge of the advertisement, his in-laws signed his name to the notice. Readers across the country saw it in papers on December 23.

> FIVE THOUSAND DOLLARS will be paid for the return, within ten days from this date, to any one of the addresses named below, of my son, CHARLES BREWSTER ROSS aged four years and seven months, who was taken from Germantown on July 1, 1874.
>
> Being entirely satisfied that his abductors were killed at Bay Ridge, L.I. on the 14th inst., I now offer the above sum for his return, or for information which shall lead thereto, promising to ask no questions.

The brothers instructed interested parties to leave Charley at one of seven different addresses between Washington, D.C., and Boston:

two belonged to the businesses of family friends in Baltimore and Washington, one to Christian's business on Market Street in Philadelphia, one to the Ross home in Germantown, and three to the businesses of the Lewis brothers in Philadelphia, New York, and Boston.

A response arrived at the Ross home after Christmas. It came in the form of another ransom note.

St. Louis, December 25, 1874

Mr. Ross—Dear Sir—You offer a reward for information that will lead to the recovery of Charley Ross. I know where he is and will tel you. I would have told you before but was afraid to, but since Douglass is dead I can tell you without fear. Last September I became acquainted accidentally with Joe Douglas and Bill Morris or Mosher (he called himself Morris then) and found out that they had Charley Ross hidden away, and they threatened to kill me if I betrayed them, but promised to pay me well to keep quiet. Now if you will give me $500 I will promise to deliver charley into your hands within three days from the time that I receive the money, or if you doubt me or my ability to do so, I will go to Philadelphia and take you to the place where he is now hidden, if you will send me money enough to pay my expenses and take me there, say bout one hundred dollars; then after you get the boy you can pay the rest. I will pledge you my life that I can do this, and would have done so before only I was in fear of my life, and it was only yesterday that I learned that Douglass was dead. If you will send the money I will do all that I have promised. Address James Cannon, care W.S. Wylie, No. 1743 North Ninth street, St Louis, Mo.

P.S. I am living six miles in the country, and Mr. Wylie is a friend, but knows nothing about this. If you send money by registered letter or money order, send it in Mr. Wylie's name.

PART FOUR:

"this is very uncertain"

(JANUARY–OCTOBER 1875)

TESTIMONY OF SARAH KERR, COURT OF QUARTER SESSIONS
Philadelphia, September 6, 1875
I was employed in Mr. Ross's family as a child's nurse in July of last
year. I remember the first day of July, 1874. I dressed the two boys,
Walter and Charley, that day. I first dressed Charley and sent him outdoors and then dressed Walter, that was between 3 and 4 o'clock. After
that I heard them talking outdoors and looking out of the window saw
Walter on the grass, that was a quarter past 4. I neither saw nor heard
anything of Charley after that.

beyond the range of possibility

MAYOR WILLIAM S. STOKLEY HAD BECOME WELL KNOWN IN
America toward the end of his first term. For the past five months, as
newspapers had recorded the nation's observations and speculations on
the Charley Ross case, an international audience had read of Philadelphia's $20,000 reward and the mayor who offered it.

On January 1, 1875, the city inaugurated Stokley into a second
term. The *Inquirer* called the ceremony "a particularly auspicious beginning of the new year" and lauded Stokley for protecting the city's
streets better than his predecessors had. Ignoring the famous crime that
the mayor's force had not, after five months, solved, writers praised
Stokley's efforts to destroy gambling halls, to prosecute thieves more

rigorously, and to pay attention to the appearance, hygiene, and vigilance of his officers.

Pennsylvania's Republicans needed this good publicity. After the November elections, when Republican incumbents had lost more seats than they had in eleven years, the two thousand members of Philadelphia's Union League met to discuss February's local elections, evaluate open positions, nominate candidates, and plan yet another implementation of Simon Cameron's weakening campaign strategy. Ulysses S. Grant's second term would expire in 1877. If his party did not reestablish itself as a political power strong enough to control the Northern states, the Democrats could very well return the whipping Grant gave them in 1872. The president had received his party's nomination in Philadelphia that year, an occasion that acquainted him with the city's newly crowned mayor.

Upon his reelection, Stokley's approval ratings appeared to be at an all-time high. Voters, however, had begrudgingly reelected him. They didn't like their higher debts and taxes, and they didn't like the way the city cut costs as it awaited the government's Centennial money. One disgruntled laborer mailed a threat to the mayor's office, warning him of hiring non-union labor.

> *Mr. Stokley*—SIR: The workingmen of this city that are almost starving to Death have formed an association to either have work or to have satisfaction out of such men as you that is robbing the city of every cent that it is worth. You have got one chance for your life that chance is this use your influence in Council and try and do something to alleviate our sufferings. Beware, for we are in earnest.
>
> BY ORDER OF THE SECRET SIX
>
> P.S. On our Centennial buildings instead of Putting citizens to work they pile in the italians because they can make them work for almost nothing.

Frustrated with political rhetoric, people wondered why their president and their civic leaders maintained ambivalent attitudes toward those displaced by the Civil War and victimized by the depression. The world knew it was coming to visit a nation still very much divided, and if Philadelphia were to embarrass America at the Centennial celebration, the Democrats could gain even more momentum—and they would have a scapegoat, a presidential acquaintance, to flaunt as the one who weakened under the international spotlight.

So as Mayor Stokley declared Philadelphia's streets safer than ever in 1875, he wasn't exactly ignoring social tensions and the unresolved Charley Ross kidnapping. On the contrary, he was "handling" them. Like any good politician, Stokley had learned how to live with uncomfortable stories: by issuing positive public statements and waiting. Only time could turn current events into memories, figments that could never be changed but always reconstructed.

Of course, if the mayor's police force could somehow initiate Charley's return, or at least uncover new evidence, Stokley would look more like the hero that the papers described.

A man from Kingston, New York, gave the mayor such hope soon after his second inauguration.

> I write to you this in regard to Charley Ross. I have not been interested, nor have I the time to bother about it. I am sure I know where he is. Now, Mr. Stokley, if you want to recover the lost boy, as I think you do, you will send somebody who knows him. You will find me in a store where I am employed, and will go with the person you send.

Stokley contacted Captain Heins and telegraphed Kingston. "Letter received. Please give grounds for your belief. Answer immediately."

"A woman is here, going to take him away," the response read. "What must I do?"

"See a justice of the peace and your district attorney, and be guided by their advice," Stokley answered. He did not forward Pinkerton's questions. "Telegraph the result."

"Send detectives at once," the Kingston office replied.

Captain Heins sent a telegram to Walling. "A man at Kingston, Ulster County, New York, professes to have important information as to the whereabouts of the boy. He has been in correspondence with our Mayor. Send an officer in Kingston in the early train tomorrow. Let your man say Mayor Stokley sent him."

Walling acted quickly.

Captain H. C. Heins, Philadelphia:—Your telegram received. Sent an officer (Selick) forthwith to Kingston to investigate. The child supposed to be Charley was a boy about 7 years of age, named Franklin P. Downer. It had been stolen from its father at New Hamburg by the mother, October 30, 1873.

George W. Walling, Superintendent

By the end of January, Stokley did have breaking news to announce. The state senate would soon approve a bill that identified kidnapping as a felony, not just a misdemeanor. Under the old law of March 1860, convicted kidnappers had faced a maximum fine of $2,000 and a maximum prison sentence of seven years at solitary confinement. The new law, which would be ratified on February 25, 1875, fined kidnappers a maximum of $10,000 and sentenced them to a maximum of twenty-five years at solitary confinement. It also provided a maximum fine of $5,000 and a maximum sentence of fifteen years for convicted accomplices.

Mayor Stokley used the impending bill to launch another public search effort. He reissued circulars listing the details of the kidnapping and the descriptions of Charley, the kidnappers, their horses, buggy, and boat. The new announcement also published the supposed route of the kidnappers, marking the first time that the mayor's office released details from the ransom letters:

After leaving Palmer and Richmond Streets, Philadelphia, about six o'clock PM, July 1, the abductors drove toward the city of Trenton, New Jersey, through which they said they passed on the night of July 2d, and on Bridge Street dropped the boy's hat—a broad-trimmed unbleached Panama, with black ribbon and without binding.

The statement continued, "After this they may have driven toward some one of the streams of water emptying into Raritan or Newark bay, or possibly as far as Newark, but this is very uncertain. The abductors returned to Philadelphia July 3d, where they mailed letters during the month."

Stokley challenged every citizen to empathize with Christian and Sarah Ross and again gather their neighbors together for a hunt. As an incentive, his office released another $5,000 reward for new information. It advised informants to contact either Stokley at Independence Hall or Superintendent Walling at New York's police headquarters on Mulberry Street.

WHEN CHRISTIAN RETURNED HOME FROM HIS MOTHER'S HOUSE in January, he received a second ransom note from the Christmas Day blackmailer, a Missouri man identified as James Cannon. Christian and his brothers-in-law contacted the St. Louis Police with what they knew about Cannon from his letters: the man claimed he was a former associate of the kidnappers, his handwriting resembled Bill Mosher's, and he said to contact him through a friend named "Wylie." Although the police had not yet released the ransom letters, newspapers had learned enough to describe them. Were Cannon not connected with Mosher, he could have read enough to imitate his penmanship.

After the kidnappers' deaths, America showed rejuvenated interest in the case by sending another surge of mail to the Ross home. Once again, writers alluded to Charley's whereabouts, offering to share secret information for the right price. The police and the family dismissed most claims as bogus. Cannon's, they accepted. His handwriting appeared suspect and his story also spoke to the authorities' latest hunch: whoever had Charley was an acquaintance of the kidnappers and kept the boy in a remote area.

Daniel O'Connor, chief of detectives in St. Louis, attempted to locate James Cannon. Failing to find a lead on that name, he and his associates traced "Wylie" to a riverboat. Officers arrested men on board and searched the premises. Inside of a desk, detectives found a stack of letters addressed to a Wylie. O'Connor shuffled through the papers and came across a note written in code.

Lgn Sxg ra abme jb yrun kmoo keber w jmroonrvb yw jm an lgxcpqo
Knab bx vxdn gry r anum qze bquan mr & nib rx wa ax lgyb gxdljw
owm gw l jamb Knix vua whion aajg bn & noxdr grv ab rw losn sv jwg
jih mnb bx ca en ny g Kn Scppwe rn Oxqxe ethn qzdn bx lztu egy &
pn xv qw Keb Xw gx&n uron dxwb ojru ca j&vm mxwh uxan lqnan
mr & jl brxwa lgw qxrnnj dn bqn h xth x bxbqn qubun bgun bgn
lrbqb qjrvm & xym lnah Xv tqc dxvax rb wx &bg bruw qxc lxyn bx
bqn G &enw bxm lvtn bqn G&& nw exjm jwm oxuaxe rb exx jKxcb
hennen rwna be&w wurbqub & rpbb x& uncb brun xxc lxyn bx bqu
on&& g G c & w bx bqu nacb bgn on & & g jwm cuny xw cy bqu ab
& nyb bbnw qxe yg aa vex bsj ma bytn bqn bqr &m Xun jam oxunxe
rb Xun Vxvn bnur gxc Qron j & crmnm lj krw ljin bon y j bg Kg bqn
ij kum rb y ny ma r w b x bqn a g y v jwn eruw bjin gxc bx hen ixcon
eqn & n bqu X xg va Keb v w wx ijan j & n gxc bx x cwyna a a ven-
bquvpqj y n j v a la ca bq n w qxc e new mx bqu Knaqb uxe Gwerbq
bqu k x g.

K. M X C P V J A

O'Connor knew that in Cannon's letters to Christian, he had said
the clue to Charley's location was hidden in such a code. The detective
handed the letter to a handwriting expert, who found a way to interpret
the cipher: it listed a set of directions leading potential searchers on a
goose chase.

The boy is still at Pine Bluff, but in a different place. We thought best
to move him. I send you these directions so that you can find him in
case it becomes necessary to remove him, or in case of any accident
to us. We may be jugged. If so, you will have to take charge of him;
but on your life don't fail us, and don't lose these directions. When
you leave the boat go to the hotel; take the right-hand road west of the
hotel; follow it north till you come to the Warren road; take the Warren
road and follow it for about twelve miles; turn neither right or left till
you come to the ferry; turn to the left at the ferry, and keep on the
straight road till you pass two roads, take the third one and follow it
one mile till you come to a ruined cabin; take the path by the cabin,
it leads into the swamp, and will take you to the house where the boy

is. But in no case are you to go unless something happens to us; then you will do the best you can with the boy.

O'Connor's final report summarized the St. Louis mystery. "By comparing the writing in the letters A and B and in the cipher letter with the ordinary chirography of the man Wylie," he wrote, "little doubt can exist that Cannon and Wylie are one and the same person; that Wylie is the inventor and engineer of the whole thing, which is nothing less than an outrageous attempt to perpetrate a swindle upon Mr. Ross."

Detectives began wondering aloud whether Charley was even alive. More than a month had passed since Mosher and Douglas's deaths, and nobody had stepped forward to claim any of the various rewards—including the one offering both $5,000 and immunity to whoever returned Charley to his uncles, the Lewis brothers.

If Charley were still alive, the detectives asked, why wouldn't he have been returned? What more could captors—particularly ones taken aback by the kidnappers' deaths—want besides money and liberty?

Their questions could have been red herrings, attempts to discourage their competition from pursuing the mayor's reward and tracking the boy. Nevertheless, once detectives verbalized what many had feared, the public allowed themselves to admit a horrible truth: their hunt could very well lead to a dead child.

Searchers slowed down. Journalists focused less on stories of lost little boys. Charley's uncles followed fewer leads to far-off places.

The *Inquirer* interpreted a quieter public as the city's collective, cynical response to the Ross family. It was wrong. Many felt just as much compassion as they had over the past several months, only they had internalized it more. Americans were still recovering from the post-traumatic stress brought on by the Civil War. When confronted with the prospect of another tragic reality, they protected themselves by turning their optimism into familiar grief. Some buried their fears under distractions. Some consciously fell silent, choosing not to further false hope. Some refused to admit failure and continued to look, accuse, and demand information. Others turned to spiritual comfort.

"Up to this hour all earthly attempts to solve the mystery have proved abortive, notwithstanding the large rewards offered," wrote one Philadelphia man. "Permit me to suggest another mode to recover Charley Ross. Our people are eminently a Christian people. Let them call their several denominations together and unitedly set apart a day or a week for prayer to Almighty God for the restoration of this dear boy to his parents."

Such an effort wasn't publicized, but perhaps it worked. A New Jersey man came forward with the most important physical clue thus far.

Back in July, he said, his little girl had found Charley's hat. She had been playing with her friends on the side of a road in Trenton when she spotted it on the ground. The girl showed it to her father when she went home, but he said he didn't make the connection between it and the description of Charley Ross's clothes until he saw Mayor Stokley's latest reward.

Sarah Ross identified the hat, and the children's nurses confirmed that it was the one Charley had been wearing when the kidnappers took him. The Trenton find was the closest that Charley's family had been to their four-year-old since he had disappeared several months before. Amid hundreds of false leads, the hat refreshed their hope. It also confirmed the theory that the kidnappers had driven through Trenton with Charley in the wagon.

Unless they had planted the hat to make it look that way.

September 2, 1875

"When your husband lay in his boat at Newark Bay, evading the police, whom he knew to be after him, where were you? Were you with him?"

"I decline to answer."

"Did you ever see Charley Ross?"

"I never did."

"Did your brother Westervelt, now testifying in Philadelphia, ever see Charley Ross?"

"No, he did not. He knows nothing at all about the case. He was just the same as kidnapped from New York to go [to Philadelphia]. He can tell nothing."

"Have you not read his testimony, given in the court today, published in the evening papers?"

"It is a lie—a base lie. He knows nothing about the case. I don't know what he testified today. He never saw the child. He can't tell where he is. I don't care what the evening papers say."

"Well, we will pass over the testimony. Are you willing to go to Philadelphia and testify to the case?"

"No, sir; there is no power on earth can make me go to Philadelphia. They tried to get me to go to my brother, telling me I could come back the next day, but I saw through their game. I have consulted with the best lawyers in New York, and I know my rights. I know that I cannot be forced to go to Philadelphia, and I won't go and they cannot make me go. I might go on my own option, but I cannot be driven there."

what have you got now?

THROUGHOUT JANUARY AND FEBRUARY, SUPERINTENDENT Walling reviewed what few reliable facts existed of the kidnapping act on July 1, 1874. The police had descriptions of Charley, the kidnappers, and the horse and buggy. Charley was missing and the kidnappers were dead, but for all Walling knew, the horse and buggy could be in plain sight. In their excitement over the chase and demise of Mosher and Douglas, the police hadn't dedicated much time to finding the getaway transportation. If he could find a caretaker for the horse, Walling thought he could learn more about the kidnappers' location in the hours following their crime.

Walling published more flyers detailing the case and instructed his men to spread them throughout New York and New Jersey. The superintendent personally asked ten newspapers in the region to carry his newest reorganization of the facts.

Within days of the reprinting, a stable keeper in Newark named Van Fleet contacted Walling's office.

Van Fleet said that in October 1874, a well-dressed young man about eighteen years old had led a scrawny-looking horse to his stables. Burs stuck to the animal's mane, its back looked sore, and its hair had turned red, a sign of poor health and bad grooming. Assuming the horse was a castoff that the boy had found roaming in the woods, Van Fleet agreed to take care of it through the weekend. The young man did return, but later than he had promised. He was accompanied by a man resembling the description of Bill Mosher. The older stranger told a black stable hand that if he could "take good care of the animal" for a while longer, he would repay him generously. He also instructed the hostler to clean reddish hairs off of the horse's black tail by washing it in salt water. One week later, a different, angrier man came to take the horse. When Van Fleet asked him for the promised money, the man swore and walked away.

New York Police Detective Titus went to New Jersey to examine the horse and interview Van Fleet. He reported back to Walling. Once he determined the story was accurate, Walling telegraphed Heins in Philadelphia and asked him to send his "best resource" to identify the horse. Heins contacted Christian, telling him to take Walter immediately to Newark. Unlike the trip he had gone on to identify the kidnappers' bodies a month before, Walter understood this particular mission.

"I shall know the horse, sure," the boy said to the press. "He has a white star upon his forehead, a white hind leg, a sore back, and there is a wind gall or wen on one of his hind legs. But I shall know him best because when the horse started he turned around and laughed." Heins and Christian both remembered Walter's giving them this last detail six months before. Because it had seemed too imaginative, they had kept it from published descriptions.

As soon as Christian escorted Walter into Van Fleet's stables, a stable hand led the horse out for Walter's inspection. The six-year-old recognized and pointed to a white patch on the horse's forehead and one on its left hind leg. He said the horse had more hair on one side than he remembered. Van Fleet told Christian that when he first saw the horse, it had a thin patch of hair on one side, but that it had grown in the past few months.

The police asked a worker to hitch the horse to a wagon so Walter could see it move as he may have on the day he was kidnapped. Once Walter sat behind the horse, somebody pulled the reins. As soon as it heard "Get up!," the horse turned its head to one side and showed its teeth.

"Look, Papa, look!" said Walter. "See, the horse is laughing at us."

Walling ordered his men to locate the young man who had first taken the horse to Van Fleet. He told the stable keeper, the Newark Police, and the local press not to intimidate the young man if he came forward. Regardless of the information the boy provided, Walling said, he would grant him immunity from any wrongdoing and "heavily" reward his cooperation.

Walling's discovery of Van Fleet's stables did not reverse the damage caused by his earlier self-aggrandizing behavior. When the superintendent took credit for tracing Mosher and Douglas, he had indirectly encouraged the press to hold him solely responsible for finding Charley. Like the millionaire Arthur Purcell, whose ransom offer the kidnappers rejected, Walling had become a failed hero when Charley didn't quickly appear.

Not only had the superintendent been unable to claim any of Philadelphia's reward money, but he also faced losing professional pay in February, when a known burglar accused Walling of arresting and detaining him without evidence for a crime he didn't commit. He was guilty, the prisoner said, only by association—the police had caught two of his acquaintances at the scene of the crime. In addition, two women registered a complaint against Superintendent Walling for using "violent language" and denying them visitation rights when they went to see the prisoners.

Walling disputed both charges, claiming he had the right to detain a thief while his officers looked for evidence and he searched for the stolen property. As for the women, Walling said, he had no way of knowing if the accused would tell them where to relocate the stolen goods, and at no time did he use inappropriate language. The press expected the Board of Commissioners to agree with Walling's justification. If it did not, then he faced a fine equal to ten days' pay or a dismissal.

The superintendent did have at least one thing working in his favor: his relationship with William Westervelt. The closest man to the kidnappers still reported solely to him. Between August 1874 and February 1875, the two men had met more than fifty times. To Walling's knowledge, Westervelt didn't communicate with anyone else in authority—even Pinkerton; the private detectives had tried to build a confidence with the informant, but Westervelt said he rejected their offer. So if the board did the unthinkable and took up the cause of a former convict, Walling could always use Westervelt's confidence as leverage.

Reporters had learned that Walling was in touch with a person close to William Mosher. They didn't know William Westervelt's name, but they knew that he had information and referred to him as one who created "renowned excitement in police circles." Besides Captain Heins, authorities in Philadelphia didn't know much more than the press.

The advisers had lost footing in the Ross case months before. After Christian fell ill, the Lewis brothers reclaimed the family's leadership role in the investigation. Philadelphia's city leaders hadn't approved of this shift in power, but the involvement of New York's force had already limited their participation, making it easier for the family to work directly with Captain Heins. Perhaps the most frustrated adviser was William V. McKean, the manager and editor of the *Public Ledger*. His paper had been the first in the world to print news of Charley's disappearance, and he wasn't about to become a member of the crowd awaiting bulletins outside of newspaper offices. McKean went to New York to offer Walling his consulting services, and to speak directly with his source. Walling acquiesced.

Although the superintendent continued to micromanage the investigation, he had gradually begun to place a greater distance between himself and Westervelt. Prior to the kidnappers' deaths, he had suspected Westervelt enough to have him followed, and now that the informant couldn't be used to track Mosher and Douglas, he was left wondering whether he had been manipulated into revealing police intelligence. Because Westervelt still believed he could earn his position back on the force, the superintendent didn't view him as a flight risk, but he did need to increase the pressure if his informant had anything else to reveal. Plus, Walling didn't have too many friends among newspaper writers, and appeasing a major editor in Philadelphia could only help his reputation.

McKean took Westervelt to the Fifth Avenue Hotel and ordered dinner for the two of them in a private room. While they ate, McKean asked questions he had prepared. The editor was confident that in this interview, Westervelt would reveal more to him than he had shared with New York's superintendent. To his frustration, Westervelt gave him the same answers he had given everybody else. At some point during the private dinner, Walling became so uncomfortable with the length of McKean's interrogation that he knocked on the door. McKean did not respond.

Eventually, McKean returned to Philadelphia—disappointed. Over the next two months, however, he would frequently visit Walling's office.

Meanwhile, Westervelt became more frustrated with Walling. He hadn't liked McKean, and he didn't like the way Walling became abrasive toward him when McKean was in the room. During one hour-long meeting of the three men, McKean had called Westervelt a "thief" and accused him of wearing stolen clothes. Instead of defending his informant, Walling let McKean say what he wanted.

Westervelt told Walling to stop bullying him. He reminded Walling that his wife, Mary, was pawning their belongings to make rent at a tenement house. He asked when he was going to get his promised job on the force back. But instead of reinstating him, Walling found Westervelt a job as a driver for the Adams Express Company. He also slipped him some money occasionally.

On February 12, soon after he began work with the Adams Express, Westervelt received a summons from Walling. He returned, once again, to police headquarters on Mulberry Street.

"You need to go to Philadelphia and meet with the city authorities," Walling said.

"No."

"You have to."

"Do you think this is necessary?" Westervelt asked.

"It must be, or they wouldn't send for you." Walling advised him to leave early in the morning.

Westervelt said he didn't have any wages yet to use for the trip.

"That shouldn't stop you," said Walling. He handed him ten dollars.

When Westervelt left New York the next morning on a 7:00 A.M. train, he planned to return at 3:00 P.M.

Captain Heins met Westervelt in Philadelphia. The two men went to police headquarters at the State House on Fifth and Chestnut Streets. There, they met Christian Ross, Joseph Lewis, Detective Wood, and two other men who took notes of the conversation. For the rest of the day, the men interrogated Westervelt about his involvement with the kidnappers. They asked him to review his interactions with the Mosher family and Joseph Douglas in the summer and fall of 1874.

"Did you ever hear of any conspiracy of this kind, of any abduction, when you were [in Philadelphia]?"

"No."

"Did [Mosher] say that Gil had given him away?" they asked.

"I guess."

"Did either or both [Mosher and Douglas] come [to your house] a few days before Mrs. Mosher came there?"

"Yes."

"Did you say to Walling several times where he could get these men?"

"I did not say several times."

"You told me this afternoon that you told Walling you could take both of them, and that Walling objected," Detective Wood said.

"If I said that I made a mistake. I meant only Douglas."

Heins disagreed. "Walling said he would not take Douglas alone. Mosher was the brains of the concern. You repeated the word 'them' many times."

"If I said that I made a mistake. I meant only Douglas."

"Can't you make a shrewd guess where the child is?"

Westervelt said he thought perhaps Charley was given to somebody Mosher and Douglas had encountered after the kidnapping.

When pressed, he responded, "You are trying to insult me. I know no more about what was done with that child than a child unborn."

The more Westervelt voiced his innocence, the more the men rephrased the same questions. Frequently after listening to Westervelt's answers, Heins asked a gentleman taking notes, "What have you got now?" Westervelt grew more and more irritated. As he listened to his testimony repeated back, he attempted to point out reporting errors. Despite his requests at the end of the day, Westervelt never heard the full transcript of his interview. He spent that night at the State House, and questioning resumed the next morning.

Again, Heins asked why Westervelt would not admit to promising Walling an arrest of both kidnappers. "Now yesterday afternoon you said to me that you told Superintendent Walling over and over again where these men could be got."

"I think you misunderstood me then."

"Why is it you told me yesterday that you had told him when he could get the men?"

"I think you misunderstood me still."

"You said to me that you wanted to make the reward of twenty thousand dollars, that you were working for the reward, and yet you know very well that you could not have made the reward by getting Douglas alone, as it could only be obtained by getting both the men and the child, and you know that as well as you are sitting in that chair."

Westervelt was trapped.

"Well," he answered, "I did not want to give Mosher away myself. If he could be taken in some way accidentally, I had no objection, but I did not want my sister to say to me if her children were brought to trouble that I done it by putting her husband in prison."

Before lunch, Heins informed Westervelt that he was under arrest. Based upon his answers, a grand jury had indicted him for involvement in the kidnapping. Heins took him to a station near Tenth Street.

Five days later, when Heins, Lewis, and another man visited, Westervelt accused them of inhumane treatment. Not only did the February winds blow through the cell's broken windows, Westervelt said, but he also had no bed or blankets, and he had to sleep with his head on a tin cup. Chief Jones transferred him to a better cell before sending the prisoner to Moyamensing, Philadelphia's county jail.

Philadelphia, September 3, 1875

"I have seen Mrs. Westervelt since her husband came to this city. I gave her a letter to some parties to assist her. I have never been to see her nor do I know where she lives. I never saw her until she came to see me and told me that she and her children were in a very bad condition."

"Did you ever tell her that you considered this prosecution an outrage and that her husband was an innocent man?"

"Objection."

The witness said he couldn't remember saying that.

"Had you any conversation with her as to the prosecution of her husband, and if so, what and whom?"

"Objection. Leading the witness."

"Have you had any conversation with Mrs. Westervelt in regard to this prosecution, and if so, when?"

"Objection. Irrelevant."

"Overruled."

"I had a conversation with her relative to her husband and his being under arrest here. She asked me about it. I don't remember the date. She came to headquarters and it was then that I spoke of."

we do right to pity Charley Ross

ONCE WESTERVELT WAS BEHIND BARS, THE DISTRICT ATTORNEY wanted to wait for more police intelligence before he began preparing his prosecution. Although the new state law had increased kidnapping penalties, the state senate had complicated the Westervelt case by adding a grandfather clause to the bill. This amendment gave Charley's kidnappers one month to present him in exchange for a lighter sentence.

The grandfather clause was necessary because less than two months before it was approved, the Lewis brothers had offered immunity to any kidnapper who returned Charley to one of seven business locations. Immediate enforcement of the new law (which sentenced perpetrators to a maximum of twenty-five years and accomplices to a maximum of fifteen) would have countered the family's claims, sending a contradictory message to the criminal community. Therefore, the senate said, acts of kidnapping would result in the punishments stated by the new bill "[. . .] provided, that this shall not apply to the detaining or concealing of any child taken or carried away before the passage of this act, where the person or persons so harboring or concealing shall, within thirty days after the passage of this act, surrender up such child to the custody of the nearest magistrate or justice of the peace, or to the sheriff of any county within this Commonwealth."

Upon Westervelt's arrest, the police had only enough evidence to charge him as an accomplice, and because Charley was kidnapped before the new act was passed, Westervelt could only be sentenced under the old law, which had no penalty for accomplices. According to it, convicted kidnappers would serve a maximum of seven years in solitary confinement and a $2,000 fine; and if the police could not find evidence proving that Westervelt directly harbored Charley, then he would serve even less time as an accomplice. By law, police could detain a suspected felon for six months after an indictment before they had to either bring him to trial or release him. So if they wanted to bring the fullest charges allowed by the new bill against Westervelt, then they needed to gather more evidence quickly. Another hitch was the grandfather clause: if Charley was returned on or before March 25, charges against Westervelt would have to be dropped.

The police kept Westervelt's name from the press after his arrest. No word of his incarceration reached the public for about a month, even though Westervelt told anybody who would listen that Walling had "kidnapped" him by sending him to Philadelphia on false premises. Such publicity would have benefitted the police, but in order to more fully make their case, they needed to actually find Charley and/or a kidnapper who would shoulder as much blame as Mosher and Douglas.

In the meantime, officials tried to protect Christian from any more false leads. When officers in Camden, New Jersey, arrested an Italian organ maker who was traveling with a young boy Charley's age, two Philadelphia detectives went to identify the child. Because of Italy's recent history of kidnappings (the Catholic church took children off the street to convert them), the American police continued to target Italian immigrants. The officers saw the Camden boy and immediately sent word to Christian—the child really did look like Charley. By 6:00 P.M., when Christian reported to the mayor's office, the town had rushed to the police station after hearing rumors that Charley Ross waited inside for his father. Hundreds of people saw the child through the station windows and the doorway.

Christian walked past the masses.

He entered the building, looked at the child, and began to cry.

"It's not him," he said.

As Christian walked out of the building and back down the street, several people in the crowd wiped their eyes.

The arrested man could not properly identify the child. Even so, the police released the boy back into his custody.

Citizens of Savannah, Georgia, thought the kidnappers had resurfaced when two men approached another set of boys aged six and four. The younger of the two men, about five feet eight inches tall, had black hair. Behind glasses, his eyes held a deranged look. His partner had gray hair, a tall, skinny frame, and a small head and neck. Eyewitnesses heard the younger man speak very quickly in a German accent to the two boys, who apparently followed the men to a train station. There, more witnesses saw the group of four, later telling police that they assumed the party was headed to Europe. Detectives never found the kidnappers or the boys.

"We do right to pity Charley Ross," the *New York Tribune* said, "taken from his comfortable home and loving father, but these other souls who have lost their way, belong by right to an honest, intelligent, virtuous life, and their father is God. Have we no outcry, no money, no pity for them?" The *Tribune* asked why the authorities of Philadelphia and New York were more committed to Charley's plight than those of other kidnapping victims or unfortunate children. The editorial pled the case of New York's street children, 25 percent of the city's adolescent population, and of the eleven thousand street children in Philadelphia, more than three thousand were "from four to eight years old . . . found in different manufactories kept at work, from ten to fourteen hours a day." As Philadelphia sent new Charley circulars to police stations and railway depots throughout America, the unsolved cases of other little ones disappeared after brief mention in the press.

Christian told the press he believed that more than half a million people were involved in the search for Charley. He said detectives, searching for his son from coast-to-coast, had spent more than $25,000 and had retained an entire group of clerks whose sole job was to pursue the leads, false information, and hoaxes spread by Americans and Europeans. Christian estimated that his team had mailed more than 700,000 circulars to police stations and train depots throughout the country. According to his count, police had interrogated more than two hundred gypsy bands for information and investigated the stories of more than six hundred children who resembled his son. By their own admission, police agreed that many of these six hundred children, misplaced themselves, were returned to the custody of adults who hadn't provided enough information to keep the children from being questioned in the first place. This number itself was only a fraction of boys and girls across America who remained on the streets or in the hands of thieves, murderers, and traffickers.

But after all of the money spent, all of the manpower exhausted, all of the circulars mailed, and all of the innocent men and women interrogated because of skin color or lifestyle choice, one lead remained overlooked. Had the advisory committee involved detectives in their initial, secretive conversations sooner, had the police and private detectives cooperated with one another, had Superintendent Walling ordered his men to arrest Joseph Douglas before tracing Bill Mosher, and had he demanded the constant surveillance of Westervelt and his family once the informant proved unreliable, authorities might have noticed important contradictions in the Mosher family's testimonies.

September 2, 1875

"Did you see the facsimiles of the letters to Mr. Ross by the abductors which were published in the Herald last year?"

"Yes, I saw them, and they are not in my husband's handwriting."

"Ross experts have pronounced them to be in the same handwriting as letters written by your husband."

"I don't care for experts. I know my husband's handwriting, and besides no letter of his has ever been found. They have all been destroyed."

. . .

"Mrs. Mosher, now tell me candidly, is the boy living or dead?"

"I do not know. I am sure he is living and will turn up before long. I am as sure that he is living as I am that I breathe. I would not believe him dead unless I should see his dead body before me."

"How do you know that he is still living?"

"I decline to answer this question."

is my child dead?

CHRISTIAN AND SARAH ROSS PRAYED THAT IN SPITE OF THE weather, somebody would respond to the Lewis brothers' reward and return Charley to the doorsteps of one of the family's seven business locations. Outside of the three designated Philadelphia buildings, during the winter of 1875 steady successions of sleet, snow, rain, and hail glazed the sidewalks. Dozens of sparrows lay dead in the town squares, gas meters froze throughout the city at night, and wind chills contributed to 373 deaths in one week.

West of Center City, an ice block threatened the residents and industrial laborers of Manayunk. The gorge sat just above the Fairmount dam, which regulated the flow of the Schuylkill River. The

River had risen five feet above its normal level. Water had flooded the Manayunk mills, causing workers to lose a week's pay and neighborhood residents to flee north or west for higher ground; they couldn't go east, as ice blocked the roads leading into central Philadelphia. The Water Department needed to break up the ice, because it kept clean water from freely flowing throughout the city's water pipes. At the Ross home in Germantown, water looked as brown as lager. It stunk, and it would only smell worse until the river could move through sunlight and aeration. The engineers, however, had to be careful—if the ice blocks broke too quickly, the heightened river would hurl them into the homes and businesses of Manayunk.

Mayor Stokley supervised attempts to blow up the ice pack. Engineers drilled holes in the ice and lowered large tin vessels full of dynamite into the water. Long tin cylinders carried fuses to the powder. The explosions were loud but unsuccessful. At most, small pieces broke away, but without enough water flow to carry them downriver, they became lodged in the dam. Because the City Council would not allot enough money for a more creative solution, Stokley and the engineers had to pray for a gentle March. Only warmer weather could aid their efforts.

A new town ordinance threatened to fine home owners two dollars for failing to remove trash, snow, and ice from the streets, but police found it difficult to uphold. Instead of insisting that officers enforce ice removal, Chief Jones cited the danger of kite flying as a public nuisance and instructed his men to fine offenders five dollars. Throughout the winter, the *Bulletin* had chastised the force for ignoring the weather-related conditions of the streets, which sent more injuries to area hospitals than did kite flying: "[The] commodious, well-paved, well-lighted, well-policed streets are not only necessary for the comfort, safety, and convenience of the population, but they give a style to any city which nothing else can give. Philadelphia is aiming at a metropolitan position, and she has many of these elements which go to make such a position."

New York papers frowned upon this "metropolitan position," questioning whether Philadelphia could handle the lodging needs of the Centennial's thousands of visitors. Slowly, successful New Yorkers had begun supporting the exhibition, signing and publishing notices that encouraged people to consider its potential for New York tourism. "All the visitors from foreign countries will land here, will find more objects of interest here than in Philadelphia," wrote the *Herald*. "It would be as great a loss to New York as to the most important of its suburbs, Philadelphia, if the Exposition should fall short of public expectation."

This is exactly what Philadelphia feared: sending elsewhere the attention that it deserved. The *Evening Bulletin* initially defended the city's accommodation plans, but after the dedication of a new Masonic hall in Center City, local critics worried about the rooming shortage as well. When more than five thousand visitors came to town for the ceremony, less than a fifth of the number predicted for the Centennial, hotels quickly ran out of rooms, and managers had to construct temporary accommodations in hallways and other common areas. Everybody knew more hotels would be needed in less than a year, but there was not enough time, manpower, or funds to construct them properly. Ignoring city ordinances and fire codes, some contractors began building temporary residences from wood.

The city leaders claimed there was plenty of lodging space available, but because so much of it was privately owned, they said home owners needed to allow familiar and foreign guests to stay in their spare rooms. "Nearly everybody is 'coming home' in the Centennial year," wrote the *Ledger*. "But after all allowances are made for these [visitors], there will of course remain a large number of dwellings with perfectly available quarters for tens of thousands of visitors." Considering that Philadelphia was still the focus of a famous kidnapping investigation, this request was an odd one to ask of citizens.

Even if families considered allowing strangers into their homes in the wake of Charley Ross's disappearance, a surge in violent domestic crimes threatened to alienate potential guests. One disgruntled man struck his wife's head with the edge of a dull axe; another sliced his wife from her throat to her lips with a razor; and a third man responded to his wife's complaints over his drunkenness by throwing their six-month-old daughter from a third-story window. When one young newlywed took a stand against domestic abuse and reported her husband to the police, he stalked her through Fairmount Park, pulled out a knife, and stabbed her in the jugular vein in broad daylight.

Police also arrested landlords and custodians for abusing their boarders. One South Philadelphia man stumbled drunk into his house one afternoon as his wife tended to their infant twins in the kitchen. After he threatened to kill her, she ran away with one baby while he poured a two-gallon can of kerosene underneath the cradle of the other. A seventy-two-year-old tenant fought to take matches from the man's hands, but he struck one on the wall behind her, lighting himself and his boarder on fire. Neighbors extinguished the flames and saved the family, but the elderly woman died from shock.

Several blocks away, neighbors contacted the police with concerns about screams coming from the home of two sisters, Catherine and Amanda Troxell. Five officers raided the house. After following an overwhelming stench to the rear of the third story, the police found fifty-year-old Mary Troxell, another sister who had recently been released from an insane asylum. Police sent Mary back to the hospital on the stretcher and reentered her room to stake out the source of the smell. Before long, they came across the corpse of the sisters' mother, who had been dead for at least three months.

Neither the papers nor the authorities attempted to reconcile the assaults with their request for citizens to offer their homes as hostels for parents and children during the six-month duration of the exhibition.

The city leaders couldn't resolve Philadelphia's social tensions, but they could distract taxpayers' concern by emphasizing the financial capital that the Centennial would bring to Philadelphia. In order to capitalize on the city's future progress, however, these leaders had to distance themselves from stories that attracted bad press. Charley Ross's name slipped from the *Public Ledger*, and an *Inquirer* editorial lamented the lack of interest in the case. "So little that seemed availing has been done recently in the Ross case that the public have, reluctantly, adopted the idea that the unfortunate Charley Ross was either dead or that, if living, his identity had by this time been forever lost."

New York, September 6, 1875

"Mrs. Mosher, you said in your interview with a Herald reporter that you were confident that the child is alive. What reason have you for thinking so?"

"Because I know my husband wouldn't have hurt a hair of his head. Mr. Walling and Mr. McKean both told me that they thought the child was living when my husband was killed, and nobody would have any reason to kill the child since."

"Did you ever see the child?"

"I never did, nor did I ever see anyone else that saw him, or knew of anyone who saw him unless it was my husband."

"Did you ever suspect that your husband might have done the stealing for a third party?"

"Yes sir. I think he would have done it if he was paid for it. I thought at times that the child was stolen for someone else. I never had any real reason for thinking so, though. My husband wanted money. He intended, if he could get enough, to get up a floating palace for the Centennial."

she is a city

MARCH 25, 1875, THE LAST DAY OF IMMUNITY GUARANTEED BY the new kidnapping act, came and went without any developments in the case. Only when the *Inquirer* noted the significance of the date did it introduce the public to William Westervelt. "Some days ago, Westervelt, the brother-in-law of Mosher, the burglar who was shot and killed at Bay Ridge, Long Island, was induced to come to this city for a conference with the police authorities relative to the case. Today he occupies a cell in Moyamensing Prison, and it is reported that there is a bill of indictment against him, based, it is said, on admissions made by him in some of his statements implying a knowledge of the abduction." The note ran at the bottom of a paragraph reviewing slow case progress, and city papers did not publish follow-up articles providing details on the indictment.

The Philadelphia *Public Ledger* may not have released information about Westervelt's arrest because it was a mouthpiece for the Republican advisers. It is curious, though, that neither the *Inquirer* nor the *Evening Bulletin* mentioned the detention of a man who authorities deemed partially responsible for Charley's disappearance. The papers may have become more judicious about printing speculation about Charley, but they hadn't wavered from reporting other confirmed progress in the investigation around the time of Westervelt's arrest— like the hat discovery in Trenton or the horse at Van Fleet's stables. The only logical explanation for the omission is that journalists' connections in the police department must not have disclosed the importance of William Westervelt. Yet confidential case information—like the content of the ransom letters—had moved fairly consistently to reporters from their sources at police headquarters. It makes sense, then, that the press didn't know details about Westervelt because the police didn't know.

Chief Jones, Captain Heins, and Detective Wood were the Philadelphia officers most entrenched in the investigation. Had they kept Westervelt's information to themselves, and had they given Westervelt the incentive to keep his mouth shut in prison, then it was plausible that the public would not realize that the biggest lead in the Ross investigation was in custody in Philadelphia. The question was why. Why wouldn't the Philadelphia police have wanted to publicize the arrest after hearing accusations of incompetence? Westervelt was clearly involved with Mosher and Douglas. This information alone could have earned public approval. Even a few details about Westervelt's familial relationship with one of the kidnappers could have calmed parents a bit more, and made the city appear safer in the midst of Centennial plans. But for some reason, the advisers were keeping Westervelt's story secret, and Captain Heins, who acted more independently than anybody else in the investigation, agreed with them.

So, unaware of Westervelt's story, Philadelphia continued to turn its attention away from what was taken from it toward what was coming to it.

Visitors journeyed to the Centennial grounds through snow showers at the beginning of April. They donned their spring best for the occasions—men dressed in white suits and ladies wore high, round hats decorated with ribbons and ostrich feathers. Parading around the freshly, constructed custom house and ticket office, visitors saw gardeners preparing flower beds and pruning shrubs. Before the winter's first storms, the head contractor had insisted upon covering the grounds with building materials like granite and bricks; his foresight prevented the ground from freezing completely, and his men had continued erecting Memorial Hall, the centerpiece of the grounds, throughout the cold weather. Once the builders laid the foundation to Horticultural Hall, a second exhibition building, the city held a week-long fund-raiser called the Bazaar of Nations at the site. There, artisans and caterers sold crafts and food, orchestras played, scholars spoke, and African-American waiters sang spirituals.

The Centennial Commission solicited proposals from photographers and continued encouraging civic groups to hold private and public fund-raisers in neighborhoods around the city—the press called these events successful, but planners were frustrated that European countries had expressed more interest in financing displays than did any of America's states other than Pennsylvania and New Jersey. Partnering with the Pennsylvania Railroad, local businessmen organized an all-expenses-paid tour of the grounds for their colleagues in New York and New England. The visitors walked through the construction sites, commented on the diligent work of the planning committee, and noted the camaraderie of the builders. They were especially pleased to see two of the five main buildings already occupying 3,300 square feet of ground. Before the train returned the delegation to New York at 8:00 P.M., many agreed to sponsor exhibits highlighting the soil sciences, the mines, forestry, craftsmanship, education, metals, and manufactories.

May and June passed without any publicized progress in the Ross investigation. One year after Charley's disappearance, three thousand school children participated in a concert on a makeshift stage inside

Machinery Hall. Twenty-two thousand parents, neighbors, and other guests sat in the midst of international flags, streamers, and banners bearing each state's coat of arms. Onstage, the children held flowers and wore medals inscribed with "Liberty to All Americans, July 4, 1776."

Not only did those out-of-state businessmen who had pledged support uphold their promises, but more western states paid to reserve display space, and city financiers received funds a year overdue from the national government. The *Inquirer* boasted of the money flowing into Philadelphia from around the world. "Those who have been accustomed to regard her as a sort of suburb or appendage of New York . . . will be apt to form a different idea of her when they learn that she is a city with a population of nearly 890,000."

you need not ask more questions

Toward the end of August, 1875, the Ross case began to dominate the headlines again. By then, Philadelphia's district attorney had to either try Westervelt on conspiracy charges or allow him to walk. Believing there was sufficient evidence to link Mary Westervelt to her husband's activities, Captain Heins also wanted her to stand trial for conspiracy. Superintendent Walling came to her defense. Even though Mary had admitted to housing Bill Mosher's family and to periodically meeting with the kidnappers, Walling said she was ignorant of her husband's behavior.

Christian Ross and his family hoped that after six months in prison, Westervelt would tire of responding to the same questions and contradict his previous answers. More than once, Sarah Ross had visited him at the Moyamensing Prison in South Philadelphia. Through tired tears, she had begged him to tell her where Charley was hiding, but Westervelt insisted on his innocence. Once, he even began crying with her, kneeling to pray with her as she asked God to return her little boy.

The trial began on August 31, 1875, in a courthouse behind Independence Hall. On the first day, there was room for all of the onlookers inside of the courtroom. Sitting on benches behind the docks holding the defendant, the defense lawyers, and the prosecutors, they saw Westervelt turn as his wife, their eight-year-old daughter and their six-year-old son rushed up the aisle to join him in the docks. When he kissed his family, he cried. As the case continued, spectators also filled the aisles and the back of the courtroom. Those who stood could see

Westervelt's large frame sitting next to Joseph Ford and Newton Brown, two respected Philadelphia attorneys.

Every day but Sundays, the crowd sat or stood in oppressive heat, leaning forward to hear testimonies full of details that the police and the city advisers had kept from them over the past fourteenth months—months in which they had searched for Charley, suspected their neighbors of taking him, prayed for the Ross family, and restricted their own children's outdoor play. They watched Westervelt take notes and exchange smiles with his wife during the testimonies of Walter and Christian Ross. They then watched this confidence wear away as Westervelt listened to colleagues testify against his character, and as he heard eyewitnesses tell of his walks and conversations around Germantown. What thrilled the audience most, though, was the reading of the twenty-three ransom letters that they had begged to see for more than a year.

During the fourth and final week of Westervelt's trial, a reporter from the *Inquirer* visited the Ross family at their home in Germantown. After Christian finished his dinner, he walked into his library, lit the gas, and sat in a chair. His children stood around him.

"What I want from Westervelt is for him to give me a clue if he has the knowledge," he said. "I want him to tell me if he knows my child is alive or dead. I want that question settled. If he is dead, I want him to tell me how and when he died, and where I can go to get the body."

Since the start of the trial in August, the Ross family had received twenty additional ransom letters doctored to resemble the descriptions of the original twenty-three. Christian handed two of the fakes to the reporter. One author identified himself as a West Philadelphia detective. He had printed neatly in pencil, "I knew Mosher and Douglas and also Westervelt and have seen them together. I have seen your boy." The handwriting on the other letter was messy, and ink blots marked the page around the words, "ros your boy is alive and is nearer your home than you have any idea." Both letters had misspelled words, and the trained eye could see that the same hand composed both.

The reporter asked Christian if he blamed Captain Heins and the Philadelphia Police for prolonging the family's torture by failing to arrest the kidnappers before they died. Ross refused to speak badly of Heins. Instead, he placed the blame on New York's police department.

"If Superintendent Walling had followed the ideas of Captain Heins there would have been different results. He wanted Walling to put another man on the case, but the latter desired to detail the officer who had given the first information of the Douglas and Mosher clue, and did it, yet this man was incompetent to handle a case like this that required brains. I believe Walling committed fatal errors and bungled the case in many particulars."

Philadelphia's District Attorney Furman Sheppard began his final argument to the jury on Thursday, September 16. In it, he recalled the testimonies of Westervelt's former police colleague Henry Hartman and the defendant's bartender Charles Stromberg, men who had witnessed Westervelt in the company of the kidnappers and heard him boast of his intimate knowledge of the crime. Sheppard also reviewed the testimonies of eyewitnesses who saw the kidnappers and Westervelt in Germantown, pointed to contradictions in Mrs. Westervelt's alibi for her husband, and charged the jurors with considering how important an accomplice like Westervelt was to the kidnappers.

"What relations of perfect conduct subsisted between this man and the abductors?" Sheppard asked. "They took him to see the horse and wagon with which they were to commit the crime. He was entrusted with the care of Mosher's family, because Mosher knew his visits to them would be covered up. Constantly they furnished him with money, trusted him, conferred with him, and put themselves completely within his family: there was such trust and companionship as was utterly inconsistent with any other theory than that of a common purpose and a common interest among them. His part in the business was to control the police while the other two kept up their batteries upon the distressed family. This was the heart of the mystery, the true nature of the prisoner's connection with it."

The attorney for the defense began his closing statement at about 10:00 A.M. the following morning. He defended Westervelt against conspiracy charges, insisting that the kidnappers had contacted him only after the kidnapping occurred. He blamed the prosecutors for building a case on inferences and for trusting eyewitnesses whose testimonies contradicted one another in time and place. Finally, he criticized the treatment his client received from the police and blamed the continued disappearance of Charley Ross on corrupt police officers seeking reward money.

"The Commonwealth asks you to convict this man upon a statement made to unauthorized parties, and in an unauthorized manner. Now what was the nature of the defendant's agreement with Walling? It was as he states it, only to report to Walling himself. He could not arrest these men, or have them arrested, on account of the agreement, for if he did he and the policemen who made the arrest would get the glory of the twenty thousand dollars, not Walling, who desired to secure them himself."

Westervelt looked down, and the judge turned to address the jury.

"Review the testimony with calm judgment, and fear not to apply every test to its accuracy. You are to decide by the testimony; if to find the prisoner guilty, it must be beyond a reasonable doubt or he goes free. Give him that doubt if it be an honest, manly doubt, derived from the whole testimony; but do not manufacture it from weakness or sympathy, either for himself or his family, for this is no hour for sympathy. Whilst you have gazed upon that scene of misery surrounding that prisoner's dock for three weeks, you must recollect that if there be guilt upon that brow, that for one year and two months the voice of Charley Ross has been lost to his home, and that, while the prisoner has his children in life around him, another father mourns his son through this terrible crime."

The judge ended his charge at 7:15 P.M. and announced a recess. Westervelt raised his head to look at the jury members. His fate rested with two manufacturers, five artisans, a grocer, a merchant, a gentleman, a tobacconist, and a clerk. Westervelt's children stopped playing quietly behind him and hugged their mother. While the jurors filed out of the courtroom, lawyers and the foreman gathered the ransom letters and indictment papers for the jury's perusal, and spectators stretched and spoke loudly. Exiting the building for the courtyard, they left Westervelt and his family alone.

The jurors' debates continued throughout the weekend and into the early hours of Monday morning. Journalists waiting inside the *Public Ledger* building across the street could look down from their offices and see jurors pacing in the deliberation room after 2:00 A.M.

Several hours later, a large crowd gathered in Independence Square to hear the verdict. For more than the past one hundred years of Philadelphia's history, the square had been a constant scene of meetings, rallies, and demonstrations; most recently, it had served as the grounds for Civil War recruiters working out of tents. Men, women, and children entered the square through one of several gates and walked down gravel walkways that weaved through one hundred young elm trees. By the time the State House bell tolled at 9:00 A.M., the jurors had reached a decision, and the crowd huddled against the courthouse doors had begun to sweat under the sunlight.

When the doors opened, arms and elbows pushed forward. Children, storekeepers, reporters, and drunks shoved their way to seats or spots in the aisles. At 1:00 A.M., the judge arrived, and Westervelt walked to the dock. Reporters read despair in his posture, walk, and pale face. He barely kissed his wife and shook his children's hands. The foreman read the verdict. Guilty on all charges of conspiracy. Westervelt pushed his head into his hands and cried.

On October 9, he appeared one last time before Judge Thomas Robert Elcock. The judge explained the delay between the verdict and the sentencing.

"I had hoped ere this I should have been appealed to for a light sentence by some merciful cry revealing something of the fate of Charley Ross," the judge told him, "but I have heard not even a whisper, nor held a ray of hope, and if the knowledge of his fate rests with you, then you become your own executioner. Justice calls loudly for your severe punishment, and it remains but for me to announce its sentence. By an act of Assembly on the 25th of February, 1875, the kidnapping of a child under ten years of age is made a felony, and punishable by a fine not exceeding ten thousand dollars and an imprisonment of not less than twenty-five years. Harboring and concealing a child is likewise made a felony, and punishable by a fine not exceeding five thousand dollars and an imprisonment not exceeding fifteen years. This act was passed since the commission of your offense, and there was no evidence in the cause which would justify a punishment to you of harboring and concealing the child, or of conspiring to do so since the passage of the act. The sentence of the Court is that you pay a fine of one dollar, the costs of prosecution, and that you undergo an imprisonment at solitary confinement, at labor, in the Eastern Penitentiary for the term of seven years, and that you stand committed until that sentence be complied with."

Westervelt breathed deeply and sat down. Leaning forward, he put his head down and pulled at his beard.

we fear being traped
in our own game

THE SCHUYLKILL RIVER TWISTED PAST THE GROUNDS OF THE
Centennial construction sites, flowing east through the WaterWorks
falls before continuing past Center City toward the Delaware River.
On the river's east bank, walkers straying from the footpath came to
the bottom of a small hill that peaked past the grounds of a fortress.
From the riverside, the building resembled a castle at the edge of the
industrial town. Thirty-foot stone walls surrounded eleven acres of
land, and notched parapets crowned five octagonal towers along the
front wall. Spaced evenly between the towers, fourteen narrow, vertical
embrasures angled toward the inner grounds, inspiring thoughts of
archers defending a king. But the protectors of this building held guns,
not bows, and instead of keeping the enemy from entering the fortress,
they kept him from leaving it.

Philadelphia's Quaker fathers had planned this building as an
alternative to the city's Walnut Street Jail; like the Revolutionary-era
jailhouses before it, the Walnut Street penitentiary had served as a holding tank more than a prison. Inside of it, male and female inmates intermingled and the warden tended bar. Disgusted with these
conditions, a group of Quakers met in the late eighteenth century to
discuss penal reform. The group took their ideas to the Pennsylvania
state legislature, and for the next forty years, they petitioned the government to fund an experiment that centered on rehabilitation through
meditation and hard labor. In 1821, after receiving a $100,000 grant
from the state, the Quakers purchased a cherry orchard on farmland

north of Center City for $11,500. They then solicited plans for the world's first prison entirely given to solitary confinement. Architects competed to provide the template that most successfully coordinated the twenty-four-hour surveillance of 250 inmates with the prisoners' exercise, food, labor, plumbing, and ventilation needs. The winning proposal belonged to a British architect named John Haviland.

Haviland envisioned seven one-story cell blocks that radiated around a circular hub. Standing at the hub's center, prison guards could see down the corridor of each cell block, which held two rows of eighteen cells; each cell had a stone floor, one bed, a toilet, a water tap, a desk, and a small skylight. To ensure anonymity and enforce silence, authorities planned on blindfolding the men as soon as they entered the prison walls, disorienting their sense of direction and discouraging them from communicating with guards. Meal servers would also minimize noise: before serving food and water through slots in the cell doors, they would pull wool socks over their shoes and attach leather straps to wagon wheels. Even exercise would be conducted quietly— Haviland planned for each cell to have a small yard behind it, enclosed by ten-foot walls. Guards arranged exercise so that prisoners in adjoining cells were not in their yards at the same time. And to frustrate prisoners from tapping codes against the pipes, Haviland looped hot water cyclinders from each cell into the corridor.

Although the Quakers believed their system offered mercy, many people disagreed. No prison had ever fully practiced solitary confinement, and prison reformers in America and Europe called the Philadelphia experiment cruel—accusations that started a pamphlet war between officials in Philadelphia and reformers in New York, New England, and Europe. Despite the controversy, however, tourists praised Haviland's work in 1830. Although the first three cell blocks were occupied and operating as the Quakers had intended, it was the front entrance building, an expensive exercise in Gothic detail, which earned these rave reviews. Because of its initial success, the Eastern State Penitentiary, or the "prison at Cherry Hill" as the locals said, would influence more than three hundred prisons worldwide, becoming the most imitated American building in Europe and in Asia in the nineteenth century.

But by the time of William Westervelt's trial, Haviland's plans had failed. At the end of 1875, there were 1056 inmates sharing 585 cells.

In their monthly reports, wardens over the years had complained of odors, overcrowded conditions, and carbon monoxide poisoning. The walls surrounding each exercise yard had blocked air circulation, and heating stoves in tunnels underneath the cells had warmed sewer pipes, releasing sewage odors. Frustrated with Haviland's spending, state commissioners had demanded that the architect alter his plans for the last four cell blocks so that the prison could house more prisoners. As a result, these four blocks had two floors, exercise yards disappeared, and prisoners shared cells. The warden was charged with pairing inmates who would not be tempted to talk, which sometimes meant placing the sane with the insane.

After Judge Elcock sentenced Westervelt on October 9, he returned to Moyamensing Prison in South Philadelphia. On April 20, 1875, a wagon delivered the prisoner to the doors of Eastern State Penitentiary. Guards escorted him underneath the tall arch and through the vestibule, two oak doors, and a gate. At the physician's office, Westervelt took a bath and had a haircut and shave. He met with the doctor and the warden, and he received his summer clothes: cotton pants, two handkerchiefs, two pairs of socks, leather shoes, and a shirt with the number 8082 sewn into it. For the next seven years, 8082 would also be his name. Placing a hood over Westervelt's head, a guard led him through the prison yard to his cell block, put his number on his cell door and reviewed the rules posted by a sign on the wall. The whale-oil lamp attached to the wall would stay lit until 9:00 P.M. After a few days of good behavior, he could ask for a Bible. Until then, he was left with his thoughts.

Philadelphia, September 9, 1875

I think that I again saw Mosher and Douglass after Mrs. Mosher came to our house. It was on the morning of the 20th of August. She and her four children came [. . .] It was three or four days after Mrs. Mosher came when Mosher and Douglass came together. It was very early in the morning. I could not say positively whether they came both together or not. Mosher came to see his wife, I suppose. He was never invited by me to come and see us. I could not say when I next saw either Mosher or Douglass. I do not think that I have any recollection of either Mosher or Douglass coming to the house after that. Mrs. Mosher and her four children occupied the same room I did. Their names are Willie, Charley [Lovey Dove], Georgie, and the baby. The latter was five weeks old then. Georgie has since died. With the exception of the baby, they were the same children that she had that I saw in Monroe Street when I was living there. Charley [Lovey Dove] had blue eyes, light hair, a round full face, very rough, coarse skin. The hair was very light.

INTERVIEWS WITH MRS. ALBERT MOSHER

New York, December 16, 1874

"I am a sister-in-law of William Mosher, the dead man whom I have just seen in the coffin [. . .] He has left a wife and four children—he had six children, the oldest boy is eight years, and his name is William. Then there is George and another boy, whose name I forget, and a little girl."

"I am only surprised his wife has not come here yet. They have four children living and two they buried. The two eldest of the living ones are William and Georgie. Willie only four years old."

INTERVIEW WITH OFFICER CHARLES WOOD,
THE *PHILADELPHIA INQUIRER*

Philadelphia, December 15, 1874

"Are you nearer the child now than before?"
"I don't think they can keep it out of the way. Either the 'two other men' have got it or Mosher's wife has it. I don't think she can keep it

out of the road. She has no means—neither have the other two men—for we know that the whole gang were reduced so low that they had to make forays into the town and commit house robberies. It was while upon such an errand that last night Mosher and Clark were killed. They had to steal to live, and to steal to be able to hide the child."

the whole gang

FROM THE BEGINNING OF THE INVESTIGATION, POLICE HAD believed that by tracing the kidnappers' horse and buggy, they could recreate whatever pieces of the journey occurred after the kidnappers released Walter and left Philadelphia. However, the only evidence stating the kidnappers left Philadelphia with Charley the night of the kidnapping (July 1, 1874) came from the ransom notes.

Within a month of the search, Chief Jones of the Philadelphia Police had ordered his men and concerned citizens to search every building within the city. To the authorities, it made sense that Charley could be hidden within Philadelphia, but at the same time, they believed that he had been taken from the city through Trenton on July 1. For their theory to be true, the kidnappers would have risked a return to the city with Charley Ross after the kidnapping.

Mosher and Douglas were seasoned criminals. They knew that Mosher had recognizable features, and they knew from Walter's questions that he was a smart little boy. Their ransom letters also revealed their avid interest in the Philadelphia papers, and since they closely read the reports beginning on July 6 that detailed the crime and their descriptions, they surely would have understood the danger of returning Charley to Philadelphia.

On July 9 or 10, Kate Morgan, the boarder, moved in with Martha

Mosher on Monroe Street in South Philadelphia. Later, Kate told authorities that the Moshers had four children: Willy, Charley, Georgie, and Mary. Martha, Kate said, called Charley "Lovey." Kate told police that Martha and the four children left for New York on a Saturday in August. Just prior to Martha's departure, police announced their intentions to search every home in the city; she left the city one week before this search began.

As Joseph Douglas bled to death on the lawn outside of Judge Van Brunt's house, he told the sailor who gave him water that Bill Mosher had "five or six" children. And during the viewing, Al Mosher's wife told the *New York Herald* that Bill and Martha had four children. She said she couldn't remember their names and ages, but in a separate article, a *Herald* reporter wrote that she identified the older two as Willy and Georgie and said the oldest was four. Another time, she said the oldest was eight. Even though Al's wife claimed that she and her husband hadn't spoken to Bill's family in a while, she knew about the newborn baby girl, and she knew about the recent death of their third son. According to Kate Morgan, Mary Westervelt, and Martha Mosher, three women who lived with the children, Charley was the name of the second oldest son, and Georgie, the boy who died, was the third son.

The kidnappers repeatedly reminded Christian in the ransom letters that they had expected the ransom to be quickly paid. Eyewitnesses placing Westervelt in Germantown the month after the abduction remembered his asking about the wealth of the Ross family, and in one note, the kidnappers admitted they had assumed Christian had more money than he did. Bill Mosher was a veteran criminal with a family to support and an established alias—Henderson. He would not have wanted to attract attention to himself, and in order to make a quick exchange, he would have wanted to keep Charley close. So instead of driving north from Philadelphia toward Trenton after abandoning Walter in Kensington, it would have made more sense for him to take Charley back to his—the Mosher—Monroe Street home after dark. He and Douglas had spent more than a month coming and going to and from the countryside on sales trips, and neighbors were used to seeing the men loading and unloading supplies and products from the buggy. They also would have seen Mosher's sons and neighborhood children running in, out, and around the "Henderson" home on Monroe Street. The addition of one more boy to the household at nighttime could have gone unnoticed.

"Charley" was the only Mosher son mentioned as having a nick-name. If Martha Mosher harbored Charley Ross, she wouldn't have anticipated keeping the child for longer than a couple of days, and she certainly wouldn't have wanted the neighbors to hear a child screaming uncontrollably from behind her door. Treating the boy kindly with the names "Lovey" and "Lovey Dove" made sense—Charley had already proven to her husband in the wagon that harsh sounds made him cry, and candy kept him quiet.

Once Mosher and Douglas realized the Ross camp was stalling and the exchange would take longer than they thought, they did flee the town. Martha stayed in Philadelphia with the children, but she was also nine months pregnant. Kate Morgan, who moved in just before the birth, wouldn't have known whether the Henderson family had two boys or three the month before, and she wouldn't have expected a bedridden nine-months pregnant woman to be harboring the child that America searched for. Once Martha had her baby and Mosher read that the police planned to search every household, he told his wife to move the family to New York and live with her brother, William Westervelt.

Right around this time, Gil Mosher named his brother to the police in the hopes that he would earn Philadelphia's $20,000 reward. West-ervelt agreed to cooperate, because communicating with Walling allowed him to keep an eye on where the police were snooping. West-ervelt knew Walling needed him, and he could manipulate the super-intendent by threatening to abandon the investigation if he found himself under surveillance. Walling played into his stratagem. Even when Walling admitted to Heins in a telegram that he suspected West-ervelt of double-crossing them, Walling did not order his men to keep the suspect's apartment under constant watch. Walling's primary goal was to orchestrate the perfect arrest of William Mosher and become a hero. Regardless of Westervelt's ethics, Walling needed his help—unfortunately for the superintendent, he had underrated his informant's involvement.

The night before Mosher and Douglas died, the whole group met at the home of Madame Morrow in New York. Mary Westervelt had complained to her husband about allowing his sister Martha and her children to stay in their small lodging-house rooms, but she was more frustrated when Martha moved out with only her two younger children, leaving her with the older two. On the night of the meeting at Madame Morrow's, Mary thought she would finally get rid of the Moshers' older two boys—presumably Willie and Charley—but Westervelt insisted that she take them home, leaving Martha and the two youngest children—presumably Georgie and Mary—with Morrow, the mother of Ike and Ed Morris, two of Mosher's old colleagues.

When the kidnappers were killed, everybody was thrown for a shock. Walling now had to answer for his stalled investigation, and there was no better person for him to blame than Westervelt. Prior to the deaths, Westervelt had maintained some privacy, but after the Bay Ridge shootings, he was watched more closely. If Charley Ross was with Westervelt's family, Westervelt would have had to make the boy truly disappear. It was the day after Mosher and Douglas died that Mosher's sister-in-law, Al's wife, claimed the only two living sons were named William and Georgie—which would mean that their son Charley, or "Lovey," had died. In later interviews, Mary Westervelt and Martha Mosher said that it was Georgie, and not Charley who had died "since" Bill Mosher's death.

Twelve years after Westervelt's trial, Superintendent Walling wrote, "I think [Charley Ross] is dead. I can conceive of no possible reason why, after the two kidnappers had been killed and Westervelt was in prison, Charley Ross should not have been returned had he been alive. The promised immunity from punishment and the reward offered by the Mayor of Philadelphia are good reasons for supposing that the child, if alive, would have been returned to its parents." It is possible that the "son" who died after Mosher's death was the real Charley Ross, murdered after being disguised for the previous five months as a Mosher child. If the Mosher family or their colleagues silenced the real Charley Ross, Mary Westervelt and Martha Mosher would have attracted less attention by saying the deceased child in the Mosher household was named Georgie, not Charley.

The Mosher boys were used to using an alias—for the entire year they lived in Philadelphia, they had identified themselves as Hendersons. If Martha Mosher began referring to her biological son Georgie as "Charley," it is likely that he and her older son William would cooperate without revealing the family secret.

Mayor Stokley announced the state's new kidnapping bill just before Westervelt was taken into custody in Philadelphia. Therefore, the Philadelphia authorities could only indict him on charges of complicity, not kidnapping. If Westervelt were to tell them everything he knew, and had Martha Mosher harbored the child as Detective Wood suggested, then Westervelt's recently widowed sister and mother of three would go to prison for potentially twenty-five years, the maximum amount of time allowed by the new law. Westervelt knew the newspapers questioned the loopholes Walling had allowed in the investigation. If he kept his mouth shut, he also knew that Walling would help him and the Mosher family as much as he could without sacrificing his position or his popularity. This meant that it was possible Westervelt would serve only seven years at most. Walling, however, would serve the rest of his career knowing that the Mosher family and their criminal friends knew just how much more he could have done to recover America's lost child.

East Washington Lane,
Present Day

GERMANTOWN AVENUE IS STILL A THOROUGHFARE FOR COM-
muters traveling between Center City Philadelphia, and its northwestern suburbs. Drivers slowly pass along it as they approach the center of
Germantown. True to its history, the two-lane road is especially rough
in the vicinity of Market Square, and tires skid over trolley lines in the
broken pavement, bumping against potholes, cement, cobblestones—
layers of failed street construction.

As the industrial age entered the twentieth century, more African-
American and immigrant laborers found employment in Germantown's
factories and moved into its neighborhoods. The community enjoyed
economic prosperity into the 1940s, escaping the initial economic dev-
astation of the Great Depression, but over the next two decades, two
factors transformed the neighborhood: Germantown's wealthier families moved back into Center City, and factory closures took jobs away
from thousands of blue-collar workers. House values dropped, lower-
income families moved in, and the economic decline intensified racial
hostility. Many white homeowners joined the "white flight" from the
city into the suburbs, but over the years, Germantown has remained a
somewhat racially heterogeneous section of Philadelphia. Although several of its blocks are undergoing gentrification, the neighborhood's low-
income population lives mainly in row homes, and most of the mansions
that once housed Philadelphia's elite have been either torn down, abandoned, or converted into apartments. The lawns of those that still stand,
however, are lush and green.

About a mile down East Washington Lane, the Zion Hill Church of Christ sits on the former Ross property. The stone wall that Walter and Charley played behind is still intact, but only a few bushes remain in the yard. Next to the church, blocks of row homes stretch up the hill toward Germantown Avenue, and across the street, part of a disintegrating mansion has been converted into a daycare center. Beech trees line this specific block, but they bend under telephone wires, and their branches have been cut. With the exception of cars passing on the road, it is quiet today, a Sunday afternoon. And even though a small street two blocks northeast of here is called Ross, generally the people here have never heard about Charley, or this piece of Philadelphia's history.

William Westervelt was released from prison on January 18, 1881. He gave at least one interview to the *New York Tribune* soon after his return to the Lower East Side, and in the article he maintained that he had had nothing to do with the Charley Ross kidnapping. Westervelt stayed out of the newspapers until his obituary appeared in 1890. His sister Martha Mosher and at least two of her nephews gave sporadic interviews through the end of the nineteenth century; in her statements, Martha voiced her innocence and her belief that Charley was alive. In 1897, Gil Mosher's son Ellsworth came forward with the news that his father, on his deathbed, said the bones of Charley Ross were buried inside of a saloon on Grand Street once leased to Bill Mosher. Although the bones of a child had been found in the wall when the building was torn down, they were those of William, Bill Mosher's oldest son, who had died years before Charley's kidnapping.

Not much is known about the life of Captain William Heins after 1875. Over the next two years, his name disappeared from records of captains who served under Mayor Stokley. Mayor William S. Stokley held office until 1886, when voters denied him a fourth term. While some historical records of Philadelphia honor Stokley for noble service, newspapers of the day accused him of "scandal breeding" as a member of the Philadelphia Buildings Commission, the group responsible for the construction of City Hall. Refusing audits, the Commission made personal demands on the city budget and awarded contracts without advertising for bids; under their watch, City Hall cost 12 million dollars more than expected and was finished twelve years later than estimated.

Newspapers referred to the building as "the temple of Philadelphia's folly."

Three months before the Centennial opened, the government released 1.5 million dollars to satisfy its financial commitment to the exhibition. Although investors did lose money, the celebration was considered successful. More than one in five Americans visited the Centennial grounds in Fairmount Park, participating in the effort to heal civic pride and American business. Foreign visitors admired America's industrial and agricultural displays, paying particular attention to Samuel Colt revolvers, Cyrus McCormick reapers, and the Corliss engine. Philadelphia's execution encouraged foreign trade and inspired creative minds, visionaries who organized six major fairs around the nation within forty years of the Centennial.

In spite of his frustration with the superintendent, Christian Ross met with George Walling in New York as late as 1887, the same year that Walling penned a memoir chronicling his thirty-seven-year career as a New York police officer (he retired in 1885). In his book, Walling said the case of Charley Ross affected him more deeply than any other.

Christian Ross never stopped searching for Charley. Within two years of the kidnapping, his dry-goods business failed and he went bankrupt. Through continued personal hardship, he sifted through the statements of those saying they were his son—at first the stories of adolescent boys, and then teenagers, young adults, and finally, grown men.

In 1876, following the advice of friends who recommended he clarify erroneous information and defend his own integrity, Christian penned a memoir entitled *The Father's Story of Charley Ross, the Kidnapped Child*. Although there was commercial interest in the book, Christian did not make much money from it.

In June 1878, Governor Hartranft of Pennsylvania gave him a title and the position of "Harbor Master." The job, a token position, paid a small salary. That same year, P. T. Barnum contacted Christian, offering to give him $10,000 if he would agree to display Charley on the Barnum tour once the child was found. Christian agreed, provided that he could return the money and cancel the deal if he ever found his son. He died at home, following an illness, in 1897.

Sarah Ross lived in the family home in Germantown until 1912, when she dropped dead of heart failure after entering her pastor's home one day. At the time of her death, five children survived her: her sons Henry and Walter, and her daughters, Sophia, Marion, and Anne. In 1926, her children sold the property on East Washington Lane, and the home was razed. Since then, three different churches have held services in a building on the lot.

As an adult, Walter Ross lived a few miles north of Germantown, in the Chestnut Hill neighborhood. Both he and his older brother Henry became very successful businessmen. Throughout his career, Walter worked in Philadelphia, moving from the position of clerk to investment banker before establishing his own firm, one that gave him a seat on the New York Stock Exchange. In 1931, his son Walter Jr. was killed in an auto crash on his way from Newtown, Pennsylvania, to Walter Sr.'s home in Chestnut Hill.

Over time, the Ross story has been forgotten, but the case received small bursts of media attention in the twentieth century. In 1924, Nathan Leopold and Richard Loeb, schoolboy kidnappers and killers, said in court documents that they were influenced by Mosher and Douglas's behavior. And in 1932, news of another stolen child shocked America. About thirty miles northeast of Germantown, in the town of Ewing, New Jersey, Charles Lindbergh's baby was taken from his crib.

Throughout the first half of the twentieth century, men claiming to be Charley Ross continued to come forward. Perhaps the most famous was Gustave Blair, a man in his sixties who first publicized his story in 1931. Blair said he had been taken from the Ross home and raised in Illinois as "Nelson Rinear" until his adopted father, attempting to conceal "Nelson's" true identity, tried to kill him. Blair said he then fled to Canada, changed his name, and returned to Illinois years later, when an older adopted brother confirmed his identity.

Walter and his siblings immediately dismissed the man's story, saying it was the kind of tale that had bankrupted their father. In 1934, Gustave Blair took his case to a civil court in Arizona, and a jury believed him, enabling him to legally change his name to Charley Ross. He then contacted the media and asked people to donate enough money to send him to Philadelphia, where he would reunite himself with his long-lost family. When they raised enough, Blair and his fiancée traveled to Germantown, aiming to marry in Walter's church—Cliveden Presbyterian. The pastor refused to marry them, and the family refused to meet them. In 1939, Blair filed a civil lawsuit against Walter Ross, demanding to be recognized as an heir. Rejecting the court papers, Walter moved to his New York home. He spent most of his time there until he died four years later, in 1943.

Charley Ross was never returned home to East Washington Lane, and a body was never identified. Regardless of whether he was killed, Charley Ross died the day that Mosher and Douglas parked their wagon on Washington Lane and offered him candy on a summer evening. Social historians have attempted to trace Charley Ross into the twentieth century, studying stories selected from the hundreds of those who wished to end the mystery with their tales of woe—and perhaps, somewhere in that pile of discarded leads, the real Charley was dismissed, denied his own identity.

When Mayor Stokley watched the Masons drop the day's newspapers into a vault on July 4, 1874, he was ensuring that his world, if perhaps lost in history, would never disappear. Two centuries later, all that is really known about Charley is cemented in that cornerstone of City Hall, underneath the statue of William Penn that still defines Philadelphia's skyline:

300$ REWARD WILL BE PAID TO THE person returned to No 5 North Sixth Street, a small Boy, having long, curly, flaxen hair, hazel eyes, clear, light-skinned round face, dressed in a brown linen suit with a short skirt, broad buttoned straw hat and laced shoes. This child was lost from Germantown on Wednesday afternoon. 1st lost, between 4 and 5 o'clock.

The End

acknowledgments

Tшis воок is a work of faith.

The faith that my family, Bill, Dianne, David, and John Alexander have had in my storytelling.

The faith that I put in my writing mentors, Suzannah Lessard, Richard Todd, Laura Wexler, Philip Gerard, and Steve Luxenberg.

The faith that my agent, Ethan Bassoff, had in my proposal, and that my first editor, Peggy Hageman, had in the manuscript.

And finally the faith of my partner, Jeff, who believed that one day, he would again have a couchmate for Thursday night TV.

I am grateful to Stephanie Gorton, my current editor, for her wisdom, optimism, and investigative eye. I also appreciate Ellen S. Leach for her thorough and attentive eye as copy editor.

I thank Dr. James Butler of La Salle University, an expert on Germantown's geography and Victorian culture, who guided my Philadelphia research and reading. The Wister Collection at La Salle University's Connelly Library holds joyful details of life in nineteenth-century Philadelphia. It was a pleasure to read through these archives.

I have spent hours in the archives of the Historical Society of Pennsylvania, the Germantown and Chestnut Hill Historical Societies, the New-York Historical Society, the National Archives, the City Archives, and in the Map Collection and the Microfilm Reading Room at the Philadelphia Free Library. The librarians, historians, and archivists have been nothing but supportive and enthusiastic about this project. Early on, the New-York Historical Society put me in touch with Richard Mc-Dermott, a passionate researcher who provided early enthusiasm for the project and suggested readings that helped me recreate the Five Points neighborhood. Special thanks goes to Alex Batlett and Judith Callard of the Germantown Historical Society. Both guided me through minutiae in the final hours of my research.

Many people volunteered their areas of expertise to advise my research endeavors. I wish to remember three of them here. Bill Fleisher of the Vicdoq Society commented on the psychology of criminals, the police, and private investigators during a particularly busy week. His words confirmed my instincts and encouraged my confidence. Dr. Morris Vogel guided early stages of my reading on Reconstruction America and offered a helpful critique of my bibliography. I also thank Jean Walker, chair of archives, First United Methodist Church of Germantown, whose thoroughness saved me hours of research.

This project began as a series of interviews with people who grew up in Germantown at different times in the twentieth century: Bill Alexander, Terry Alexander, Joe Beal, Rosemary Morris, Margaret Smith, and Rick LeFevre. Their memories furthered my interest in this neighborhood, and through a series of coincidences, led me to the Germantown Historical Society, where I first read about Charley Ross.

And to my writing friends, Jill Sisson Quinn, Brian Spadora, Lori Lichtman, Patrick Walters, Kelly Christ, Sharyl Covey, Diana Morris-Baver, Colleen Clemens, Denise Loock, and Kitty Chism—I am most at home during our late-night talks, gossip, bizarre bets, bottles of Talese wine, and long letters. You are gently yet painfully honest, and because of this, I appreciate your encouragement, friendship, and feedback all the more.

illustration credits

1. Christian Ross: Courtesy of Germantown Historical Society, Philadelphia, PA

2. Washington Lane: From Ross, Christian. *Charley Ross, the Kidnapped Child: The Father's Story.* Philadelphia: John E. Potter and Company, 1876.

3 and 4. The first ransom letter: From Ross, *Charley Ross, the Kidnapped Child.*

5. The first ransom envelope: From Ross, *Charley Ross, the Kidnapped Child.*

6. Pinkerton pamphlet: Courtesy of the Historical Society of Pennsylvania.

7. Pinkerton flyer: Courtesy of the Historical Society of Pennsylvania.

8. Pinkerton pamphlet: Courtesy of the Historical Society of Pennsylvania.

9. Superintendent Walling: From Walling, George W. *Recollections of a New York Chief of Police.* New York, N.Y.: Caxton Book Concern, Ltd., 1888, c1887.

10. Main Street (Germantown Avenue) at Rittenhouse: Courtesy of La Salle University's Connelly Library. Plate 12 of Richards, John. *Quaint Old Germantown in Pennsylvania: A Series of Sixty Former Landmarks of Germantown and Vicinity Drawn on Zinc During the Years 1863-1888.* Philadelphia: 1913.

11. Main Street (Germantown Avenue) at Manheim: Courtesy of La Salle University's Connelly Library. Plate 27 of Richards, *Quaint Old Germantown in Pennsylvania.*

12. Main Street (Germantown Avenue) Life: Courtesy of La Salle University's Connelly Library. Plate 31 of Richards, *Quaint Old Germantown in Pennsylvania.*

appendix

Letter 1

July 3 – *Mr. Ros:* be not uneasy you son charley bruster be all writ
we is got him and no powers on earth can deliver out of our hand. you
wil have two pay us before you git him from us, and pay us a big cent to.
if you put the cops hunting for him you is only defeetin yu own end.
we is got him put so no living power can gets him from us a live. If
any approch is maid to his hidin place that is the signil for his instant
anihilation. if you regard his lif puts no one to search for him yu mony
can fech him out alive an no other existin powers. dont deceve yuself
an think the detectives can git him from us for that is imposebel. You
here from us in few day.

Letter 2

PHILADELPHIA, July 6 – *Mr. Ros:* We supos you got the other
     leter that teld yu we had yu child all saf and sond.
   Yu mite ofer one $100,000 it woud avale yu nothing. to be plaen
with yu yu mite invok al the powers of the universe and that cold not
get yu child from us. we set god—man and devel at defiance to rest
him ot of our hands. This is the lever that moved the rock that hides
him from yu $20,000. not one doler les—impossible—impossible—
you cannot get him without it. if yu love money more than child yu
be its murderer not us for the money we will have if we dont from
yu we be sure to git it from some one els for we will mak examples of
yure child that others may be wiser. We give yu al the tim yu want
to consider wel wat yu be duing. Yu money or his lif we wil hav—
dont flater yu self yu wil trap us under pretens of paying the ransom
that be imposible—d'ont let the detectives mislede yu thay tel yu thay

can git him and arest us to—if yu set the detectives in search for him as we teld yu before they only serch for his lif. for if any aproch be made to his hidin place by detective his lif wil be instant sacrificed. you wil see yu child dead or alive if we get yu money yu get him live if no money yu get him ded. wen you get ready to bisnes with us advertise the folering in *Ledger* personals (Ros. we be ready to negociate). we look for yu answer in *Ledger.*

Letter 3

PHILADELPHIA, July 7 – *Mr. Ros:* We se yu anser in *Leger* the question with yu is be yu wilin to pay for thosand ponds for the ransom of yu child. without it yu can never get him alive if yu be ready to come to terms say so. if not say so. and we wil act acordinly. We take yu anser either way as granted and wil act on it. we care nothin bout yu schemin and plotin to detect us. that is only childrens play with us. this thing is wel understod with us and is taken out of the power every humin bein to detect us. yu wil find it so at the end of this bisines. the only answer we want from yu now is, be yu wilin to pay $20,000 to save Charley. if yu love yu mony more than him his blood be upon yu and not us fo wil show him up to yu either dead or a live (it is left with yu) anser the folering in *evnin herald* or *star. Ros.*—wil come to terms. *Ros.*—wil not come to terms. omit either line yu pleas try the experiment. offer $100,000 reward se if it avales any thing. use the detectives as yu pleas but don't let them mislede yu to the sacrifice of Charley. dont concent to any thing only in good faith. we wil act upon yu word, if yu prove faithles we will prove to yu heart's sorow that wil keep our word to the very letter.

Letter 4

PHILADELPHIA, July 9 – *Ros.* we is set your price. We ask no more. we takes no les we no the extent yu bility. how mucht time yu want to obtain this money. yu is only in part answered our question. the only question for yu to answer is is u got it and be wilin to pay it then we wil proceed to bisiness at once. is it necessary to

repeat the fatle consequences of delayin to give time to detectives to find
his hidin place. we teld yu it be posible to find his place, but imposible
to find him. no aproch can be made to it without a known signal
and any stranger forcibly comin to it wold be the signal for his instant
anihilation were he wold never be herd of. this makes our party safe
and shows yu that if it come to extremes we wil spare not the child.
thus yu se al the detectives in the country could avale yu nothing only
Jeopodisin his life Ros this undertaken cost us $1000 to prepare the
machenery to perform the work therefor consider wel befor yu consent
to pay it. for pay it you have to or sacrifice yu child. we want no other
anser but this and on the fath of yu word his lif hang. Ros i is got it
and be wilin to pay it. this anser or omition it satifies us.

Letter 5

PHILADELPHIA, July 13 – *Ros*: Yu say yu be redy to comply. we
presume yu have wel considered be for yu maid this promis we take yu
at yu word and we hold the lif of yu son to the strictest performanc of
yu word. we want yu mony. yu want yu child. the question between
us is do yu mean to give the mony or do yu think by holdin out a fals
promis to ensnare us into the hands of the authority. i want to explane
this mater to yu so yu wil not deceve yu self for it is imposible for the wole detective force combind to put even one of us in the power of the
law. in transfering yu mony to us be for yu get yu child yu have got
to rely entirely on our word. we ask no more money. we wil take no les.
if we wanted more we wold ask it now. in 5 ours after we receve the
mony and find it corect, yu wil se yu child home saf. Aft we gets the mony
we has no further use for the child, an it is our interest then to restor him
home unharmed, so that others will rely on our word. if we don't get the
mony from yu the child's life wil an shall be sacrificed. consider wel, then,
wat yu be doin, for any promis yu mak us we hold the life yu child to
bind you to it. Ros, it would be more satisfact to yu to give this mony
to the detectives than us, but if we git it yu git yu child—if not yu child
must die, that we can sho others that we mak no threths wich we don't
kepe. Ros, it is our place to dictate, yues to comply. be you redy to
pay it as we dictate. if so, have the $20,000 in United States notes. in denom-
ination not excedin "tens." have yu money were yu can git it

any moment wen cal for, the detectives, wen they read this, wil tel yu
they have now got the key that opens the secret, but don't be misled by
them (we alone hold the lock wich is yu child, if they open the dor for yu
it wil only revele his (ded body) if yu regard his life let a fatherly love be
yu gide. Ros, yu have inevitably got to part with yu mony or yu child,
wich is certain as death itself. any fals act on yu part seals the fate of yu
child an closes any further bisiness with us. consider wel, an if these
terms agre with yu anser the folerin. Ros, it is redy, yu have my
word for it. we look for the answer in the *Evenin Star.*

Letter 7[2]

PHILADELPHIA, July 16 – *Ros:* The reason we did not respond to yu
answer was we had to go a bit out in the country an the blasted old
orse give out so we could not get back in time. We went as much as
anything to se how Charley was. Yu have our word that he is yet
safe—in health an no harm done him thoug he is uneasy to get home
with Walter. he is afraid he won't get home in time to go to Atlantic
City with his mother when Saly comes back. Ros, yu understand the
condition the money was to be given us. We wold gladly give yu
Charley befor we got the mony but that wold be imposible under the
existing circumstances. Yu must satisfy yuself that yu wil git him
after we git the mony an find it corect and no sly marks put on the
notes. We told yu we wold place him in yu hands in 5 ours after we
fond the mony corect but that we can not do but our word for it that yu
shall have him insid of 10 ours an may our blasted sols be eternaly
damed if we do not keep our word with yu—as we said befor after we
gits the mony we have no further use for the child but we have a big
object in restoring him to yu safe and sound. We shall be redy we think

---

[2] While Christian Ross mentions that Letter #6 was mailed from a postal box in
Philadelphia, there is no record of the text of the letter in his memoirs or in newspaper
accounts of the trial. The police and the family spoke of 23 ransom notes in total, and
the next to last note was marked #22 ½. The kidnappers did not place numbers on the
letters, and at times appear confused as to how many notes had been written. It is possible that early published versions of the letters simply skipped from #5 to #7, and upon
arriving at #23 too early, used the #22 ½ as a marker.

by Saturday to efect a change with yu (the child for the mony). Ros—
we want to impres upon yu mind the grate danger in efecting this change
—the danger lies intirely with yuself if yu wish to make a change an
absolute certainty yu most comply in every particular as we instruct yu
then a failure is imposible. the first place, yu must not let the detectives no how yu are to setle this bisiness (not that we fear them at all) in
aresting one of us for as we told yu that is imposible—but they wil
secretly interfear in this bisines in some underhanded way to prevent the
mony from findin its way to us—we were going to deal with yu alone an
yu only, an if yu call in any others to give you a counter advice from ours
then yu mistake wil be yu own misfortune. let yu friends advise yu
and not the detectives they study their own interest an the interest of
society. yu have a duty to perform to yuself that stands paramount to all
else in the world an if yu ever expect to regain yu child a live, yu alone
with the advice of yu friends must perform it. we wil give you this much incite
into our bisiness—that if any arest is made it wil be an inocent
person who wil be ignorant of the part he is actin. but it is imaterial with
us wether it be an inocent person or one of our own party the moment
any arest is made or any clandestine movements in tramsiting this
mony to us it will be conclusive evidence with us that yu have broken yu faith
with us an that our we pledge our selves befor all the gods in the
universe if there be an god exist that yu child shal die an we wil give yu an
oculd prof of it an then all further business with us ceases. (yu have answered
al that is necessary at present. we have yu word for it.) we want yu to nail this
mony up in a smal strong ruf box an have it were yu can git it at a minutes notice. mark on it (Drugs for H H H.

Letter 8

PHILADELPHIA, July 18—*Ros:* we be at a los to understand yu a week
ago yu used yu had the amont an was wilin to pay it the editorials seme
to speak as if the mony wus yet to be contributed befor yu could pay
it. this wold be a terable mistake for yu to have it caled for an yu had
it not to hand out for it wold never be solicited the second time. if yu
mean square bsiness with us we wil do al we promis yu. if yu mean
stratigem it is imaterial wether yu hav the mony or not yu can try the game
as wel without the mony as with it. if yu trap any one it wil be some one

we care nothin abot aonly we lose the mony (yu lose the child) we be
redy to test it soon as you say mony is redy. we se the pealers has coped
a lad an grate prase is given them for their efficiency but we care nothin
for him but if it was one of our chums they had, yu child wold have dide
within an our after it, an al further negotiations wold cease at once. yu
wil find in the end that the cops can do nothn for yu in this case, thay
are as far of the track now as the day they started in persuit of the game.
we cautioned yu against setin the peelers or cops as som here cal them
lookin for the chilld. don't yu believe us when we tel yu that they only
search for the child's life. The blasted editorials have got the city in
such a feve bout the child that we can hardly do anything. i tel yu they
endanger the child's life at every stroke of the pen. one editor wants to
kno why we dont give yu some prof that we ever had the child by sendin
some of his close or a lock of hair we have our reason for not sending
them. to satisfy yu we have him yu remember his striped stockins are
darned in two or three places were they had holes in. ask Walter if we
did not put the blanket up in front of him an Charley in behind to hide
them. ask Walter if we did not say we wold go down to aunt Susans
befor we went out on the mane street to buy torpedos. Ros——if yu ever
want yu child restored to yu a live yu have got to act with us alone yu
and yu friends only. we tel yu positivly if yu love yu child the detectives
are yu worst enemies. if yu have them in yu service they will be the
means of yu losin yu child forever. if yu interfea in our bisines we
can never efect the change an death inevitably will be the result. we
can not keep the child forever. we don't want to keep him any longer than to
give yu time to procure the mony we thought yu were better
fixt for money or we would never took yu child but since we hav him
we shal cary out our plan with him. tis corosponence with us must
stop short we wil not keep it up longer. befor yu git this we shal join
our friends at a distance but we wil notice al yu have to say either in
ledger star or *herald* or *sunday dispatch* anything you wish to communicate to us head it C R R instead of Ros. dont let yu wife be foolishly
led by the Spiritualist to think they can tel her anything bout Charley,
there is but one thing on earth outside of us that has the power to tel yu
an that is the money. yu wil find in the end that we speak truth for
once, This man Woster is innocent he has nothing to do with us, do as yu
please with him an make the most out of him yu can. our advice to yu
is an we hope yu will take it for once that is dont yu state in personals

that yu have the mony until yu have it naled up in the box we described
to you an redy to give wen caled for. the brokers we se have had a metin
an think they can restor yu child an bring us to justice—they mean wel
to yu but they be actin under a great delusion—if they be friends to yu
let them make the mony up which is the only thing can restor the
child—if they will not do that yu drop them unless yu want to cut yu
child's throat—if they want revenge let them git it after yu get yu child.
this is a friendly advice do as yu think best—yu hear no more from us til
we no yu mind—we have told yu that yu will se yu child again but it
depends with yu an yu only in what condition you se him. We thought
we would be ready to setle this bisines to-day but it must be delayed.

Letter 9

BURLINGTON, July 21. –*Ros.* yu statement in Monday Star is so con-
flictin with yu statement in this morning personals that we are yet unable
to comprehend yu nevertheless we wil act upon yu promise as if it was
made by an angle. in monday Star yu say yu can have no faith in us
neither do we have any faith in yu from the nature of this bisines it is to
be presumed neither can have implicit confidence. the way this bisiness
stands is this yu pay us the money yu are left without anything to bind
us to our promis but our own word which yu say yu do not believe. then
on what ground can we efect the change. we have seen yu own statement that yu would not comply with our terms an yet yu say (the money
is redy how shal I no yu agent) the fact of us having yu child and you
having paid us every dollar we demanded what further use could we have
for him? He has answered the end for which we took him; this is one
reason why we should give him up. The next reason is, if we should
ever play the same game in any other part of the country, who would
have any confidence in getin their child after they had paid the ransom
if you should lose yu child we don't say we shal ever play this trick in
this country again, for the popular outcry is a most to great. It has been
stated that since the great outcry of the people that we would gladly surrender the child without a ransom. Do not deceive yuself on that, for
we could set the child at liberty at any moment, but we never wil alive
without the money, no never, never, never! Ros, in order to ever get
yu child alive there is but one way left yu an that is the way we point

out to yu. Yu must comply with our terms in every particular, and met
our agent step by step as we instruct yu. If yu mean to act in faith to
us yu can have no objection to this course. The fair an the faulce part is left
with yu to chose, for it is with yu alone we shal presume to act an
the life of Charley shal bind yu to yu word. do not deceive yuself an
think this is only to frighten yu. we appeal to the highest power exist
on high to bear us witness. (we solomly swear befor the twelve houses
of heaven so sure as the sun rises in the east an sets in the west, so sure
shall Charly die if yu brake yu promis with us an may the same curse
fal upon us if we do not keep our promis with yu. Ros we want to
caution yu stil more for this is a question involves the life or death of
yu child. do yu desire to make a change of yu money for the child if
yu are sincere take advice from us who yu think are yu worst enemies
but in the end yu wil find we were yu best advisers the advice is that if yu
want to regain yu child drop the police entirely have nothing to do with
them while yu are transacting this bisines with us or the whole thing wil
prove a failure an yu child must died if yu mean to ensare us then our
advice is enlist al the power yu can invoke but be sure yu prove successful for one false step seals the fate of yu child. We have told yu it is
impossible to ensnare one of our friends. Do yu not believe us, or are
yu wilin tu put the life of yu child at issue an test it with us. In all of
our letters we have told yu the life of yu child shal be the bond that bind
 yu tu yu promise; any stratagem or false promise on yu part must an
shall seal the fate of your child and you have none to blame for yu be his murderer an not us—for one reason from yu we shal stop at
nothing until we haveing given yu a prof that we can keep our word
even unto blood. i repeat if yu want yu child yu comply with our terms
in every particular. One false step on yu part will make yu and yu
family weep tears of blood but if yu act in faith with us al wil go wel
with yu. What have the authorities done towards findin yu child. They
have done nothing yet and they are as far from his hidin place to-day as
they were on the 6th day of July (yu money alone can find him) if these
terms suit yu answer the followin in the *Ledger* personals.
C R R. i will agree to the terms in every particular.
P. S. –have the money ready as we described we wil send prof with
him so yu can no him when he comes.

Letter 10

PHILADELPHIA, JULY 24—Ros. we have seen yu reply in personal
(yu agree to the terms in every particular) we accept yu offer for we
consider yu fuly understand the great an momentus obligation yu place
youself under when you assented tu this agreement. we be sory that
we cannot effect the chang to-day. our creed is such that it forbids us
to any bisines of this kind only at a certain quarter of the moon an the
phace of the moon has just passed over so we have got tu wate one week
befor we can transact any bisines between us. this delay may be a great
sorce of torture tu yu but it cannot be avoided. we pledge ourselves in
the mean time yu child shal not suffer for any thing only the close confinement which is necesary for his safe keepin. we have him so that
we feel at ease against all the detective force in the country ever feritin
him out. the authorities have offered $20,000 for the recovery of the
child an detection of us if they had yu interest at hart this would be the
worst thing they could do. this is only oferin a reward for the sacrifice
of yu child, We told yu at the beginin that yu child could never be takin
from us a live that he was so situated that we could destroy him in one
instant. an forever out of al prof against us but yu seam to have no
faith in our word. neverthesless yu have nothin to fear on that point
for he can never be found by any detective force. neither can any reward no matter how large be any temptation to us to peach one on the
other for we are sworn an blood bound unto death tu never give each
other away. Ros. one week must intervene befor we can negotiote for
the restoration of Charley by that time there will be an $100,000 reward
yu will se by that time the detectives can avail yu nothing or yu wil se
that we spak trought from the beginin. that there was no earthly hope
left yu only in payin the ransom in good faith an then yu get yu child.
what we mean in good faith is tu set no trap. We no it is not posible
for yu to trap us. but by any stratigem on yu part or connivance it
wil thwart our perposes an the money wil never come to us. if this
result takes place through any act or connivance of yuse then yu lose yu
(child forever.) If yu do as we instruct yu an this money gits lost (it
shal be our los and not yuse) an yu shall git yu child just as if we got
the mony. no matter what our instruction is for yu to do with the mony
yu do it an yu child shal be restored to yu. if we tel yu to burn it up
do so, if we tel yu to throw it off the dock do so, if we tel yu to give it to

any one do so, an yu child wil be restored yu wether the mony gits
lost or not through any act of ours. Ros. the whole contract is sumed
 up in these words. yu pay us the mony in good faith in denominations
from 1s to 10s in U.S. notes an no private marks fixed on them, then we
consider yu have fulfilled yu part and yu shal have yu child restored
safe to yu. if we do not fulfil our part in good faith to yu, we invoke the
vengeance of hell, if there be an hell, to be our eternal portion. we have
told yu that we wil transact this bisines with yu and yu friends only. we
know a true friend wil not advise yu rong if he has the interest of yu
child at heart we shall no nothing about detectives in the bisines if yu cal
them in for advice or asistance it wil be at the peral of yu child's life for
in their eigerness to arrest us, which they never can do, they will surely
be the means of sacrificing yu child. we shal never cal on yu but once
for the mony so it is yu part to have it at a minute's notice. but yu have
plenty of time yet. due notice wil be given yu when to have it at hand
(we request no answer tu this) till yu hear from us again which perhaps
wil be one week. in the meantime yu and yu family console youself that
yu child is wel an safe tu yu. an to us against al detective power.
nothin surprised us more after we had told yu the imposibility of findin
the child an the risk it wold be tu the child's life tu find his hidin place
yet yu in disregard of this advise persisted in havin the detectives search
for him. time wil tel yu that we do not lie in every word we write. the
reward signifies nothin, with us wether it be $20,000 or $20,000,000 it
wil accomplish nothin with us an the authorities wil fail on that point tu
bribe one of us as yu wil se in the end of this bisines. Ros our word for
it no harm shal befal yu child intentionaly til yu hear from us again 7
days by that time yu must be prepared for his ransom if yu ever expect
him alive. Ros mark the selfishness of Mr. Stokley an his committe
of brokers what do they say. not one cent for ransom but millions for
conviction. do they have yu interest at heart. no it is a selfish motive.
they are wilin to sacrifice yu child that theirs be safe. why do they not
pay their money to have yours restored first, an then offer a reward for
our conviction

Letter II

PHILADA., July 28.—Ros are yu not convinced by this time that the
detectives can render yu no service whatever. are yu agoing let them
keep yu under the delusion that they can yet recover yu child an bring
us to justice. we tel yu the thing is imposible we fear them not—
neither do we fear they wil ever find charley until we find him for yu.
We se in the personals that Mr. Percll a milionaire of New York offers
to pay the required amount to redeem yu child an ask no questions, but
we have no confidence in him neither would we treat with him if he offered one milion in hand an no questions asked. in the transaction of this
bisines we are determined to no no one but yu, an if yu suffer these letters
to go out of yu hands so that they can personate yu in effectin this change
 we shal hold the child subject to the fulfillment of yu promise an one
fals step by yu or by any one acting for yu, yu may consider the bisenes
is at an end, an the trap has sprung that render further negotiation useles
to yu. At the end of this week must end this bisenes; it must place him
in yu hands safe an sound or must place him in the grave; it is left
entirely with yu. if yu have not the mony to redeem him an ask for an
extension of time we wil keep him for yu but under no other circumstances we wil not. We are not afraid to keep him for we set the whole
force at defiance to find his hidin place. No matter how grate the reward
is, it signifies nothin with us—they are goin to search every house in
the city. we wil give yu the satisfaction to tel you he is not in the city
nor ever has been since the day he left home, nor he never wil be again
unles we return him to yu for the ransom, we wil give you the satisfaction
of knowin that he is within 100 miles of this city an yet we defy al the
devels out of hell to find him. we tel yu sincerely we have prepared
this place for every emergency an it is death for yu to find him
while he is in our custody. we told yu in our last letter we could not
transact any business for one week. we are now prepared to effect the
change as soon as yu be redy, but under no circumstances say yu be redy
when yu be not able to put yu hand on it, an hand it out. rest assured if
our agent cals for it an he does not get it without waiting, he will never
come again an the our of redemption is forever gone by with you. from
you former promises we take it as granted that yu be agoin to redeem
yu child in good faith, it is unnecessary therefore to repeat the consequences
of any perfidey or fals step on yu part. we teld yu to put the mony in

a box, but we now tel yu to put the mony in a strong, white, leather valise, locked an double straped an be prepared to give it or take it wherever we direct yu. if yu are directed to cary it yuself yu may take al the friends yu pleas with yu—but don't let the cops know yu bisines nor go with yu unles yu want the bisines to turnout a failure. if yu want to trap take the whole force with yu an then be sure yu know what yu be doin—for we know what we be doin. this is al the caution necesary for yu to save yu child alive. if you can have all things ready as we have directed yu by thursday the 30th insert the *folowin in the ledger* personal (John—it shall be as you desire on the 30th.) Ros you may fix any other date that is convenient for you. Rosy u have sed yu had no confidence in these men an would not do as they requested yu. now we say yu must do as we request yu, or there is no earthly hope left yu to save yu child alive. this is the only alternitive given yu an yu wil find we are prepared for every emergency. detection is impossible if yu do not ransom him, he must die. if yu attempt to arrest any of our agents, he must die. If yu fail to comply with the terms after promising – he must die.

Letter 12

PHILADELPHIA, July 30—*Ros:* from yu answer this day you signify everything is redy. everything is redy with us. we now give yu a wide margin for preparation to make an arest if yu be pleased to do your actions this day desides CHARLEY's fate it is left with yu alone wether he shall live or die. we caution once, an the last time do not think we are trifling. Ros. you are to take the 12 P.M. train to-night from West Philadelphia for New York. it arrives at New York 5.05 A.M. take a cab at Cortland or Disbrossers streets, N.Y., an ride directly to the grand central station at 4 avenue and 42d streets. take the 8 A. M. northern express by way of hudson river (take notice) you are to stand on the rear car and the rear platform from the time you leave west phila depot until arrive at jersey city—you are then to stand on the rear platform of hudson river car from the time yu leave the grand central at New York until yu arrive at Albany. if our agent do not meet yu befor yu arrive in Albany yu wil find a letter in post office at Albany addressed to C. K. Walter directing yu where yu are then to go. Ros—the probability is yu may not go one mile before our agent

meets yu and yet yu may go 250 miles before he intercepts you but be it
where it may yu must be prepared to throw the valise to him regardless
of all risks. the risk of being lost we assume an yu get your child without fail. these are the signals: if it be dark the moment the rear car
passes him he wil exhibit a bright torch in one hand an a white flag in
the other hand but if it be light he wil ring a bell with one hand and a
white flag in the other hand. the instant yu see either of these signals
yu are to drop it on the track an yu may get out at the next station, if the
cars continue on their course we consider yu have kept your word, and
yu child shal be returned yu safe but if they stop to arrest our agent then
your child's fate is sealed. this letter ends all things in regard to the
restoration of yu child.

Letter 13

PHILA 31 July.—*Ros:* Yu seem to have no faith in us whatever. we
told yu to be at yu store on thursday and this bisines would be all settled
up but yu seem to pay no attention to it. at the time we supposed yu wer
gitin redy to effect the change yu were as the *Evening Star* stated on you
way to potsvill to see some child there. if yu ever expect to git yu child yu
must look to us and no one else for there is no other existin powers that
can restore him we have told yu to let the detectives take their own way
an do as they pleas for they wil do yu no good and we don't think they
can do much harm if yu had done as the last letter instructed you and let
the potsvill affair alone yu would now have the plasure of seeing yu child
safe at home after we had seen that yu had gone to potsvill we did not
instruct our agent to meet yu from the fact we thought it was no use.
if yu are trifling with us yu wil find we are not the right party to be trifled
with but if yu mean squar bisines with us although we are perhaps the
worst men in the world we wil act honorably with yu in this affair. we
told yu the last letter was the only one yu should ever reseive from us an
we would keep our word but we are inclined to think yu did not get it
befor yu started for potsvill. to save yu al further trouble an vexation in
runing around to false reports that yu child is found here, and found there,
we tel yu candidly that yu child is not in the possession of any woman or
family or that his hair is cut off short. to save yu further troble pay no
attention to any telegrams of that description for it is only trouble in vain

for yu. your childs hair is the same length that it ever was an there is
no disfigurement whatever in him but he is kept where no human eye
can behold him yu have expressed the opinion that we would git tired of
keeping him an turn him over to some charitable institution. dont
flatter yuself with such an idea we have told yu what his end is, if yu do
not redeem him we shal never digress from that. he wil never be taken
from the place he is now concealed unless he is brought out to be restored
to yu. Ros. if yu want to redeem yu child yu must come to us. you can
reach us through the personals of the *Ledger* or *Evening Star*. our
address is John. a change can be easily accomplished if yu desire it.
remember yu have our word in 10 ours the whole thing shall be con-
summated yu git yu child an we git the money

Letter 14

 PHILA. Aug, 3.—Ros—in not keeping our apointment with yu was
entirely a mistake from the fact of havin seen a statement in evening
star that yu had gone to potsvill on the day you was to setle this bisines
with us. we saw the mistake but not in time to communicate with our
agent or to notify yu not to go as we directed yu. Yu say yu want us to
point out some sure way by which this money can be transmited to us—
of course we can not call on yu personally neither can we receive it by
letter. Ros—We will make the followin proposition to yu and if yu
comply with the terms propounded we wil settle this bisines in very
quick time satisfactory to both parties concerned so far as the restoration
of your child is concerned. We assure yu that yu child is now well and
in as good health as when he left yu home—do yu consent to the followin proposition and stake the life of Charley on the faith of yu
promise.
    Proposition 1st. Yu wil hand the box with the amount in to our
agent when he calls to yu store.
    Proposition 2d. Yu wil hand him the box, ask him no questions—
not follow him—not put any one to follow him—not tel him what the box contains—not notify the detectives so they can follow him—not do anything that wil interupt its transit to us.
    Do yu agree to the first and second proposition while we hold the life
of Charley to bind yu to yur promise. Remember when yu promise

your word is life or death to yu child. If yu consent to these terms answer the folowing *Ledger* or *Evening Star* to save time. (John i agree to the 1st and 2d propositions.) The reason we have warned yu in al our letters about the detectives to keep them ignorant of this compromise bisines is not that we fear detection but we now they wil interfear and baffle us from receiving the money and yu from giting yu child. we told yu in our last this corrospondonce must end but it was a mistak on our part therefore we be wilin to give yu a fair opportunity to redeem yu son if you wil. when our agent call on yu he will give yu a symbol of which yu wil previously receive a facsimilar so there wil be no posibly mistake in him, if there be it shal be our loss and not yours providing yu do as instructed. if we lose the money through our agent yu get yu child just as if we got every dollar.

Letter 15

PHILADELPHIA, August 4.—*Ros:* we saw yu ansur. yu say it is imposible to agree to the terms, then we say emphaticaly yu can never redeem yu child from us. yu requested a more sure way of paying yu money for yu child we agreed to give yu a satisfactory way which would have made the change sure and safe for yu and safe for us, the way we propounded was the sure test of your sincerity and yu answer implies distinctly that yu son is not worth that amount to save him, yu may be entertaining the idea that if the money is not paid we will turn him loose. yu wil find when it is to late that this was a grate mistake. we tel yu plainly and positively that the chances of yu ever geting yu child again is ninety-nine out of an hundred against yu. if yu do not redeem him he is just as good as the money to us for we have him for reference though we may never work this thing in this country again. be where it may we have the Ros child to show that we do about what we say when we told yu your child should stand responsible for our word to us we ment just what we said and any perfidy on yu part would have brought instant death on his head. now we are convinced that you would not keep faith with us, if yu could violate it with impunity to yu child and yet we do not blame yu for that, and yet do yu suppose that we would produce the child and hand him over to you the instant yu paid the money to us. the thing is absurd to think of such a change, we are not

redy yet to have chains put on us for life. we did think once that we
might effect the change in canidy in that way, but we find that cannot be,
for yu could hold us there on robbery and extortion until yu could get
us here and then yu would have us on the whole. Mr Ros the way
the case stands now, it looks as if yu dont want to redeem yu child, or
at least yu must redeem him on yu own terms. That is impossible;
we repeat it, that is absolutely impossible. If yu ever get him from
us, and we are sure yu never will get him from any other than us,
yu have got to come to us on our own terms and our terms wil be more
stringent than ever. One has suggested to redeem yu child with counterfeit money; another to mark all the money, and then we could be
traped after with the money. We say if yu had redeemed yu child
with counterfit money, or with money privately marked, we would not
restored yu child till yu had replace the marked money double-fold.
A woman has proposed to Tagget to produce Charley and his abductors
for $5,000. This will be by far the cheapest way for yu to git yu child,
for we wil never restor him for one dollar less than the amount we first
named. when we found out yu circumstances was not good, we were
goin to throw off one-half the amount an accept $10,000 but the public
have raised hell so, and sympathised for yu in offring such large rewards
that we shall have the whole or none. but they took good care in offering it in such away that they would never have to pay one dollar of it.
if they ment bisines why did they not offer so much for the child and so
much for the abductors. the reason is they thought one or the other rewards might have to be paid. but we don't think they would ever have
to pay a dollar for either child or us. yu wil find the truth of this in the
end (if I no myself). Mr. Ross we leave the city to-night. we shal not communicate with yu any more unless yu can satisfy us yu want to redeem yu child on our terms which wil be $20,000 and not one dollar
less and it must be paid to us as we prescribe. when yu receive this we
shal be at least 200 miles from here we leave the detectives of phila and
Mr tagget to work out their clues. we think we have left no clues
behind us. Charley wil remain where he was taken the second night
after he left home. If Mr tagget can find a clue to that place he wil no
doubt get the reward we have no feminines into that place. charley will
never come out of there. it shal be his everlasting tomb—unless the
ransom brings him out. we are not destitute of a few dollars yet, charley
shal never starve to death if death it must be, it shal come upon him as

instant as the lightning strock itself. Mr Ros, if you have anything to say to us it must be through the personals of New York *Herald*. we can see that, where ever we are and no doubt every day, we shal notice nothing only from you. no matter what propositions others may make they wil receive no attention. yu say the action must be symultanious from the nature of this bisines that can never be, so that ends the bisines we told yu in 10 ours after the receipt of mony if we found it genuine, and not secretly marked al up, yu would then get yu child in our way of passing him over to yu. this does not suit yu so we wil leave yu to yu own way of giting and the detectives to work out their clues.

Letter 16

NEW YORK, August 21.—*Mr. Ros:* we have heard nothing from yu since we wrote yu about 3 weeks ago. we then told yu if yu had anything to comunicate to us to do it through the New York *Herald* personals. we have seen nothing but these words (Christian K. Ross, 304 Market street). we know not what to make of that. we have therefor come to the conclusion that yu don't mean to redeem yu child on the conditions which we proposed. yu must bear in mind we would never agree to any other terms. the fact of yu saying the action must be symultainous is absolutely imposible. we would require at least a few ours to examine the mony and see if it were spurious or all marked up and then but a few ours more would be necessary to place yu child in yu possession for he is not so far off as yu may imagin. the folowing is the way we had intended to return him to yu. we was going to put a labill on his back and take him to a respectable house at night rouse them up. tell them to take this child as directed pay them for their trouble, this arrangement does not me with yu concent so there is no other alternitive left yu. now we demand yu anser yes or now as we are going to urope the 24 Sept and he has got to be disposed of one way or the other by that time. if you say redeem him it has got to be on our terms alone if yu do not answer we shall take it as granted that yu dont mean to pay yu money. we shall act accordingly. address (John New *Herald* personals.) you are listing to old womans visions and dreams which wil never find yu child. we could have told yu it was useless to go to illinoise to look for charly but yu would not have believed us.

Letter 17

ALBANY, August 26.—Mr. Ros—Your timely answer saved yu child.
we had determined if yu did not care to save him we would not swerve
one jot or tittle from the fate we had designed for him—not that we
delight in blood but it was inevitable with our selves in order to carry
out our plan of action yu ask for no more prof that we had him or that
we have him—that is right—yu should have prof that we are the identical ones who kidnaped Chaley—we thought that yu were well satisfied
that we were the kidnappers—we wil first prove to yu we took Charley—
ask Walter if one of the men did not hold him between his legs an
partly on his knee with the cloth in front of him while Charley set
behind us both entirely out of sight—ask him if he did not want to go up
on main road to git fireworks and we told him we would first go to ant
Susy's that she kep a shop we could get them cheaper. ask him
if we did not keep givin him pieces of candy as we rode along.
ask him if we did not go from your house west to Morton street and then
south instead of going towards the depot on Washington lane as it has
been stated in the papers these remarks we think are suficient to prove
to yu that we are the men who took him if yu have received any other
letters headed other than Ros or Mr. Ros they are forgeries, we have
sent you 8 or 10 letters in all, if you had accepted the proposition we
made yu some four weeks ago yu would now without doubt have yu
child safe in yu own house but yu rejected the offer and left us without
the means to negotiate with yu. Mr. Ros if yu ever expect to recove yu
child yu have got to in a measure rely on our faith. in dealing with us
yu must be satisfied that yu child was taken for a ransom. we have set
the price and asked the ransom of yu. do yu think if yu paid the ransom once that we would ever ask it the second time. no man would be
foolish enough to pay ransom the second time for a thing he had paid
for once and did not get. if we wanted more money from yu we would
ask it now, instead of asking more we would rather throw off some. but
the public have interfered so much in this busines that we are determined every dollar shall be paid or not one cent Yu have asked that
the action between us should be symultainous Yu must know from the
nature of this business that is impossible—first we would have to give
yu Charley when we receive the mony yu git yu child, We might git a
bundle of brown paper and a chain around our necks No sir Mr. Ros

We must have at least 4 or 5 hours to examine the money to see if yu have delt faithfully with us what we mean is yu must give the mony in good condition unscarified or not at all, then yu have performed yu part in good faith When that is done we have no further use for Charley he has answered the whole end for which we got him and we as vile as we are would be working against our own interests if we did not return him to yu as we promised we only wish it was posible to effect the change symultaniously but as that cant be done yu must accept the best we can offer yu, do yu open this correspondence with the intention to pay yu money on our terms and git yu child or is it the foolish advice of some of yu friends again with the idea of entraping us. do you want to daly along and keep your child month after month living in a place where the strongest could not live over one year. we would not let him unnecessarily sufer but this exteriordary search has made it necessary to keep him where the light of the sun has never shown upon him since the 2d day of July. we have seen Charley about 4 days ago his whole cry is he wants Walter to come see him and he is afraid he wil not go to Atlantic City with his mother. don't think this is only an appeal to your affection as a farther it is symply the words that he used when we saw him last. Mr. Ros. one word more—do you want to redeem Charley or not on our terms. if yu do yu must make up you mind that the money must be paid in good faith. don't deceive yu self that if the ransom is not paid that we will set yu child at liberty. we can never do that our whole plan would be frustrated at one blow and our work would come to naught. as yu deal with us so shal we deal with you in return. we saw yu personal in *Herald* of 26. whatever answer yu have to make to this let it be in Albany *Argus* no put it in New York *herald* personals as we wil leave here to-day and drop this somewhere on OUR WAY to New York. we can see the New York *herald* any part of the United States.

(Address as be for John.)

P.S.—yu acted wisely in refusing these letters until yu got yu child —if yu had published them, no doubt it would have been the means of sacrificing you child.

Letter 18

NY. Sept 6 –Mr. Ros we cannot see how yu can resist the proof that we have got him notwithstanding Walter's contradictory story, yu must admit he was

taken by some one yu must admit he was taken for a ransom now if we
have not got him who has got him—has any one else asked yu for a
ransom we think not. mr. percell that benevlent man who offered to
pay the ransom now says yu have never lost yu child—we know percell
lies because we have positive that we have him and yu have positive
proof that yu lost him. Mr. Ros in order to convince yu that we have
him yu require some of his cloths sent yu. it was hinted some six weeks
ago in one of the editorials to send yu some of Charly cloths in answer
to that we said we would never do anything of the kind because we
could give an irrestible proof without it—if we sent you any cloths we
have got to expres them which we wil never do we don't know for certain wether his cloths have been saved up to the time we dont go near
him often for we have nothing to do with guarding him though we have
seen him three or fourtimes since 2d of July we told you in one of our
letters that Charley had never been in any way whatever disguised nor at
that time he had not been but since then he has had his hair cut short
and girls clothes put on him now wether they have kept his cloths or
not we cannot say and we cannot send them if they have them the
probibility is they have destroyed them for every possible precautionary
measure has been taken since we have seen what great efforts have been
made to find his place of concealment we were surprised to think yu
would make such efferts to find him when we told yu that to search for
him yu was only searching for his life and any approach by a detective to his
hiding place would be a certain sign for his destruction yu either
don't believe this or yu don't regard the life of yu child where he is
now confined wil be his tomb unles yu bring him out with the ransom
yu detectives can never do it your friends who advise yu that we wil
set him free should you not ransom him wil be the worst advise yu ever
had. your friends yu say ask for more proof that we ever had him they
are as foolish as percell for he says you never lost him. your detectives
have never had the slightest clue or trace of him since the our he was
taken but in order to convince these sceptical friends that we had him
and have him we will now give the detectives a small clue to work upon
but it will serve no other end only to convince these sceptical friends or
yours that we have him. on the night of 2d July at 11 o'clock we passed
through Trenton, N.J. Charley lay in my arms asleep. after we had
passed about 2 squares up bridge st Charley's hat drop off and we did
not notice it until he woke up and asked for his hat we would not go

back for it. you can get this hat by advertising for it there if it is not
worn out. if it should be worn out you can find out who found one that
night or the next morning. now ask one of your domestics or Mrs. Ros
if charley did not have on the afternoon of the first of July a narrow faded
pink ribbin tied around his head to keep the hear out of his eyes. if yu
find this a fact which we have no doubt yu wil and as it was never d-
scribed in the advertisement, we think no human being could mention it
but the party who took him. if this does not satsfy yu and yu friends
that we have him then yu must go unsatisfied. This clue of the hat will
end there when you find it and it wil avail yu nothing more. Let the detectives work it up much as they please, the clue will end there we know
or we would not told of it. Mr. Ros we don't know wether yu ever mean
to ransom yu child yu certainly dont act much like it. but we do know
yu will never get him without it unless you arc fortunate enough to ketch
us knapping and take him by stratagem. there is not one chance in
10,000 of ever getting him that way. yu must not delude yuself with the
idea that if we go to europe this month that we wil set yu child free or
take him with us and then will be the time to find him. that wil never
be Mr. Ros we have told yu befor if yu ever expect to get yu child yu
wil have to ransom him and to the full amount we named. if you deal
fair with us we wil deal fair with yu if yu play any tricks with us we
shall do likewise with yu. whatever you do with us we shall do likewise with yu. whatever yu do with us yu must do it in good faith or
not at all then yu get yu child safe and sound. we shall not keep up this correspondence much longer, whatever yu mean to do must be soon. we
see the New York herald every day whatever yu have to say we wil notice it. we are now in lansingburg above Troy New York we dont know
where we shall post this letter yet we leave here to-day.

Letter 19

NEW HAVEN, Sept. 23—*Mr. Ros.*—we did not see yu last answer til
to day. we was in new brunswic british province and cold not see the
New York *herald* we went there to se if the law would permit us to
make a symultaneous change with yu but we find no such change can
be efected with safety to our selves. you ask to transact the bisiness
through an attorney this is to absurd to think of for one minute that man

does not exist that we cold trust to receive that money but one of our own party and we are not wiling that one of our party shall become recognizable by any living person. as we now stand we can confront any one with impunity and are determined to keep so. if you be convinced that we have him and want to ransom him why did you not agree to our proposition. we have told yu if the money was lost in transit tu us it would be our los should yu folow our instructions and yu get yu child.

 Mr. Ros we cannot show the child to yu and we cannot give you any more proof than we have; yu must expect this as the only alternitive left you to ransom him or murder him, for one or the other wil and shal take place before many days. Yu as his father have been mor cruel to him than we have. We told yu that his place of concealment was such that no living being could find it and that it was not a fit place for any one to be in the length of time he has been there. We do not keep him there to punish him; your detectives have made it much worse for him than he would be had they not such a close search for him; he has kept his health wonderful considering his close confinement. We do not see him often or even hear from him. The last time we se him he had been ailing with pain from stoppage of urin he would go 24 and 30 ours without making water and then he would cry with pane when he would urinate, but his custodian got him som medicine which helped him. we tel yu positively Mr. Ros his hiding place must be his tomb unless you bring him out with the ransom for we have a settled plan to act upon and we shal never digress from it and that is death or ransom. Yu will find we speak truth in this for once if yu compel us to put him to death yu shall receive a letter in 24 ours after, wher yu wil find his body. as soon as we cop another kid and it wil be a millionaire this time your child must die. we wil then see if he wil be so heartless as to let his child die. you detectives perhaps tel yu that yu wil pay yu money and get no child then but we dont do bisiness in that way we dont want him much longer neither dead or alive. if yu pay for him yu shall have him safe and sound. if not yu shal have him dead. so you can rest assured yu wil get him soon one way or the other. if die he must yu shal se that he has been dead but a few ours when yu git him then yu can thank yu friends for their kind advise. Ros this is the last advise we wil offer yu if yu reject it yu can make up yu mind that the day of grace is forever lost to save your child. Ros if yu want to save yu child yu must comply with our terms and yu yourself be our Attorney for we wil have no other and we are absolutely determined on that point. when yu see fit to change yu money for yu child in the way we direct yu can answer this through the *herald* personal New York. we shall keep up this unnessary correspondence no longer your asking for more evidence that we have him looks to us as if it was a scheme of Mr. Haines to entrap us, but mr hains will never have that pleasure Mr Ros you must be convinced by this time that no reward however large can effect or influence our party we told yu this at the first and we tol yu how hopelessly it was for yu to search for him when we had taken such great labor to find a suitable place to conceal him and the imposebility for any one to find him in our possession when we have it fixed so we can lanch him into eternity at an instant's warning, and yet yu consent that a reward shall be offered to induce some one who has no right to approach his hiding place but perhaps yu look upon this as romance or fiction yet fiction is sometimes more stranger than truth. Ros—yu should be your own councilor in getting yu child and then let the detectives council yu how to get us, take our advice for once and se if we do not give you the best council—that is get yu child at any price on any terms we offer yu regardless of all other advise—we have told yu and now repeat it that this thing is drawing to a final crises. Mr Ros when yu conclude to act as our atty and meet us on our terms then yu can answer this as directed we shal henceforth notice nothing else from yu.

Letter 20

NEW BRUNSWIC. September 30. *Mr. Ros* : yu have at length agreed to our terms. how much better would it have been for yu had yu complied at first. we told you at first there was no other alternitive left yu but to part with your mony or yu child for one or the other yu must, we told yu before it shal not exceed 10 ours from the time we receive the mony til yu receive yu child and yet it may be a few ours longer. we must have time to examine the money to see that yu have not got it secretly marked up. we tel yu for your own interest not to mark the notes in any way whatever for if you break the terms of agreement with us we shal then break it with yu and yu had much better keep your money for we tel yu positively we would not keep our word. we would not liberate the child. but on the other hand if yu come to us in good

faith with the intention of parting with yu money for the sake of getting
yu child and saving him from death then we pledge ourselves by all the
powers that be sacred in heaven and earth yu shall have yu child saf and
sound as soon as we can get him to yu with safety to ourselves we think
we told yu once how we would return him tu yu. but this is the way
we propose to do. we will take him to some ministers house at night
put a label on him stating this is Charley Ros take him immediately to
304 Market st phil or washington lane germantown yu will find a sufficient sum in his pocket to pay yu for yu trouble no reward will be paid.
we have sent word to his parents stating where he is. Mr. Ros we do
not intend the party where we leave him shall see us at all they will be
perfect innocent so you should not give them any trouble. we will send
you word immediately stating where he is left. but the probability is he
will be brought home long before yu the get letter but this will make it
perfectly safe and sure for yu to get him. Mr. Ros it is true yu have
got tu rely entirely on our honor for the fulfillment of this part of the
contract but you can rely with implicit confidence. bad as we are and
capable of the blackest deeds yet we have some honer left. your large
rewards have in a measure proved this there are 4 of us to divide the
$20,000 among and either one of the 4 could went and got the whole
amount to himself if he had been without principal. how easy could any
one of the 4 went on the sly and had us all coped and revealed where
the child was secreted but yu see we have not done it. we have no fear
of one another though it were a million dollars. we have told yu for
your own interest not tu mark the money which yu intend tu ransom
your child with. keep faith with us and we will keep faith with yu and
yu shal have yu child safe and sound in 10 or 12 ours. provide yourself
with the amount in United Sates notes from 1 tu 10 in denomination.
not national bank notes when yu are all prepared with this and are ready
to meet us drop a word in the *herald* New York yu can take as many of
yu friends as yu choose but do it quietly if yu want tu get yu child. Mr.
Ros first get yu child then let the detectives assist yu. yu see they have
not the power to do anything. time has proved this and if yu rely upon
them so it will ever prove. Mr Ros put yu child when yu get him on
exhibition and yu wil relize all your money back in 6 months for there is
not a mother in phila that will not pay a dollar to see him.

Letter 21

NEWBURG, N.Y. Oct. 11.—*Mr. Ros:* You say the money is ready how is it then we can't come to a speedy compromise if yu was anxious to get yu child and wiling to pay yu money then there is no troble about it we are anxious to give him up but only on the conditions we have before told yu you ask again how we are to deliver him to yu we told yu in our last letter plainly how we would return him to yu is not that way satisfactory yu don't want us surely to turn him loose on the road at the ded our of night we wil never bring him to you personaly nor wil we ever take him to any one you appoint but we will take him to a strange family where it is least expected and where you will be sure to get him if the way of delivering him is not satisfactory to yu then we cannot come to terms for we are determined in delivering him to yu that no person shal see our face when we do go with him we shal be completely disguised yu ask to state plainly how yu are to pay the money that is imaterial to yu what disposal is made of it so long as yu comply with our demands which you already know   all you have to do now in order to have yu child restorded to yu is to make up yu mind that yu have got to part with so many dollars and it maters not to yu what becomes of the money so long as it satisfies our demand we return yu the child. yu may have a doubt that yu may not then get yu child. we cannot give yu the child before we get the money for then we part with every compulsion to make yu pay it. we cannot hand you the child as yu hand us the money for all the power and all the law is on your side. the thing is all embodied in a nutshell. the child is of no entrensic value to us whatever, any further than to compel yu to ransom him if yu pay the ransom and we do not give him up to yu would any one else give a dollar for their child when they would have no assurance whatever of getting him. you certainly would not be full enough to pay the ransom the second time when we had not kept faith with yu the first time but yu ask he might be dead and then we could not give him up— yes he might have been dead a dozen times through your neglect to redeem him but as it hapens he has lived in spite of his close confinement again yu say we might hurried his death as we have threatened it so many times. That is true—we might but it has not come to that crisis yet so long as the inducement is held out of geting the ransom he is in a measure safe but there wil be a time when the inducement wil exaust itself when this death takes place it wil be our policy and interest to make it know n to yu at once that others may be wiser than yu—if yu should pay the ransom and then not get yu child would any one else have faith enough in us to pay a ransom when Ros did not get his child after paying for him—Mr. Ros you can rest assured with all confidence when yu pay yu mony yu wil get yu child but it wil be imposible unless you do. yu have ben living in hope of geting him without the ransom but the detectives in the case are powerless. yu get a clue every few days or rather a false clue. only a few days ago yu child was seen in New Haven. i tel you positively and tu save you trouble and anxiety that yu child has not been seen by any human being since the third day of July other than the party who have been in charge we could not take him five miles without being arrested; when we return him to yu it will be in the night time if at all when yu hear yu child is seen here or there yu can have no faith in it. for he wil not be see by any one while we have him that yu can rest assured of. yu say yu money is ready. are your eady to take a short journey and have this thing set- tled. Mr. Ros this continual correspondence looks to us as if it was but a ruse to get a clue to our whereabouts. We tel yu positively should they succeed in capturing one of us it would certainly prove death to yu child. Do you believe it or not—whether or not it wil not alter our decree. If yu banish all hope of ever getting yu child til yu ransom him and drop the detectives yu wil then take a rational view of the thing and see it in its true light. We told yu we were going to urope last month; part of us did go, but we expect them back in few days and then we can settle the business if yu are ready. We wil see the personals in the New York *herald*.

OCTOBER 15—we had almost concluded after writing this not to send it for you ask questions that answered planly—but we wil see what you want now—if yu are ready to pay we are ready to return the child to your satisfaction.

Letter 22

PHILA Oct 31 Mr Ros we told you at the beginning of this bisnes we would deal with none but you   the reason of this must be apparent to yu   the fate of your child would depend upon your actions in dealing

with us we know you would not intentionally sacrifice your child in
breaking faith with us we told you in dealing with us you must act in
good faith and any breach of faith on your part would be meeted out in
 crtain death Mr Ros if you have any relation or friend that you can
delegate to this important bisines then we are ready to deal with him
we care not who he may be if it be mr hines or the states attorney—we
are willing to negociate with him but mr Ros we want you not to deceive
yourself in this bisines for we tell you plainly his acts will involve the
life or death of your child we shall regard him as your substitute in
every particular and hold the life of your child responsible for his actions. Mr Ros from your answers we understood you agree to the terms
we previously dictated. send your substitute to New York tuesday 3rd
november with the means to settle this bisines. remember the money
must be in every particular as we directed for you can accomplish nothing
with us in using any stratagem for we will not release the child under
any other circumstances then your carrying out the terms in good faith
with us it is unnecessary for us to pledge ourselves in any way in regard
to the child being immediately returned to you. all we can do or say is
—it shall be our first move to restore the child after we see the money is
all right. we shall spare no trouble or expense in returning the child to
you safely. though it cost us five thousand we would not hesitate to use
it in order to return the child. but it will not cost us ten dollars and you
shal have him as safe and sound as he was on the first day of July last
when he was playing in front of your door with Walter. your substitute on arriving in new York must put a personal in *herald*. say. John i am
stoping at _____ hotel with his name in full. Mr Ros you say the money
is ready and your substitute. and we are ready. then Novemer the
3d wil prove or disprove the sincerity of your action. Mr Ros you see
by this we have come among you once more.

Letter 22 ¹/₂

NEW BRUNSWICK, November 3—*Mr. Ros*. it looks very strange to us
that you should quible about the name to address us. is your object to
keep the detectives informed of our whereabouts by having us writing
you so often. it looks so but time will prove all things. our advice is to
you and it is better than all the detectives combined can give you is to act

squarely in this bisnes if you have any regard for your child. we think
we have cautioned you enough on this point. we are satisfied the detectives are working the thing up to their interest we know all about their
doings and how they are bleeding you and Mr louis out of your money
you will open your eyes to their games. by the by we could tell you much
about them but our place it to keep mum and yours to investigate before
you give more money out. it makes us jealous to see you pay out your
mony foolishly when they can give you nothing in return but a parcel of fabricated lies. we confes we are bleeding you to—but we have an
equivalent to give you in return, if you child is any equivalent. you will
find sooner or later that there is no other earthly party in this world to
deal with than ourselves if you want to recover your child. Mr. Ros
why could not your relative give any name so that we could have a name
to address him?   it matters not what the name is we shall regard him
as yourself in every sense of the word so look to whom you appoint to
transact this business for you. we tell you positivey and absoluty that
on his acts right or rong square or crooked in dealing with us the life or
death of yu child shall hang now. Mr. Ros you may appoint any one
you please to transact the bisines with us but we want you to bear in mind
that his acts are your acts and it shall be consumated just as you will it –
and if you want your child safe and sound this is the final day of salvation.
we have been at least under $15 a day expensive since we had him but that
is our own affair. you may have been under five times that expense for
what we know. Mr Ross you must not be deceived from this because we
are under expenses from keeping him that we will turn him loose should
you not meet our demands. we tell you positively we could not do it
we would not do it should it benefit us the whole amount of $20,000
than for the redemption of your child. you may think from this should
you pay the demands. we might not then return your child. Mr Ros
when you have paid our demands in good faith you have answered all
we can ask of you and we tell you as we have told you before that your
child is not worth one cent to us after that ony to return him to you and
we would not fail in any event to return him to you for $10,000.
Strange as this may appear to you yet it is our interest to do so. should
you not come to our terms it is our interest that you never get him and
you may rely on it you never will alive. you may think this is to cruel
for any sivelized person to perpetrate but we tell you positively it is the
lot of one of us to perform it if it comes to this crises. you will not be

able by any quibbling to stay the hand of fate much longer from him.
we have kept him over one hundred days longer than we expected.
now it is for you alone to say whether he shal live or die. this is the
last letter we shall we ever send you till we send you the final one revealing to you whether he is either alive or dead just as you will it to be.
you need not ask more questions for they will not be noticed no answer
will be returned. if you appoint anyone to conduct this business for you
let him come to New York make it known through personal with any
address he choses. this address will do (John Johnathan is stopping at
so and so. Johnathan or who he may be must not leave the hotel till he
hears from us. if you mean square bisiness have your personal in
Friday's *Herald* (N.Y.) and be in New York on Saturday morning.
Mr. Ros bear in mind this is the last and final letter you ever receive
from us unless you come to New York to close this bisiness.

Letter 23

PHILA., Nov. 6. – *Mr. Ros:* we told you in the last positively we would not
write you any more. this dozing about puts us to no small amount
of trouble we had left phila for New York thinking you were ready
to close up the business. we told you positively procrastination is dangerous. had we accomplished what we have been fishing for the last
three months your child would now have been dead but we have not yet
caught the fish we wanted. yours is but a small item compared with
something else. Walter said you owned the two new houses right opposite you or we should never troubled you. Mr. Ros you have asked to
keep this negotiation a secret between ourselves it is a wise policy in
your doings not that we fear being traped in our own game. This is
positively the last from us. if you are sincere you would be anxious to
settle this business if you regard the life of your child. we mean to fulfil
every promise we made you in good faith. the result depends entirely
with yourself whom you appoint to transact this business for yu we want
at least two days notice before you come to New York for we may be
500 miles off and we ask for time to get there yu can say tuesday no 10.
Saul of Tarsus. (choose your own name say i will be stoping so and so all day.
do not leave the hotel wherever you may be stoping for one
minute during the day). this thing must come and shall come to a close
in a few days.

we is got him

p. 17   *Their shoes got caught*: Wister, Frances, 23; Callard, 54.
p. 17   *Travelers had complained*: Wister, Frances, 24; Clemens, 47;
           The Germantown Guide, July 25, 1874.
p. 17   *They lived in caves*: Callard, 13.
p. 17   *the community earned enough money*: Weigley, 25, 62, 327.
p. 17   *During the winter*: Wister, Frances Anne. "The Great Road," 23.
p. 17   *General Howe's men*: Switala, 5.
p. 17   *runaway slaves found their way*: Ibid.
p. 18   *After Philadelphia absorbed*: Wister, Jones, 24; Weigley, 24.
p. 18   *Often, salesmen and charlatans*: Callard, 101, 113.
p. 18   *In the early summer evenings of 1874:* Coffin, 25; Zimmerman, 1, 3, 24.
p. 18   *on Wednesday, July 1, Peter Callahan*: *PI*, September 1, 1875.
p. 18   *Earlier that day,*: Ross, 27.
p. 18   *Laughter had echoed*: *The Germantown Guide*, June 27, 1874.
p. 18   *Just after 5:00 P.M.*: *PI*, September 1, 1875.
p. 18   *It was drawn by a brown horse*: Ibid.
p. 18   *The driver's face was partially hidden*: Ross, 33; *INA*, July 23, 1874; *EB*,
           December 16, 1875.
p. 19   *the men spread a dirty, ripped lap cover*: Ross, 33.

you wil have two pay us

p. 21   *Before they went out to play*: Ross, 28.
p. 21   *Charley had light-brown hair*: Ross, 34.
p. 21   *Charley looked up to him and put Walter in charge*: Ibid.
p. 21   *If somebody he didn't know approached him*: Ibid.
p. 21   *Neither boy shied away*: This is based on the court testimonies of
           Mary Kidder and Peter Callanan.
p. 21   *Walter asked why*: Ross, 31.
p. 21   *"No, we will take you to Aunt Susie's"*: Ibid.
p. 22   *He asked the men to identify features*: Ibid.
p. 22   *Charley began to whimper*: Ross, 32.
p. 22   *If somebody snapped at him*: Ross, 34.
p. 22   *"Faster, faster!"*: Ross, 32.

p. 22   *The passenger added liquor to it*: Ibid.

p. 22   *The forefinger on his left hand*: Zierold, 148.

p. 22   *"Slower, slower"*: Ross, 32.

p. 22   *the wagon turned again, again, and again*: PI, July 17, 1874.

p. 22   *John Hay, a young tobacconist*: INA, July 31, 1874.

p. 22   *Walter ran to the intersection*: Ross, 32.

p. 23   *He had a receding hairline*: Photo of Christian Ross, Courtesy of GHS.

p. 23   *The Panic of 1873*: Beers, 432; Foner, 512.

p. 23   *Philadelphia's commercial and industrial*: Beers, 433.

p. 23   *causing neighbors to wonder*: INA, July 28, 1874.

p. 23   *Christian looked forward*: Ross, 27.

p. 23   *and their two older brothers*: Ross, 26.

p. 23   *Walter and Charley knew*: Ross, 27.

p. 23   *Germantown and Philadelphia ordinances*: The Germantown Guide, July 4, 1874.

p. 23   *Christian said they needed*: Ross, 27.

p. 23   *Between one and ten acres*: Ross, 25.

p. 23   *Christian owned a smaller plot*: Philadelphia Public Library, Map Division.

p. 24   *"Are your boys likely"*: Ross, 28.

p. 24   *Christian stared*: Ibid.

p. 24   *Four days earlier*: Ross, 27.

p. 24   *"No, Sir"*: Ibid.

p. 24   *Mrs. Kidder hurried*: Ross, 28.

p. 24   *That week, a local paper had addressed*: The Germantown Guide, July 4, 1874.

p. 24   *kidnapping in America was a misdemeanor*: INA, July 31, 1874.

p. 25   *"Where have you been, Walter?"*: PI, September 1, 1875.

p. 25   *he had seen and heard a terrified Walter*: INA, July 30, 1874.

p. 25   *"a man had put him out of a buggy"*: Ibid.

p. 25   *It had served as*: Callard 59, 68, 100.

p. 25   *The central office dialogued with*: Berman, 86; Harring, 49.

p. 25   *Buchanan, a large, thirty-eight-year-old Irishman*: GHS, Ross folder, "Buchanan."

p. 25   *Thirty minutes later, Buchanan reported*: Ross, 29.

p. 26   *The Ross and Lewis families had known*: Biographical Encyclopedia of Dauphin County, 1896.

p. 26   *Christian's grandfather was a German immigrant*: Ibid.

p. 26   *the Lewis brothers owned three successful*: PI, December 23, 1874.

p. 26   *Joseph Lewis owned more property than*: Philadelphia Public Library, Map Division.

p. 26   *Joseph and his son Frank Lewis listened*: Ross, 29.

p. 27   *Christian noticed how unusually quiet*: Ross, 30.

p. 27   *The men arrived around 11:00 P.M.*: Ibid.

p. 27   *repeated their belief that drunken fools*: Ross, 35.

p. 27   *A thunderstorm loomed*: Winner, Septimus, Diaries.

p. 28   *"head-aching weather"*: Ibid.

p. 28   *men often gathered to sit*: *INA*, July 31, 1874.

p. 28   *In search of eye witnesses*: Ross, 36.

p. 28   *His memory shocked both men*: Ross 37, 42.

p. 28   *Only one paper*: *PL*, July 3, 1874.

p. 28   *the community gathered to pray*: Ross, 39.

p. 29   *A local doctor reported that*: *INA*, July 23, 1874.

p. 29   *A handyman remembered*: *PI*, September 1, 1875.

p. 29   *A couple of people in town*: Ibid.

p. 29   *Mr. Johnson*: Ross, 40.

p. 29   *Readers of the Philadelphia* Public Ledger: *PL*, July 3, 1874.

p. 30   *because Christian feared disturbing Sarah*: *Germantown Guide*, August 15, 1874.

p. 30   *"suspicious persons"*: Ross, 40.

p. 30   *Residents had told Lieutenant*: Ross, 42–43.

p. 30   *Several women were watching*: Ibid.

be not uneasy

p. 33   *On the morning of July 4*: *PL*, July 6, 1874.

p. 33   *hoping that the detectives were right*: Ross, 46.

p. 34   *His constituents numbered close to 800,000*: Keels, 136; Whiteman, 114.

p. 34   *more than 20 percent of whom worked*: *PI*, July 6, 1874.

p. 34   *in the 8,000 factories*: Bell, 203.

p. 34   *almost five times*: *Manual of the Councils of the City of Philadelphia*, 1874-1876.

p. 34   *Ulysses S. Grant accepted*: *NYT*, October 18, 1874.

p. 34   *William Stokley had also been*: Sprogle, 152–153.

p. 34   *His first political act was to*: Wolf, 211.

p. 34   *the immigrant community*: Beers, 422.

p. 34   *He immediately fired*: Sprogle, 151–152.

p. 34   *other city wages dropped 10 percent*: Marshall, 204.

p. 34   *thousands of railway workers*: Ibid.

p. 34   *Five days before July 4*: Sprogle, 154.

p. 35   *four million Americans had settled*: Brown, 16.

p. 35   *into 40 million people and*: Brown, 16.

p. 35   *600,000 soldiers, had died and freed slaves*: Faust, xi; Hendrickson, 229.

p. 35   *Stokley greeted his honored guests*: *PL*, July 4, 1874; *PI*, July 6, 1874.

p. 35   *Together, they exited*: *PL*, July 4, 1876.

p. 35   *The mayor's carriage went directly*: Hepp, 82; *PL*, July 6, 1874.

p. 35   *Trees lined both riverbanks*: Philadelphia Public Library, Photo Collection.

p. 36   *He arrived at the excavation site*: *PI*, July 6, 1874.

p. 37   *William Penn had designed*: *PI*, July 6, 1874.

p. 37   *Nobody spoke*: Ross, 46.

p. 37   *had delayed his plans for 180 years*: PI, July 6, 1874.

p. 37   *Five thousand attendees*: PL, July 6, 1874. Details in the following
scene are drawn from this article and an article appearing in the
Ledger on July 2, 1874.

p. 37   *"We have a manly local pride"*: PI, July 6, 1874.

Yu be its murderer

p. 39   *standardized development had chafed*: Beers, 419, 421; Warner, 50, 52.

p. 39   *On a normal weekday, shoppers*: Callard, 39.

p. 39   *Jimmy Jones . . . from floor to ceiling*: Haines, 16–22; Callard, 39.
Jimmy Jones was also the name of a descendant of this shopkeeper,
one who operated the family business into the middle of the twentieth century.

p. 40   *Weeping willows cast*: Clemens, 19, 23, 34; Wister, James, 82.

p. 40   *parents had heard:* Haines, 2. The archives and Wister collection at
La Salle University, organized by Dr. James Butler, were particularly helpful in reconstructing life in Victorian Germantown.

p. 40   *Families picnicked*: Coffin, 64–66; Clemens, *Quaint Old*, 6, 9; Haines,
98.

p. 40   *Germantown's children were used*: Coffin, 39–40; Clemens, *East
Germantown*, 33–37.

p. 40   *monks had awaited*: Zimmerman, 1, 4.

p. 40   *two men with bushy beards still roamed*: Coffin, 34–36; Clemens, *East
Germantown*, 35.

p. 41   *"See the ghost!"*: La Salle University Library, Campbell Collection,
Germantown Data #41.

p. 41   *Sarah Lewis Ross had given*: EB, September 23, 1874.

p. 41   *Sarah had no idea*: Ross, 47.

p. 42   *Christian's neighbors suspected that*: INA, July 28, 1874.

p. 42   *"Why did you not bring Charley"*: Ross, 52.

p. 43   *"No harm has come to Charley"*: Ross, 63.

p. 43   *"Surely you have not heard rightly"*: Ibid.

his lif wil be instant sacrificed

p. 45   *he went home to Germantown*: Ross, 64.

p. 45   *the efforts of Simon Cameron*: Foner, 485–486; Hoogenboom, 830-839.

p. 45   *Prior to the Uniform Elections Act*: Hoogenboom, 830–839.

p. 46   *"There was no plan of any importance"*: Ross, 92; Bell, 204.

p. 46   *pushed Christian closer toward*: Ross, 85.

p. 46   *the police had relied upon*: Ross, 40.

p. 47   *the authorities summoned citizens*: Ross, 73.

p. 47   *"suspicious-looking"*: Ross, 73.

p. 47   *to ships on the Delaware, factories*: Bell, 202, 204; Warner, 50, 52.

p. 47   *"No one outside of"*: Ross, 88.

p. 48   *a third-generation businessman*: *Biographical Encylopedia of Dauphin County*, 1896.

p. 48   *the advisers encouraged Christian*: Ross, 86.

p. 49   *He noticed the stamp*: Ross, 72.

p. 49   *Jewish communities in the Middle Ages*: *INA*, July 16, 1874; *The Germantown Guide*, November 7, 1874.

p. 49   *"kidnapping" wasn't coined*: Fass, 10.

p. 49   *one hundred years later, the definition had evolved*: Fass, 11; *EB*, July 21, 1874.

p. 50   *many European slave traders*: Fass, 10–11; *PL*, August 4, 1874.

p. 50   *Children also fell victim to:* Fass, 13.

p. 50   *hundreds of "street urchins" disappeared*: Ibid.

p. 50   *a solely Italian problem*: Fass, 44; *EB*, July 14, 1874; *INA*, July 20, 1874.

p. 50   *no organized police force*: Monkonnen, 31; Philadelphia Public Library, Police Department Inventory Part 4, 79.

p. 51   *when more than eighty thousand acres were*: Warner, 50; Monkonnen, 36.

p. 51   *The corps' initial efforts*: Monkonnen, 36.

p. 51   *"The detective force of Philadelphia"*: *EB*, July 14, 1874.

he is uneasy

p. 53   *"I felt that it was a fearful risk"*: Ross, 97.

p. 53   *After authorizing public citizens*: Ross, 55.

p. 54   *close readers had noticed*: *PI*, July 22, 1874.

p. 54   *Jones wrote to the city's weekly and daily papers*: *EB*, July 14, 1874; *PL*, July 17, 1874.

p. 54   *The city was outraged*: *PL*, July 17, 1874; *PI*, July 22, 1874.

the danger lies intirely with yuself

p. 55   *A family named Henderson*: Walling, 204.

p. 55   *Mr. Henderson worked*: *PI*, December 21, 1874.

p. 56   *searchers walked through alleys*: *PL*, July 23 and August 10, 1874.

p. 56   *Throughout the city*: Ross, 54-55.

p. 56   *clapboard houses:* Warner, 52.

p. 56   *a stable keeper named*: *INA*, July 18 and July 20, 1874.

yu child shal die

p. 57   *the* Ledger *had had a reputation for:* Supplement to the *Philadelphia Inquirer*, July 16, 1962. Page 16.

p. 57   *the* Ledger *staff was the first in*: Ibid.

p. 57   *prompt reporting been more in demand:* Summers, *The Press Gang*, 15.

p. 57   *Nearly 3 million men:* Faust, 3.

p. 57   *elevated journalistic standards:* Summers, *The Press Gang*, 15.

p. 58   *every major American city:* Summers, *The Press Gang*, 15.

p. 58   *the* New York Herald *alone sent forty:* Ibid.

p. 58   *Readership in more than one hundred metropolitan:* Summers, *The Press Gang*, 12.

p. 58   *George W. Childs:* Supplement to the *Philadelphia Inquirer*, July 16, 1962. Page 18.

p. 58   *The* Ledger *developed:* Ibid.

p. 58   *readership of 400,000:* Summers, *The Press Gang*, 12.

p. 58   *chief editor was a man named William V. McKean:* Supplement to the *Philadelphia Inquirer*, July 16, 1962. Page 18.

p. 58   *"For what may be done in one instance":* EB, July 14, 1874.

p. 58   *"The journalists of this city":* EB, July 16, 1874.

p. 59   *"a particularly useless and expansive body":* EB, July 14, 1874.

p. 59   *Both the* Ledger *and the* Evening Bulletin: *EB*, July 16, 1874.

p. 59   *Inspired by the success of London's Crystal Palace:* Rydell, 8.

p. 59   *The centerpiece of London's Crystal Palace:* Rydell, 15.

p. 59   *Riddle's risk cost the city:* Rydell, 17.

p. 59   *By 1874, Europe had hosted:* Ibid.

p. 60   *"There must be no compromise with thieves":* PI, July 9, 1874.

p. 60   *It attacked Christian's integrity:* Reported by *The Germantown Guide*, August 8, 1874.

p. 60   *"No man with any soul":* PI, July 27, 1874.

p. 60   *His friends loudly defended:* PI, July 27 and September 25, 1874; *PL*, July 28, 1874.

p. 60   *"No possible good could result by":* Ross, 86.

he is yet safe

p. 63   *"Tramp Acts" were being passed:* Harring, 201.

p. 63   *Sarah Ross's friends responded:* Ross, 110.

p. 63   *She sought the help of:* Ross, 100.

p. 63   *search parties conducted:* Ross, 54–55, 72–73.

p. 63   *strangers showed up at the Ross home:* Ross, 102.

p. 64   *blamed Charley's disappearance on:* Ibid.

p. 64   *"Now you have broken the spell":* Ross, 105.

p. 64   *as far away as California:* Ross, 81.

p. 64   *one letter sent to police advised:* Ross, 93.

p. 64   *On July 17, Joshua Taggart:* EB, July 17, 1874; *PI*, July 17, 1874.

p. 64   *Police detectives earned:* HSP, Folder, Plan of Police for the History and County of Philadelphia, 1874.

p. 64   *"thief catchers":* Monkonnen, 36.

p. 64   *Through the 1870s,:* Monkonnen, 31, 80.

p. 65   *Editorials complained about*: *PL*, July 23, 1874; *PI*, July 22, 1874.
p. 65   *picking up undertones of gossip*: *EB*, July 17, 1874.
p. 65   *And then he arrested*: *EB*, July 17, 1874.
p. 65   *For the past twenty years, the authorities had*: Ibid; *INA*, July 18, 1874.
p. 65   *he had a black eye and a*: *EB*, September 7, 1874.
p. 65   *According to an act of 1860*: *PI*, July 18, 1874.
p. 66   *"Oh no," responded the solicitor*: Ibid.
p. 66   *Christian Ross didn't think Wooster*: *PI*, July 22, 1874.
p. 66   *"a man of considerable education"*: *EB*, July 17, 1874.
p. 66   *parents demanded that Stokley*: *PI*, July 22, 1874; *EB*, August 10, 1874.
p. 67   *A man in West Philadelphia*: *PI*, July 27, 1874.
p. 67   *ten-year-old Elizabeth Coffin*: Coffin, 20.
p. 67   *"candy and other nice things"*: Ibid.
p. 67   *Germantown's parents*: Ibid; Haines, 2.
p. 67   *"Look after that youngster of yours"*: *PI*, July 20, 1874.
p. 68   *"I would be liable to"*: *INA*, July 20, 1874.
p. 68   *"I don't believe it does"*: Ibid.
p. 68   *City solicitor Charles Collis*: *EB*, July 18, 1874.
p. 68   *"Do you think Taggart"*: Ibid.
p. 68   *Prison guards in South Philadelphia*: *INA*, July 24, 1874.

we wil send prof

p. 71   *"Does not the fact that"*: *PI*, July 21, 1874.
p. 71   *"the same handwriting"*: Ibid.
p. 71   *"shock and incense the community"*: Ibid.
p. 71   *"shameful and unbearable"*: *EB*, July 22, 1874.
p. 71   *"easily committed"*: Ibid.
p. 71   *"the whole detective force of the country"*: *PI*, July 22, 1874.
p. 71   *Twenty-four hours later*: *PI*, July 23, 1874.
p. 72   *"every newspaper in the United States"*: *PL* and *INA*, July 23, 1874.
p. 72   *Clerks in the mayor's office*: *PI*, July 24 and 25, 2874.
p. 73   *He insisted that*: Ross, 112.
p. 73   *much of the public agreed*: *PI*, July 22, 1874.
p. 73   *"You must excuse the looks"*: *INA*, July 24, 1874.
p. 74   *He asked why he was locked up*: *PI*, July 21 and 22, 1874.
p. 74   *"And even if I was,"*: *PI*, July 21, 1874.
p. 74   *"getting gloriously drunk"*: *INA*, July 24, 1874.
p. 74   "had no hard feelings" and "to lead a different life": *PI*, July 24, 1874.

they are goin to search every house in the city

p. 77   *after the arrival of each one*: Ross, 64.
p. 77   *he had been accepting "hush" money*: Walling, 273.
p. 77   *chastened the police for releasing*: *NYH*, July 27, 1874.

p. 77   *Street children of all ages*: Ross, 169; *PI*, July 28 and July 30, 1874; *INA*, July 31, 1874; *NYT*, August 5, 11 and 12, 1874; Fass, 47.

p. 77   *Poor parents and fortune seekers*: *PI*, July 31, 1874; *PI*, August 10, 1874; Ross 102, 152.

p. 77   *Western Union extended a free wire*: Ross, 60.

p. 78   *One mother was stopped so often*: *EB*, August 4, 1874.

p. 78   *In North Philadelphia,*: *PI*, July 20, 1874.

p. 78   *Authorities also mistakenly arrested*: *PI*, July 27, 1874.

p. 78   *A Philadelphia detective traveled*: Ross, 122.

p. 78   *"Fancy Bill"*: *PI*, July 30 and August 3, 1874; July 30, 1874.

p. 78   *Neighbors in Germantown remembered two foreign couples*: *INA*, July 31, 1874; *PI*, July 27, 1874.

p. 78   *they did discover stolen silks and jewelry*: *PI*, July 29 and 30, 1874.

p. 78   *"every Philadelphia property for the child"*: *PI*, July 28, 1874.

p. 78   *An ex-detective echoed*: *PL*, July 24, 1874.

p. 79   *Editorials disagreed, arguing that*: The Evening Standard, August 8, 1874.

p. 79   *Benjamin Franklin, the*: *EB*, July 24, 1874.

p. 79   *his doctor confined him temporarily to his bed*: Ross, 224.

p. 79   *Without contacting Christian Ross or*: *PI*, July 27, 1874.

p. 79   *"compromise a felony"*: Ibid.

if you want to trap

p. 81   *Frederick S. Swartz, a postal agent*: *PI*, July 31, 1874.

p. 81   *"My God, that's Charley Ross!"*: Ibid.

before he intercepts yu

p. 83   *Christian received*: Ross, 122.

p. 83   *"I have the child and the parties"*: *PL*, July 31, 1874.

p. 83   *By 11:45 A.M.*: *INA*, July 31, 1874.

p. 83   *The* Inquirer *later reported*: *PI*, July 31, 1874.

p. 83   *Track repairs delayed the train*: Ibid; *INA*, July 31, 1874.

p. 83   *Hundreds gathered around*: *INA*, July 31, 1874.

p. 83   *"The child is not Charley Ross"*: *PI*, July 31, 1874.

p. 84   *At midnight, an undercover officer*: Ross, 131.

p. 84   *He shivered as the train moved*: Ibid.

p. 84   *"This of course kept up"*: Ross, 133.

p. 84   *He arrived*: Ibid.

we think we have left no clues behind us

p. 89   *a former cow path called Mulberry Street*: Bernard, 475; Riis, "Preface."

p. 89   *the city's most infamous slum*: Ibid.

p. 89   *Locals knew this area as*: Ibid; McCabe, "Preface" and "XXVII./ Life in the Shadows."

p. 89   *old, rotten slabs of meat*: Riis, 50.

p. 89   *sleeping on lager-drenched wood shavings*: Kingsdale, 475.

p. 89   *rented a spot on the floor for a nickel*: Kingsdale, 477.

p. 89   *who yawned and stretched away*: Riis, photos.

p. 89   *children stepped over sewage*: Gilfoyle, 19.

p. 89   *Some walked west to Newspaper Row*: Riis, 216.

p. 89   *others meandered north*: Ibid.

p. 89   *for a spot to polish boots or sell flowers*: McCabe, "LXXXVII. Street Vendors."

p. 89   *If the oldest boys made enough money*: Kingsdale, 477.

p. 89   *Posters of sports stars*: Kingsdale, 475.

p. 90   *men propped tired feet*: Kingsdale, 474.

p. 90   *saloon keeper's oily head and*: Kingsdale, 475.

p. 90   *could look through the wrought-iron windows*: Kingsdale, 474, 485.

p. 90   *Charles Stromberg had owned*: TW, 52.

p. 90   *even a poor man could scrape*: Kingsdale, 474.

p. 90   *had some time to himself between*: Kingsdale, 475.

p. 90   *Stromberg knew one of the man*: TW, 52.

p. 90   *blamed the dismissal on his refusal*: TW, 47.

p. 90   *his wife had sold some of their furniture*: TW, 69.

p. 91   *they peddled an insect repellent*: TW, 34.

p. 91   *he began to record their visits*: TW, 53.

p. 91   *Hartman asked Westervelt one night*: TW, 60.

p. 91   *saloons turned into community centers that*: Kingsdale, 476, 478-479.

p. 91   *the patrons shared Irish heritages and*: Kingsdale, 483; Asbury, 119; Harring, 182.

p. 91   *"wife pacifiers"*: Schlereth, 227.

p. 91   *sang about lost loves or*: Kingsdale, 480.

p. 91   *and left letters*: Schlereth, 227.

p. 91   *whenever a chalk mark appeared*: TW, 60.

p. 91   *Stromberg kept it despite*: TW, 43.

p. 91   *"I can tell you confidentially that I…"*: TW, 52.

p. 92   *"two shillings"*: TW, 60.

p. 92   *paid a few cents for*: Riis, 64.

p. 92   *Kerosene lamps cast small shadows*: Riis, 59; Brace, 93.

p. 92   *smells of unclean bodies and*: Barnard, 6.

p. 92   *lay with at least a dozen sleeping*: Barnard, 6; Riis, vi; McCabe, "XXVII: The Five Points. 2. The Cellars."

we know not what to make of that

p. 93   *"Chief of Police of Philadelphia:"*: Walling, 200.

p. 93   *in 1847 at age twenty-four*: Walling, 33.

we have heard nothing from yu

p. 100   *"In the good old times"*: PI, August 28, 1874.

p. 100   *pushed northern Republicans*: Beckert, 225.

p. 101   *they facilitated the arrival of*: Beckert, 146; Harris, 14, 17; Harring, 51.

p. 101   *they emphasized Christian education*: Tholfson, 99, 108–109; Foner, 482; Miller, 219; Hilkey, 10; PL, August 15, 1874.

p. 101   *Officers in Denver, Colorado,*: PL, September 21, 1874.

p. 101   *A police chief in St. Paul, Minnesota*: EB, September 4, 1874.

p. 101   *"bright, intelligent face"*: Ibid.

p. 101   *"rough-looking" man*: Ibid.

p. 101   *Officers in North Philadelphia*: PI, August 11, 1874.

p. 101   *"Charley Loss"*: Ibid.

p. 101   *A man named Murkins in Odell, Illinois*: NYT, August 20, 1874.

p. 102   *the New York–based Children's Aid Society*: EB, August 11, 1874.

p. 102   *it did not keep consistent, acceptable records*: NYT: May 25, 1883.

p. 102   *In New York City, eight-year-old*: EB, August 4, 1874.

p. 102   *"Wait! Wait!"*: Ibid.

p. 102   *Reporters in Albany, New York*: PI, August 4, 1874.

p. 102   *Seven-year-old Joe Harlen*: EB, August 11, 1874.

p. 102   *In Newport, Rhode Island*: EB, August 25, 1874.

p. 103   *"No,"*: Ibid.

p. 103   *"But there has been much that would"*: EB, August 11, 1874.

p. 103   *"A search like this can of course"*: PL, August 10, 1874.

p. 104   *"The stealing of little Charley Ross"*: Ibid.

p. 104   *prior to this article, they hadn't known*: Ibid.

p. 104   *In early August, Chief Jones*: EB, August 7, 1874; Ross, 47.

p. 104   *"Citizens should be careful as"*: Ibid.

p. 104   *"Nobody, except a policeman"*: INA, August 8, 1874.

p. 104   *neighbors more thoroughly explored old coal mines*: PL, August 13, 1874; EB, August 7 and 9, 1874.

p. 104   *did uncover contraband and numerous thieves*: EB, August 7, 1874.

ask him no questions

p. 105   *Christian Ross disagreed with police*: Ross, 112.

p. 105   *Christian did join investigators*: PI, August 10, 14 and 25, 1874; Ross, 152, 202.

p. 105   *by formulating a list of questions*: Ross, 161; PL, July 31, 1874.

p. 105   *Crowds of hopeful helpers greeted*: Ross, 162.

p. 105   *MR. C. K. ROSS—Dear Sir*: Ross, 148.

p. 106   *until the middle of the nineteenth century*: Henkin, 44.

p. 106   *People avoided high postage costs*: Henkin, 43.

p. 106   *"transient newspaper"*: Henkin, 47.

p. 106   *in 1845, the postal service lowered*: Henkin, 46.

p. 106   *the postal service changed dramatically*: Henkin, 88.

p. 106   *In 1864, sixty-six American cities*: Henkin, 90.

if death it must be

p. 109   *On Saturday, August 10*: Ross, 178.

p. 109   *Walling greeted Christian*: Ibid.

p. 109   *That night, tragedy struck*: *EB*, August 10, 1874.

p. 110   *he tightened the flow of information*: Ross 179.

p. 110   *"No, sir, never,"*: Ross, 178.

p. 110   *"I did not think he was one of"*: Ross, 178.

p. 110   *Walling also identified the man*: Ibid.

now we demand yu anser

p. 111   *Mosher had grown up on a*: *PI*, December 16, 1874.

p. 111   *His father had been a somewhat*: Zierold, 140.

p. 111   *older brother Gil taught him*: Ibid.

p. 111   *a cask fell on Mosher's left hand*: *EB*, December 15, 1874.

p. 111   *the brothers weren't speaking*: Zierold, 146.

p. 111   *Their parents had died, as had*: Ibid.

p. 111   *Gil's crime of choice had*: Zierold, 141.

p. 111   *They had disowned him years*: Zierold, 146.

p. 111   *Bill Mosher joined a successful gang*: Walling, 141; *PI*, December 16 and 17, 1874.

p. 111   *Between 1850 and 1852,*: Walling, 143.

p. 112   *In 1853, a ship watchman*: *PI*, December 16, 1874.

p. 112   *Unfortunately, someone had beaten the*: *PI*, December 16, 1874.

p. 112   *took on woodworking jobs*: *PI*, December 21, 1874.

p. 112   *failed business ventures*: *NYH*, December 20, 1874.

p. 112   *Once, he secured a financier*: *PI*, December 21, 1874.

p. 112   *Six months later, the business*: Ibid.

p. 112   *opened a saloon, where he lived*: Zierold, 146.

p. 112   *the little boy died*: *PI*, December 24, 1874.

p. 112   *they buried his bones in the wall*: Everly, 387.

p. 112   *Mosher also worked for "fencers"*: Asbury, 214–215.

p. 112   *recruited a young teenage thief*: *PI*, December 16, 1874.

p. 112   *Mosher introduced Douglas to a*: Ibid.

p. 112   *a part-time piracy practice along*: Ibid.

p. 112   *built a shack on Berrian's Island*: Ibid.

p. 112   *hid their bounty until*: Ibid.

p. 112   *they set out on a trip by boat*: Ibid.

p. 113   *after filling their boat with fancy clothes*: Ibid.

p. 113   *The thieves were tied by their necks*: Zierold, 147.

p. 113   *Cutting through a wall, Mosher*: Ibid.

p. 113   *Douglas moved to Brooklyn*: *EB*, December 15, 1874.

p. 113   *The police next heard about the two men*: Ibid.

p. 113   *Gil's wife, Liz, began visiting*: TW, 43, 46.

p. 113   *Westervelt wrote to Bill Mosher* : TW, 103.

p. 113   *Bill Mosher and his accomplice*: TW, 30.

p. 114   *"What does he want?"*: TW, 88.

p. 114   *Three blocks away from the store*: Ibid.

p. 114   *"Is Gil Mosher here?"*: Ibid.

p. 114   *Westervelt and Douglas walked to the corner*: Ibid.

p. 114   *Her sons Ed and Ike*: TW, 78.

p. 114   *Mosher stood up and then rushed*: TW, 88.

p. 114   *Fifteen minutes later*: TW, 88.

p. 114   *"Tell Gil I did not see"*: TW, 28.

p. 115   *She asked again for Bill Mosher*: TW, 89.

p. 115   *Westervelt read the letter out loud* : Ibid.

p. 115   *far enough away that the bartender*: TW, 52.

p. 115   *By now, Stromberg had noticed*: Zierold, 201.

p. 115   *"If she is fine, and nobody is looking"* and following quotes: TW, 89.

p. 115   *changed his shirt*: TW, 81.

p. 115   *Her landlord didn't appear*: TW, 67.

p. 115   *a neighbor named Mrs. Mary O'Leary*: Ibid.

p. 115   *He, his wife, and their two children*: Ibid.

p. 116   *She saw her boys playing around the house*: Ibid.

p. 116   *noticed that the boy Charley*: Ibid.

p. 116   *Before taking the train back to New York*: TW, 57.

p. 116   *Westervelt asked him if*: Ibid.

p. 116   *"Yes," McDowell said,* and following conversation: Ibid.

p. 116   *Westervelt chose not to post*: TW, 89.

p. 116   *Westervelt met a former police colleague*: Ibid.

p. 117   *The Thirteenth Precinct*: Ibid.

p. 117   *Captain Hedden met him and took*: Ibid.

p. 117   *Most of the office spaces at headquarters*: Walling, 181.

p. 117   *Two floors above them*: TW, 89.

p. 117   *Both demanded that Westervelt undergo*: Ibid.

p. 117   *he later took Westervelt to*: Ibid.

p. 117   *stood watch at the superintendent's front*: Ibid.

p. 118   *He asked if Westervelt knew that his*: TW, 42.

p. 118   *"Bill Mosher wouldn't have taken a child"*: Ibid.

p. 118   *Walling repeated that*: TW, 90.

p. 118   *Westervelt contacted Walling with a*: Zierold, 167.

p. 118   *Walling immediately contacted*: Ibid.

p. 118   *Moran had grown up in Douglas's neighborhood*: Zierold, 167.

p. 118   *"felonious assault"*: Ibid.

p. 119   *By the time he got the message and arrived*: Ibid.

ask Walter if

p. 123   *Walling interpreted the kidnappers' repetitive*: Walling, 203.

p. 123   *"I am more confident than ever"*: Ibid.

p. 123   *He agreed with all of the kidnappers' answers*: NYH, August 26, 1874.

p. 123   *They asked why the authorities*: PI, July 17, 1874.

p. 124   *They also wondered why Mayor Stokley*: Ibid.

p. 124   *"We refer to the absurd and reprehensible"*: EB, August 11, 1874.

p. 124   *"County district attorneys cannot"*: PI, August 28, 1874.

p. 124   *A private group of citizens*: INA, July 18, 1874.

p. 124   *"The above reward will be paid"*: EB, August 31, 1874.

p. 125   *"the wisest and most eminent of our citizens"*: PI, September 17, 1874.

p. 125   *They also sent a private memo to the nation's*: HSP, Folder, Charles B. Ross, Pinkerton flyer.

p. 125   *"With whom is he?"*, etc.: Ross, 420.

p. 128   *Christian had refused to release a photograph*: INA, August 18, 1874.

p. 128   *"Those who desire to aid in these renewed"*: PI, September 17, 1874.

p. 128   *ED. PHILADA. INQUIRER:* PI, September 12, 1874.

p. 128   *The* Public Ledger *warned readers against*: August 13, 1874.

p. 127   *"I, Kennard H. Jones,"*: INA, August 8, 1874.

p. 127   *"The time has fully come for the mayor"*: EB, August 11, 1874.

p. 127   *the* Evening Bulletin *suggested the mayor*: August 5, 1874.

p. 128   *"running after any and every shadow that"*: EB, August 12, 1874.

p. 128   *"Do you want to talk?"* and following conversation: Ibid.

p. 129   *"I advertised more than one month ago"*: EB, August 31, 1874.

this thing is drawing to a final crises

p. 133   *Philadelphia entered the fifth week of*: EB, September 10 and 12, 1874.

p. 133   *"The change from week to week at"*: EB, August 12, 1874.

p. 133   *"Every portion of the work is pushed"*: Ibid.

p. 133   *Crowds gathered behind a large fence*: Ibid.

p. 133   *It would also be the first world's fair to dedicate*: Rydell, 21.

p. 133   *people watched engineers and masons*: EB, August 12, 1874.

p. 134   *The artisans worked rapidly to build railroads*: Ibid.

p. 134   *approved by Congress to cover 50 percent of*: Brown, 23; Whiteman, 118.

p. 134   *The Centennial Commission had planned*: PL, September 24, 1874.

p. 134   *City Council agreed to advance a loan*: Brown, 21.

p. 134   *Philadelphia had already needed to assume*: Ibid.

p. 134   *A three-month-old baby disappeared from*: PI, September 11, 1874.

p. 135   *Police could also not find a three-year-old boy*: EB, September 10, 1874.

p. 135   *Near Washington, D.C., neighbors observed*: EB, September 8, 1874.

p. 135   *"And if the fact that the boy has brothers"*: Ibid.

p. 135   *Townspeople in Orange County, New York*: EB, September 7, 1874.

p. 135   *"Where did you go from when you went away?"*: Ibid.

p. 135   *"Success in this inquiry may atone somewhat for"*: PI, September 14, 1874.

p. 136   *Police also located Charlotte Wyeth*: EB, September 18, 1874.

p. 136   *"Godspeed"*: Ibid.

p. 136   *"The chief mystery in regard to the difficulty"*: *EB*, September 9, 1874.

p. 136   *"If the New York detectives are so superior"*: *EB*, August 5, 1874.

p. 136   *the NYPD released no statement*: This comment is based on my study of Philadelphia and New York papers from July of 1874 through September 1875.

p. 136   · *Walling bribed Westervelt's cooperation*: Walling, 204.

p. 136   *He also began regularly inviting*: Walling, 203.

p. 137   *Walling's men followed Westervelt to*: TW, 96.

p. 137   *within forty-eight hours of an authorization from*: Ross, 221.

p. 137   *"In view of the threats contained in the letters"*: Ross, 220.

p. 137   *"We will have them both,"*: Ibid.

p. 137   *He wrote Heins on September 11, finally*: Ross, 193.

p. 137   *DEAR SIR. – Since writing you this A.M.,*: Ross, 193.

p. 138   *Heins pursued the lead on the stable*: Ross, 194.

others will rely on our word

p. 141   *the newspapers indirectly attacked*: *PI*, September 27, 1874; *EB*, August 7 and 28, 1874; *PL*, August 10, 1874.

p. 141   *the 620,000 deceased*: Faust, xi.

p. 141   *one of his wife's brothers showed Sarah a*: Ross, 64.

p. 142   *he sought the advice of a German psychic*: Ross, 206.

p. 142   *The eighteenth-century Swedish mystic*: Cox, 12.

p. 142   *Spiritualists were fascinated with electricity*: Sargent, iv.

p. 142   *To thousands of Americans,*: Faust, 82.

p. 142   *"planchettes"*: Faust, 182.

p. 142   *led to the popularity of daguerrotypes*: Cox, 112.

p. 142   *"Get out of this, go into the next room, I'll soon"* and details from the following scene: Ross, 208.

p. 143   *one of which offered a German witchcraft recipe*: Ross, 209.

p. 143   *Christian had tried to shield five-year-old Walter*: Ross, 172.

p. 143   *The* New York Herald *suggested Walter had been*: reported in *INA*, August 8, 1874.

p. 143   *The paper wondered whether Christian kept the ransom*: Ross, 171.

p. 143   *the net worth of Catherine Ross, Christian's mother*: *Biographical Encyclopedia of Dauphin County, PA*, 1870 Census of Middletown, PA.

p. 143   *"The parties who actually made away with the infant"*: as reported in p. *EB*, August 7, 1874.

p. 144   *"We have not heard of anything being accomplished"*: *EB*, August 5, 1874.

p. 144   *Libel laws did govern newspapers*: *EB*, October 14, 1874; *PI*, October 15, 1874.

p. 144   *In 1874, new legislature redefined libel law*: *EB*, October 14, 1874.

p. 144   *"matter proper for public information, provided that"*: *PI*, October 15, 1874.

p. 144   *a man identifying himself as "G"*: PI, September 23, 1874.

p. 145   *"The following is the theory of those who knew"*: EB, September 23, 1874.

p. 145   *"of a character to injure me in my said business"*: Ibid.

p. 145   *James V. Lambert, Christian's colleague*: PI, September 25, 1874.

p. 145   *"Were [the kidnapping] a humbug"*: Ibid.

p. 145   *He encouraged Christian to bring libel charges*: Ibid.

p. 145   *The writer "G" was really named Milford N. Ritter*: Ibid.

p. 146   *"the common talk of Mr. Ross' neighbors"*: PI, September 25, 1874.

p. 146   *"in a store on Columbia Avenue, where women"*: PI, October 14, 1874.

p. 146   *All parties involved testified at the fall*: Ibid.

p. 146   *"He is in a very prostrate condition"*: EB, September 29, 1874.

p. 146   *"I said I hardly knew what to say about it"*: PI, September 30, 1874.

p. 146   *Milford N. Ritter admitted to authoring the*: PI, October 15, 1874.

p. 146   *The publishers of the* Reading Eagle *said they*: EB, October 14, 1874.

p. 147   *"malicious intent"*: EB, October 14, 1874.

p. 147   *"Can an article containing the foulest aspersion"*: Ibid.

p. 147   *After deliberating for only a few minutes*: PI, October 15, 1874.

p. 147   *the publishers paid a $1,000 fine*: PI, December 7, 1874.

p. 147   *The doctor told Sarah to keep him confined*: EB, September 29, 1874.

p. 147   *he retreated to his mother's house*: Ross, 267.

p. 147   *Christian would remain bedridden in central Pennsylvania*: Ross, 223.

p. 147   *She asked her brothers to pay the full*: Ross, 241.

keep faith with us

p. 149   *Heins's working relationship with the superintendent*: PI, December 10, 1874.

p. 149   *local merchants appeared uninterested*: PL, September 10, 1874.

p. 149   *"profound and prevailing apathy has discouraged"*: as reported in EB, November 17, 1874.

p. 149   *The western states had pledged quick support*: EB, November 17, 1874.

p. 150   *"What is most desirable now is that Massachusetts"*: Ibid.

p. 150   *"It is time now that the doubt will be settled"*: Ibid.

p. 150   *the Centennial Commission targeted local business*: EB, October 14, 1874.

p. 150   *Fifty years after two mechanics proposed the idea*: EB, October 23, 1874.

p. 150   *twenty-six showcases*: Ibid.

p. 150   *lasting six weeks from mid-October through mid-November*: EB, October 17, 1874.

p. 150   *The exhibition earned the Franklin Institute*: EB, October 6 and 17, 1874.

p. 150   *The press praised the police for maintaining*: EB, October 14, 1874.

p. 151   *"The condition of the streets will be marked"*: PL, November 19, 1874.

p. 151   *The city planners authorized funds for*: PL, November 12, 1874; PI, November 18, 1874.

p. 151   *solicited bids for repairing roads*: PI, November 18, 1874.
p. 151   *Police spread circulars with "No Refuse Allowed"*:
p. 151   *A group of men in one corner bar beat*: EB, September 18, 1874.
p. 151   *Street thugs fought one another with blackjacks*: EB, October 26, 1874.
p. 151   *They beat a seventy-five-year-old man to death*: EB, November 17, 1874.
p. 151   *"feminine-looking" man*: EB, October 12, 1874.
p. 151   *attacked women*: EB, October 14, 1874; PI, November 18, 1874.
p. 151   *shot one man in the eye*: PI, November 4, 1874.
p. 151   *another in the throat*: EB, October 12, 1874.
p. 151   *assaulted officers for arresting their friends for rape*: EB, October 14, 1874.
p. 151   *Police locked up twelve-year-olds*: EB, October 14, 1874.
p. 151   *a fireman who threw a cat*: EB, October 6, 1874.
p. 151   *an angry drunk who stabbed a fellow drinker*: Ibid.
p. 151   *the proprietress of three brothels,*: EB, November 3, 1874.
p. 151   *the story of Mary Elizabeth Carton*: PL, September 17, 1874; EB, October 20, 1874; PI, October 21, 1874.
p. 152   *The district attorney angered the public*: EB, October 20, 1874.
p. 152   *"It is true that the use of a deadly weapon"*: EB, October 21, 1874.
p. 152   *"If so, it will be quite an inducement to murderers"*: Ibid.
p. 152   *The judge supported the district attorney's decision*: PI, November 21, 1874.
p. 152   *the jury found Francis Carton guilty and*: Ibid.
p. 152   *"Foreigners will judge the nation by what they see"*: EB, November 24, 1874.
p. 152   *foreign ministers across the globe received invitations*: PI, October 10, 1874; EB, September 12, 1874.
p. 152   *A fund-raising delegation traveled to Massachusetts*: EB, November 17, 1874.

your substitute

p. 153   *Mary Westervelt, William's wife, was growing*: TW, 74.
p. 153   *the NYPD force of 2,500 men*: TW, 44.
p. 153   *Westervelt advised Walling to keep*: Ross, 231.
p. 153   *He directed him to investigate the Astoria ferry*: Ross, 222.
p. 153   *He told him about a boating trip*: Ross, 231.
p. 153   *He described the kidnappers' clothes*: Zierold, 167.
p. 154   *Westervelt also accompanied his sister Martha Mosher*: TW, 96.
p. 154   *She often visited Madame Morrow*: Ibid.
p. 154   *Sometimes Westervelt and/or Joseph Douglas*: TW, 30.
p. 154   *Westervelt continued to frequent*: TW, 33.
p. 154   *One day in late October*: Ibid.
p. 154   *"What does Westervelt want with him?"*: Ibid.
p. 154   *The question startled Douglas*: Ibid.

p. 154   *He threatened to cease contact with Walling*: TW, 46, 96.

p. 154   *He reminded Walling that he was betraying*: TW, 96.

p. 154   *he didn't think the police commissioners would:* TW, 50.

p. 155   *Dear Sir. — I saw my informant last night:* Ross, 229.

p. 155   *while suspecting Westervelt's intentions*: This inference is based upon the content of telegraphs that Walling sent to Heins throughout the Fall of 1875. See Ross, 229–230.

p. 155   *Heins learned that the kidnappers*: TW, 52.

p. 155   *He knew they were steering a green skiff*: Ibid.

p. 155   *Using a small boat, thieves would sneak*: Walling, 141.

p. 155   *If they couldn't reach their "fencing" destinations*: Walling, 143.

p. 155   *Walling rented a steam-tug*: TW, 50.

p. 155   *"sea-faring man" who "knew all about coasting"*: PI, December 15, 1874.

p. 155   *The foursome traveled up the Hudson River to*: Ibid.

p. 156   *"searched thirty or forty islands in the Sound"*: Ibid.

p. 156   *Gil Mosher had uncovered many potential*: Ibid.

p. 156   *"Yours of yesterday received."*: Ross, 230.

p. 157   *He told them that he believed the New York Police*: Ross, 242.

p. 157   *the Ross camp decided to make the exchange as*: Ibid.

a parcel of fabricated lies

p. 159   *William Stokley anticipated a win*: EB, October 31, 1874.

p. 159   *that the Republican advisers kept Stokley*: Ibid.

p. 159   *The Republican party was changing*: Grimsted, 185; Foner, 499–500; Beckert, 225.

p. 159   *The Democrats, while still unfriendly*: Foner, 311.

p. 159   *Enough national offices were at stake*: PL, October 9, 1874.

p. 160   *Pennsylvania Republicans pushed*: EB, October 14, 1874; PI, October 26 and 28, 1874.

p. 160   *"a movement against American industry"*: EB, October 21, 1874.

p. 160   *"the doctrine of protection"*: EB, November 2, 1874.

p. 160   *"If the wall is broken down so that British"*: EB, October 21, 1874.

p. 160   *Philadelphia Police expected*: History of Philadelphia, 837; EB, November 4, 1874.

p. 160   *Chief Jones prepared two omnibuses*: EB, November 4, 1874.

p. 160   *the election reform of 1874 had led to more*: PL, October 6, 1874.

p. 160   *By 7:00 P.M., bonfires flickered*: PL, November 4, 1874; EB, November 4, 1874.

p. 160   *Hundreds gathered in the news district*: EB, November 4, 1874.

p. 160   *Telegraph lines communicated results*: Ibid.

p. 160   *when people walked home around 11:00 P.M.*: PL, November 4, 1874.

p. 160   *The district attorney had lost*: EB, November 6, 1874.

p. 161   *Nationally, Democrats had gained*: PI, November 5, 1874.

p. 161   *"General Grant ... has surrendered"*: *NYH*, November 4, 1874.

p. 161   *"The Democrats, as a national party"*: *NY Evening Post*, November 4, 1874.

we ask for time

p. 163   *Letters still arrived daily*: Ross, 112.

p. 163   *Sarah's neighbors did notice one*: *EB*, November 21, 1874; *PI*, November 23, 1874.

p. 164   *November 12, 1874*: Ross, 230.

p. 164   *He summoned Westervelt*: TW, 95.

p. 164   *If Mosher and Douglas show up*: TW, 94.

p. 164   *DEAR SIR.—Please see*: Ross, 242.

p. 165   *Henry Lewis and his son Frank*: Ibid.

p. 165   *The night of the eighteenth, they*: Ibid.

p. 165   *Walling sent an officer to arrest Westervelt*: TW, 95.

p. 165   *He confronted him in a private room at police*: Ibid.

p. 165   *Walling accused Westervelt of double-crossing him*: Ibid.

dead men tell no tales

p. 169   *Walling had repeated instructions*: TW, 49.

p. 169   *he had separated himself from*: *NYH*, December 20, 1874.

p. 169   *he had learned that a man*: *PI*, December 18, 1874.

p. 169   *"Nosey."*: Ibid.

p. 170   *the men spent days driving around*: *PL*, December 15, 1874.

p. 170   *One June day, they visited*: Ibid.

p. 170   *Douglas arrived at the cemetery*: TW, 34.

p. 170   *Another cold winter had hit New York*: Several articles in the Philadelphia papers during the winter of 1875 mention the frigid temperatures.

p. 170   *Westervelt had warned him away*: TW, 95.

p. 171   *At 9:00 P.M., he saw a figure*: TW, 34.

p. 171   *The men stopped at a saloon*: Ibid.

p. 171   *Young girls—many of whom were*: McCabe, "LXXXVII. Street Vendors."

p. 171   *"Come down as far as the ferry"*: TW, 97.

p. 171   *When Douglas reached the corner*: TW, 97.

p. 171   *They would use a black cat-rigged*: *NYH*, December 18, 1874.

p. 172   *paid the authorities $150 for it*: *PI*, December 19, 1874.

p. 172   *he tracked the boat down and stole*: *PI*, December 18, 1874.

p. 172   *"Wilmot"*: *NYH*, December 19, 1875.

p. 172   *Two months after the Ross abduction*: *NYH*, December 18, 1875.

p. 172   *most river pirates would have carved*: Chambers, 638.

p. 172   *he spread newspapers*: Zierold, 37.

p. 172   *Douglas joined him by*: TW, 97.

p. 172   *Strong winds blew through the trees*: *NYT,* December 15, 1874.
p. 172   *The men easily hid the black boat*: Ibid.
p. 172   *went to Winant's*: Ibid.
p. 172   *Each man possessed a gun and*: Zierold, 237.
p. 172   *They stopped at a widow's home*: *PI*, December 16, 1874.
p. 172   *in one of the windows upstairs*: *NYT,* December 15, 1874.
p. 172   *As Douglas searched for something*: *NYH*, December 17, 1874.
p. 172   *"There they come!"*: *PI*, December 17, 1874.
p. 173   *"I give up"*: Ibid.
p. 173   *"Look out for that man,"*: Ibid.
p. 173   *"Whiskey for him!"*: *PI*, December 16, 1874.
p. 173   *"It serves you right"*: Ibid.
p. 173   *Douglas looked up*: Ibid.
p. 173   *The girl smirked*: Ibid.
p. 173   *He told them he was single*: Ibid.
p. 173   *A sailor named Herkey*: *EB*, December 15, 1874.
p. 173   *"It's no use lying now"*: Ibid.
p. 173   *Herkey stared*: Ibid.
p. 173   *"Mosher knows all about the child"*: Ross, 248.
p. 174   *Men lifted his shoulders*: Ibid.
p. 174   *"God help his poor wife and family!"*: Ross, 249.
p. 174   *"Inspector Walling knows"*: *EB*, December 15, 1874.
p. 174   *Men dragged his and Mosher's bodies*: *PI*, December 15, 1874.
p. 174   *"Joe"*: *EB*, December 15, 1874.
p. 174   *"Take the glove off that left hand"*: Ibid.

tell C.K.R. quietly

p. 175   *Christmas displays on either side*: *PL*, December 21, 1874.
p. 175   *Farmers from New Jersey*: Ibid.
p. 175   *the silver sheens on their pastel*: *EB*, December 12, 1874.
p. 175   *The previous Thursday, a buggy*: *PI*, December 14, 1874.
p. 175   *Heins also waited on news from*: Ross, 271.
p. 175   *Heins did not brief Philadelphia's*: *PI*, December 19, 1874.
p. 176   *"Mosher and Clark were both killed"*: *PL*, December 15, 1874.
p. 176   *Heins immediately contacted*: Ross, 250.
p. 176   *"Tell C.K.R. quietly"*: Ross, 267.
p. 176   *Within two hours of receiving*: Ross, 250.
p. 176   *Once again, crowds gathered*: *PL*, December 15, 1874.
p. 176   *"For a long time"* and the following quotes: *PI*, December 15, 1874.
p. 177   *Two of Walter's uncles*: *EB*, December 16, 1874.
p. 178   *Walling himself met with Walter*: *EB*, Ibid.
p. 178   *Detective Dusenbury escorted*: Ibid.
p. 178   *"That's the man"*: Ibid.
p. 178   *"I remember him by his nose"*: Ibid.

p. 178   *Callahan also recognized Mosher*: Ibid.
p. 178   *"I am certain that he"*: Ibid.
p. 178   *The coroner walked Walter*: Ibid.
p. 178   *"Oh, that's awful like him"*: Ross, 251.
p. 178   *"He sometimes had candy too"*: Ross, 252.
p. 178   *At 2:30 P.M., a police officer*: NYH, December 16, 1874.
p. 178   *One woman wore a green dress*: Ibid.
p. 179   *Liz refused to climb down the ladder* and details from this scene: Ibid.
p. 179   *A half hour later, a woman in her*: Ibid.
p. 179   *He said no.*: Ibid.
p. 179   *"Yes, Father, there were"*: Ibid.
p. 179   *"That's the oldest one."*: Ibid.
p. 179   *"I am a sister-in-law of William Mosher"* and following quotes: Ibid.

the resemblance is most striking

p. 181   *Christian's brother James arrived*: PI, December 14, 1874.
p. 181   *a heavyset man with a lame leg named*: Ibid.
p. 182   *Sarah Ross and her brothers told*: Ibid.
p. 182   *"I do not think it is Charley"*: PI, December 17, 1874.
p. 182   *"Thomas Scott"* and *"Henry Ship"*: PI, December 14, 1874.
p. 182   *townspeople demanded that the police*: Ross, 270.
p. 182   *Citizens began writing letters*: Ross, 269–272.
p. 183   *In St. Louis, Henry Lachmueller Sr.*: Ross, 272.
p. 183   *At his mother's home in Pennsylvania*: PI, December 17, 1874.
p. 183   *"It is not him."*: PI, December 17, 1874.

Detective Silleck knew that

p. 185   *"I knew of these two men only as"*: PI, December 16, 1874.
p. 185   *"To Captain Walling belongs the"*: EB, December 15, 1874.
p. 186   *stood like a general in his uniform*: Zierold, 139.
p. 186   *"Soon after I received"*: EB, December 15, 1874.
p. 186   *"We arranged our plans very"*: Ibid.
p. 187   *"One satisfactory result comes from this"*: Ibid.
p. 187   *"That they did not find them at all"*: Ibid.
p. 187   *"Mr. Walling,"*: Ibid.

to vindicate themselves

p. 189   *On December 15, Mayor Stokley*: PI, December 16, 1874.
p. 189   *That night, New York's Detective Doyle* and the following scene details: EB, December 17, 1874.
p. 190   *"Neither the police authorities"*: PI, December 16, 1874.
p. 190   *"The New York police, for the sake"*: PI, December 19, 1874.

p. 191   *thieves had gravitated to their*: Walling, 141–144.

p. 191   *The force allotted such a small number*: "The Bride of A Pirate," 134.

p. 191   *Walling learned about a Mrs. Russell* and the following scene details: *EB*, December 19, 1874.

p. 192   *"I do not think the boy is concealed"*: *EB*, December 16, 1874.

p. 192   *Another reporter asked whether Mosher's*: Ibid.

p. 192   *"My idea is that the boy may be picked up"*: Ibid.

p. 193   *"Nothing here; coming back."*: *EB*, December 19, 1874.

p. 193   *"Did she say anything to you about Mosher* and the following quotes: Ibid.

we'll defend ourselves

p. 195   *Such a large crowd arrived at*: *PL*, December 17, 1874.

p. 195   *Due to an illness, Mr. Holmes Van Brunt*: *PI*, December 17, 1874.

p. 195   *"And scarcely have we time to wonder"*: Ibid.

p. 195   *Albert Van Brunt testified*: *PI*, December 17, 1874.

p. 195   *"Albert, go over and see what has sounded"*: *EB*, December 15, 1874.

p. 196   *Albert said he left*: *PL*, December 17, 1874.

p. 196   *"Whichever way they come"*: Ross, 246.

p. 196   *two bullets had pierced Mosher's back and*: *NYH*, December 16, 1874.

p. 196   *"We, the jury, find that the killing of the"*: *PI*, December 19, 1874.

p. 196   *New York's* Evening Telegram: reported in *PI*, December 22, 1874.

p. 197   *"I am his wife"* and following quotes: *PI*, December 18, 1874.

p. 197   *The coroner approved both requests*: Ibid.

p. 197   *A man named Munn, an undertaker*: *PI*, December 19, 1874.

p. 197   *Munn told McGuire that*: Ibid.

p. 197   *"that boy Charley will be found before"* and following quotes: *PI*, December 19, 1874.

p. 197   *he placed them in imitation rosewood coffins*: *NYH*, December 19, 1874.

p. 198   *"good-looking and genteel in appearance"*: *NYH*, December 20, 1874.

p. 198   *"No girl could get a kinder husband"*: Ibid.

p. 198   *Bill had supported her by*: Ibid.

p. 198   *"I have seen few men"*: Ibid.

p. 198   *A reporter asked if Martha remembered*: Ibid.

p. 198   *"I first heard of the Ross case"*: Ibid.

p. 199   *"If Martha Mosher don't know where"* and following quotes: *NYH*, December 22, 1874.

p. 199   *"What! Know what the police were doing?"*: Ibid.

p. 199   *"Now, there's that coroner,"*: Ibid.

serve the public

p. 203   *The* New York Herald *was the first newspaper*: December 14, 1874.

p. 203   *"While [the Herald's] investigations of"*: Ibid.

p. 203　*On December 20, Sarah's brothers*: Ross, 261.

p. 203　*he could prove the kidnappers sold*: *EB*, December 15, 1874.

p. 203　*friends and members of the Mosher family placed the men*: *PI*, December 22, 1874; *NYH*, December 21, 1874; *PI*, December 18, 1874.

p. 203　*a Philadelphia bartender*: *PI*, December 22, 1874.

p. 203　*he had allowed Mosher to pay*: Ibid.

p. 204　*Detective Heins agreed to meet a spiritualist*: *PI*, December 30, 1874.

p. 204　*receiving any New Yorker who had a*: *EB*, December 17, 1874.

p. 204　*"drop-in"*: *NY Tribune*, December 17, 1874.

p. 204　*"gentlemen"*: Ibid.

p. 204　*the superintendent praised the idea but said*: *EB*, December 17, 1874.

p. 204　*"It is stated that the contributors"*: *EB*, December 19, 1874.

p. 204　*FIVE THOUSAND DOLLARS will*: *PI*, December 23, 1874.

p. 204　*The brothers instructed interested parties*: Ibid.

beyond the range of possibility

p. 209　*Testimony of Sarah Kerr*: *PI*, September 7, 1875.

p. 209　*On January 1, 1875, the city*: *PI*, January 1, 1875.

p. 209　*"a particularly auspicious beginning"*: Ibid.

p. 209　*writers praised Stokley's efforts*: Ibid.

p. 210　*two thousand members of Philadelphia's*: *EB*, November 11, 1874.

p. 210　*Mr. Stokley—SIR: The workingmen*: *EB*, December 17, 1874.

p. 211　*A man from Kingston, New York*: *PI*, February 22, 1875.

p. 211　*I write to you this in regard*: Ibid.

p. 211　*"Letter received"*: Ibid.

p. 211　*"A woman is here, going to"*: Ibid.

p. 211　*"See a justice of the peace and"*: Ibid.

p. 211　*"Send detectives at once"*: Ibid.

p. 211　*Captain Heins sent a telegram*: Ibid.

p. 212　*Walling acted quickly*: Ibid.

p. 212　*"Captain H. C. Heins, Philadelphia"*: Ibid.

p. 212　*The state senate would soon approve*: *EB*, January 15, 1875.

p. 212　*The new law, which would*: Ibid.

p. 212　*He reissued circulars*: *EB*, January 28, 1875.

p. 212　*After leaving Palmer and Richmond*: Ibid.

p. 213　*his office released another $5,000*: Ibid.

this is very uncertain

p. 215　*writers alluded to Charley's whereabouts*: Ross, 289–290, 305.

p. 215　*Daniel O'Connor, chief of*: *PI*, January 22, 1875.

p. 216　*Lgn Sxg ra abme*: Ibid.

p. 216　*The detective handed the letter*: Ibid.

p. 216　*The boy is still at Pine Bluff*: Ross, 288.

p. 217   *"By comparing the writing in the letters"*: PI, January 22, 1875.

p. 217   *Detectives began wondering aloud*: EB, January 30, 1874.

p. 217   *The* Inquirer *interpreted a quiet public*: April 24, 1874.

p. 217   *"Up to this hour all"*: PI, January 20, 1875.

p. 218   *A New Jersey man came forward*: EB, February 23, 1875.

p. 218   *Sarah Ross identified the hat*: Ibid.

what have you got now?

p. 221   *Walling published more flyers*: EB, January 12, 1875.

p. 221   *a stable keeper in Newark*: PI, January 11, 1875.

p. 221   *Van Fleet said that in October*: EB, January 12, 1875.

p. 221   *"take good care of the animal"*: Ibid.

p. 221   *Detective Titus went to New Jersey*: Ibid.

p. 221   *"best resource"*: Ibid.

p. 221   *"I shall know the horse, sure,"*: Ibid.

p. 221   *Because it had seemed too imaginative*: Ibid.

p. 221   *a stable hand led the horse out*: PI, January 13, 1875.

p. 221   *"Look, Papa, look!"*: EB, January 12, 1875.

p. 223   *he would grant him immunity from any*: Ibid.

p. 223   *when a known burglar accused Walling*: NYH, February 14, 1875.

p. 223   *"violent language"*: Ibid.

p. 223   *Walling disputed both charges*: Ibid.

p. 223   *If it did not, then he faced*: Ibid.

p. 223   *the two men had met more than fifty times*: NYH, January 22, 1881.

p. 224   *"renowned excitement in police circles"*: NYH, December 21, 1874.

p. 224   *McKean went to New York*: TW, 58.

p. 224   *McKean took Westervelt to the Fifth Avenue*: PI, September 15, 1875.

p. 225   *During one hour-long meeting*: TW, 99.

p. 225   *McKean had called Westervelt*: Ibid.

p. 225   *Westervelt told Walling to stop*: TW, 49.

p. 225   *Walling found Westervelt a job*: Ibid.

p. 225   *He also slipped him*: TW, 46.

p. 225   *On February 12, soon after* : TW, 75.

p. 225   *he planned to return at 3:00 P.M.*: Ibid.

p. 225   *Captain Heins met Westervelt*: PI, September 2, 1875.

p. 226   *"Did you ever hear of"* and following quotes: TW, 38.

p. 226   *Frequently after listening to Westervelt's*: PI, September 15, 1875.

p. 226   *Westervelt never heard the full*: Ibid.

p. 226   *He spent that night at the State House*: Ibid.

p. 226   *"Now yesterday afternoon"*: Ibid.

p. 227   *Before lunch, Heins informed*: Ibid.

p. 227   *Heins took him to a station*: Ibid.

p. 227   *Westervelt accused them of inhuman*: Ibid.

p. 227   *Chief Jones transferred him*: Ibid.

We do right to pity Charley Ross

p. 230   *"[. . .] provided, that this shall not apply*: *EB*, February 26, 1875.

p. 231   *When officers in Camden, New Jersey*: *EB*, May 6, 1875.

p. 231   *Because of Italy's recent history of*: Ibid.

p. 231   *By 6:00 P.M., when Christian*: Ibid.

p. 231   *Citizens of Savannah, Georgia*: *PI*, June 3, 9 and 11, 1875.

p. 231   *"We do right to pity Charley Ross"*: *EB*, December 21, 1874.

p. 232   *"from four to eight years old"*: Ibid.

p. 232   *Christian told the press he believed*: *PI*, February 22, 1875.

is my child dead?

p. 233   *Outside of the three designated*: *EB*, January 4, 1875.

p. 233   *steady successions of sleet, snow, rain*: *EB*, January 4 and 19, 1875.

p. 233   *Dozens of sparrows lay dead*: *EB*, February 10, 1875.

p. 233   *wind chills contributed to 373 deaths*: *PI*, January 28, 1875.

p. 233   *an ice block threatened the residents*: *PI*, February 27, 1875.

p. 233   *The gorge sat just above the Fairmount dam*: Ibid.

p. 234   *Water had flooded the Manayunk mills*: Ibid.

p. 234   *water looked as brown as lager*: *PI*, March 30, 1875.

p. 234   *if the ice blocks broke too quickly*: *PI*, March 31, 1875.

p. 234   *Mayor Stokley supervised*: Ibid.

p. 234   *Engineers drilled holes in the ice*: *PI*, March 3, 1875.

p. 234   *city council would not allot enough money*: *PI*, March 6, 1875.

p. 234   *A new town ordinance threatened*: Ibid.

p. 234   *Chief Jones cited the danger*: *PI*, August 10, 1875.

p. 234   *"[The] commodious, well-paved"*: *EB*, January 19, 1875.

p. 235   *"All the visitors from foreign countries"*: *NYH*, January 30, 1875.

p. 235   *local critics worried about the*: *PL*, May 6, 1875.

p. 235   *When more than five thousand visitors*: *PI*, June 25, 1875.

p. 235   *Ignoring city ordinances and fire codes*: Ibid.

p. 235   *"Nearly everybody is 'coming home'"*: May 6, 1875.

p. 235   *one disgruntled man struck*: *PI*, January 19, 1875.

p. 235   *another sliced his wife from her*: *EB*, February 26, 1875.

p. 235   *a third man responded to his wife's*: *EB*, March 9, 1875.

p. 235   *his drunkenness by throwing their*: *PI*, July 19, 1875.

p. 235   *one young newlywed took a stand*: *PI*, July 5,10, and 13, 1875.

p. 236   *One South Philadelphia man stumbled*: *PI*, August 10, 1875.

p. 236   *neighbors contacted the police with*: *PI*, August 2, 1875.

p. 236   *"So little that seemed availing"*: *PI*, April 24, 1874.

she is a city

p. 237   *"Some days ago, Westervelt"*: *PI*, April 24. 1875.

p. 239   *Visitors journeyed to the Centennial*: *PI*, April 14, 1875.

p. 239   *donned their spring best*: PL, April 28, 1875.
p. 239   *freshly-constructed custom houses*: PI, May 3, 1875.
p. 239   *the gardeners preparing flower beds and pruning*: PL, May 17, 1875.
p. 239   *the head contractor had insisted*: EB, April 23, 1875.
p. 239   *men had continued erecting Memorial Hall*: EB, April 23, 1875.
p. 239   *the city held a week-long*: NYT, June 1, 1875.
p. 239   *artisans and caterers sold*: EB, April 23, 1875.
p. 239   *The Centennial Commission solicited*: Ibid.
p. 239   *planners were frustrated that European*: PL, May 25, 1875.
p. 239   *local businessmen organized*: PL, May 12, 1875.
p. 239   *They were especially pleased to*: Ibid.
p. 239   *three thousand school children*: PI, July 6, 1875.
p. 240   *Twenty-two thousand parents*: Ibid.
p. 240   *"Those who have been accustomed"*: PI, August 21, 1875.

you need not ask more questions

p. 241   *Walling said she was ignorant*: PI, September 3, 1875; PI, December 19, 1874.
p. 241   *Through tired tears, she had begged*: PI, September 15, 1875.
p. 241   *Once, he even began crying with her*: Ibid.
p. 241   *there was room for all of the onlookers*: NYH, September 10, 1875; PI, weekday reports, August 30 – September 16.
p. 242   *Every day but Sundays, the crowd sat*: Ibid.
p. 242   *They watched Westervelt take notes*: Ibid.
p. 242   *What thrilled the audience most*: NYH, September 10, 1875.
p. 242   *After Christian finished his dinner, he walked*: PI, September 20, 1875.
p. 242   *the Ross family had received twenty addititional ransom letters*: Ibid.
p. 242   *"I knew Mosher and Douglas"*: Ibid.
p. 242   *"ros your boy is alive and"*: Ibid.
p. 243   *"If Superintendent Walling had followed"*: Ibid.
p. 243   *District Attorney Furman Sheppard began*: PI, September 16, 1875.
p. 243   *"What relations of perfect"*: PI, Friday, September 17.
p. 243   *Joseph Ford, attorney for the defense*: TW, 108.
p. 244   *"The Commonwealth asks you to convict"*: PI, Friday, September 17.
p. 244   *"Review the testimony with"*: TW, 112.
p. 244   *His fate rested with two manufacturers*: EB, August 31, 1875.
p. 244   *Westervelt's children stopped playing quietly*: PI, Friday, September 17.
p. 244   *While the jurors filed out of the courtroom*: Ibid.
p. 244   *The jurors' debates continued throughout*: PI, September 20, 1875.
p. 244   *Journalists waiting inside the*: Ibid.
p. 245   *a large crowd gathered in Independence Square*: Ibid.
p. 245   *By the time the State House bell tolled*: Ibid.
p. 245   *the crowd huddled against the courthouse*: Ibid.
p. 245   *arms and elbows pushed*: Ibid.

p. 245   *Children, storekeepers, reporters*: Ibid.

p. 245   *At 10:00 A.M., the judge arrived*: Ibid.

p. 245   *Westervelt walked to the dock*: Ibid.

p. 245   *Reporters read despair*: Ibid.

p. 245   *Westervelt pushed his head into his hands*: Ibid.

p. 245   *On October 9, he appeared one last time*: TW, 112.

p. 245   *"I had hoped ere this I should have been"*: Ibid.

p. 246   *Westervelt breathed deeply*: TW, 112.

p. 246   *Leaning forward, he put his head*: Ibid.

we fear being traped in our own game

p. 247   *Thirty-foot stone walls surrounded*: Johnston, 63.

p. 247   *Philadelphia's Quaker fathers*: Johnston, 21.

p. 247   *the Walnut Street penitentiary had served*: Shearer, 11.

p. 247   *male and female inmates intermingled and*: Johnston, 26.

p. 247   *for the next forty years, they petitioned*: Johnston, 26.

p. 247   *In 1821, after receiving a $100,000 grant*: Johnston, 44.

p. 248   *for the world's first prison entirely given*: Johnston, 45.

p. 248   *The winning proposal belonged* : Johnston, 34.

p. 248   *many people disagreed*: Johnston, 24, 29, 44.

p. 248   *No prison had ever fully practiced solitary*: Johnston, 27.

p. 248   *tourists praised Haviland's work*: Johnston, 57.

p. 248   *the "prison at Cherry Hill"*: Johnston, 31.

p. 248   *would influence more than three hundred prisons*: General Overview, Eastern State Penitentiary Website, http://easternstate.org/learn /research-library/history.

p. 249   *1056 inmates shared 585 cells*: Report of the Inspectors of the Eastern State Penitentiary for 1875. February, 1876. This number differs from Penitentiary Papers, IIIB. 2. Governance, 1870-1923, 2a. Inmate population and number of cells, obtainable from the ESP archives. On page 178, it states that 801 prisoners shared 585 cells. After intense study, I am inclined to side with the inspectorss report.

p. 249   *wardens over the years had complained*: Johnston, 43.

p. 249   *The walls surrounding each exercise*: Johnston, 43.

p. 249   *state commissioners had demanded*: Johnston, 180.

p. 249   *As a result, these four blocks had two*: Johnston, 40.

p. 249   *Guards escorted him*: This scene is reconstructed from information in Norman Johnston's *Crucible of Good Intentions*, pages 43 and 49.

p. 249   *At the physician's office*: Johnston, 48.

p. 249   *8082*: Eastern State Penitentiary Commutation books. Microfilm. Pennsylvania State Archives, Harrisburg.

p. 249   *and reviewed the rules posted*: Teeters, 137, 176.

p. 249   *The whale-oil lamp attached*: Johnston, 44.

p. 249   *he could ask for a Bible*: Ibid.

the whole gang

p. 254   *"I think [Charley Ross] is"*: Walling, 208.

East Washington Lane, Present Day

p. 258   *Westervelt was released*: Eastern State Penitentiary Commutation
          Books, Microfilm. Pennsylvania State Archives, Harrisburg, PA.
p. 258   *at least one interview to the*: New York Tribune, January 22, 1881.
p. 258   *his obituary appeared in 1890*:
p. 258   *His sister Martha Mosher and at least*: NYT, November 27, 1890.
p. 258   *In 1897, Gil Mosher's son Ellsworth*: Everly 387.
p. 258   *"scandal breeding" as a*: NYT, May 13, 1893; Bell, 204.
p. 258   *Refusing audits, the Commission*: Ibid.
p. 258   *City Hall cost 12 million dollars to*: Ibid.
p. 259   *More than one in five Americans*: Foner, 564.
p. 259   *paying particular attention to*: Rydell, *Fair America*, 16; Foner, 564.
p. 259   *visionaries who organized six major*: Rydell, *Fair America*, 25.
p. 259   *Christian Ross met with George Walling*:
p. 259   *Walling said the case of Charley Ross*: Walling, 198.
p. 259   *following the advice of friends*: Ross, 17.
p. 260   *Throughout the first half of the twentieth century…*: ** Thomas Everly,
          in his article "Searching for Charley Ross," discusses twentieth
          century claims on Charley's identity. Both Everly and I cite Paula
          Fass's fascinating work, *Kidnapping in America* (1997). Fass devotes
          her first chapter to Charley Ross; her work discusses how the case
          embodies Victorian characterizations of innocence and propriety,
          and it suggests how the kidnapping served as a prototype for
          twentieth-century abductions.

bibliography

Government Publications. *1875 Annual Report of the Chief of Police.* The Philadelphia Free Library.

Adams, Peter. *The Bowery Boys: Street Corner Radicals and the Politics of Rebellion.* Westport, CT: Praeger, 2005.

Ade, George. *The Old-Time Saloon, Not Wet—Not Dry, Just History.* New York: Long and Smith, 1931.

The Life, Trial and Conviction of William H. Westervelt, for the Abduction of Little Charley Ross: the Tragic Death of the Burglars Mosher and Douglass (on Long Island, N.Y.), Who Were Implicated in Abducting the Poor Little Fellow : the Confession, the Whole Case, the Trial in Full. Philadelphia: Barclay & Co, 1875.

Asbury, Herbert. *The Gangs of New York: An Informal History of the Underworld.* New York: Knopf, 1927, 1928.

Beers, Dorothy Gondos. "The Centennial City: 1865–1876." In *Philadelphia: A 300-Year History.* Russell F. Weigley, ed. New York: W.W. Norton, 1982.

Bell, Marion L. *Crusade in the City: Revivalism in Nineteenth-Century Philadelphia.* Cranbury, NJ: Associated University Presses, 1977.

Beckert, Sven. *The Monied Metropolis: New York City and the Consolidation of the American Bourgeoisie, 1850–1896.* New York: University of Cambridge Press, 2001.

Berman, Jay Stuart. *Police Administration and Progressive Reform: Theodore Roosevelt as Police Commissioner of New York.* New York: Greenwood Press, 1987.

Brace, Charles Loring. *The Dangerous Classes of New York.* New York: Wynkoop & Hallenbeck, 1872.

Braude, Ann. *Radical Spirits: Spiritualism and Women's Rights in Nineteenth-Century America.* Boston: Beacon Press, 1989.

Brown, Dee Alexander. *The Year of the Century: 1876.* New York: Charles Scribner's Sons, 1966.

Callard, Judith and Germantown Historical Society. *Germantown, Mount Airy, and Chestnut Hill.* Charleston, SC: Arcadia Publishing, 2000.

Carp, E. Wayne. *Family Matters: Secrecy and Disclosure in the History of Adoption.* Cambridge, MA: Harvard University Press, 1998.

Chambers, Julius. "The River-Thief." In Appleton's *Journal of Literature, Science and Art.* (December 7, 1872) Vol. 8, No. 193: 638, New York: D. Appleton, 1869–1876. APS Online.

Clemens, Thomas E. *East Germantown: A New Name for Ancient Villages.* Philadelphia: Germantown Press, 1936. LaSalle University Library Collection.

———*Quaint Old Landmarks in East Germantown.* Philadelphia: Germantown Press, 1939. LaSalle University Library Collection.

Coffin, Elizabeth W. *A Girl's Life in Germantown.* Boston: Sherman, French, 1916. La Salle University Library Collection.

Collis, Charles H. T. File, Historical Society of Pennsylvania. July 25, 1862; October 12, 1862.

Costello, Augustine E. *Our Police Protectors.* Montclair, NJ: Patterson Smith, 1972.

Countryman, Matthew J. *Up South: Civil Rights and Black Power in Philadelphia.* Philadelphia: University of Pennsylvania Press, 2006.

Cox, Robert S. *Body and Soul. A Sympathetic History of American Spiritualism.* Charlottesville, VA: University of Virginia Press, 2002.

Davis, Allen F., Frederic M. Miler and Morris J. Vogel. *Philadelphia Stories: A Photographic History, 1920–1960.* Philadelphia: Temple University Press, Philadelphia 1988.

Dilworth, Richardson, ed. "Credit Unions and Social Capital in Philadelphia." In *Social Capital in the City: Community and Civic Life in Philadelphia.* Philadelphia: Temple University Press, 2006. 25–40.

Edwards, Rebecca. *New Spirits: Americans in the Gilded Age, 1865–1905.* New York: Oxford University Press, 2006.

Egle, William., and A. S. Dudley, Harry I. Huber, and R. R. Schively, eds. *Commemorative Biographical Encyclopedia of Dauphin County, Pennsylvania.* Chambersburg, PA: J. M. Runk.

Everly, Thomas. "Searching for Charley Ross." *Pennsylvania History.* (Summer 2000) Vol. 67, No. 3: 376–396.

Fabian, Ann. *Card Sharps, Dream Books, and Bucket Shops: Gambling in Nineteenth-Century America.* Ithaca and London: Cornell University Press, 1990.

Fass, Paula S. *Kidnapped: Child Abduction in America.* New York: Oxford University Press, 1997.

Faust, Drew Gilpin. *This Republic of Suffering: Death and the American Civil War.* New York: Knopf, 2008.

Foner, Eric. *Reconstruction, America's Unfinished Revolution, 1863–1877*. New York: Harper and Row, 1988.

Fox, Kenneth. *Better City Government: Innovation in American Urban Politics, 1850–1937*. Philadelphia: Temple University Press, 1977

Gilfoyle, Timothy J. *A Pickpocket's Tale: The Underworld of Nineteenth-Century New York*. New York: W. W. Norton, 2006.

Greenwood, Janette Thomas. *The Gilded Age: A History in Documents*. New York: Oxford University Press, 2000.

Grimsted, David. *American Mobbing, 1828–1861, Toward Civil War*. New York: Oxford University Press, 1998.

Gutman, Herbert. "Work, culture and society in industrializing America between 1815 and 1843." In *Essays in Comparative History: Economy, Politics and Society in Britain and America*. Clive Emsley, ed. Philadelphia: Open University Press/Milton Keynes, 1984.

Haines, Ella Wister. *Reminiscences of a Victorian Child*. Philadelphia: E. W. Haines, September 1953. La Salle University Library Wister Collection.

Harring, Sidney L. *Policing a Class Society: The Experience of American Cities, 1865–1915*. New Brunswick: Rutgers University Press, 1983.

Harris, Neil, ed. *The Land of Contrasts: 1880–1901*. New York: Doubleday, 1970.

Harrison, George L., Jr. File, Historical Society of Pennsylvania. Letter to Mayor Stokley; Correspondence between Harrison and Christian Ross.

Hendrickson, David. *Union, Nation, or Empire: The American Debate Over International Relations, 1789–1941*. Lawrence: University Press of Kansas, 2009.

Henkin, David M. *The Postal Age: The Emergence of Modern Communications in Ninteenth-Century America*. Chicago: University of Chicago Press, 2006.

Hepp, John Henry IV. *The Middle-Class City: Transforming Space and Time in Philadelphia, 1876-1926*. Philadelphia: University of Pennsylvania Press, 2003.

Hessinger, Rodney. *Seduced, Abandoned and Reborn: Visions of Youth in Middle-Class America, 1750–1850*. Philadelphia: University of Pennsylvania Press, 2005.

Hilkey, Judy. *Character is Capital: Success Manuals and Manhood in Gilded Age America*. Chapel Hill: University of North Carolina Press, 1997.

"History of Chestnut Street." *Sunday Dispatch*. 1870. Philadelphia Public Library – Photo Archives, Chestnut Street – General History Box.

Hoogenboom, Ari and Philip S. Klein. *A History of Pennsylvania*. City Archives.

Hopkins, Griffith Morgan. Atlas of the Late Borough of Germantown, Twenty-second Ward, City of Philadelphia. Philadelphia: G. M. Hopkins, 1871.

Hotchkin, Samuel Fitch. *Ancient and Modern Germantown, Mount Airy and Chestnut Hill*. Philadelphia: P. W. Ziegler, 1889. Art Museum Reference, La Salle University Library.

Jenkins, Charles F. *The Guide Book to Historic Germantown*. Germantown: The Society, 1902. Wister Collection, La Salle University Library.

Johnson, David R. "The Search for an Urban Discipline: Police Reform as a Response to Crime in American Cities, 1800–1975." Dissertation. University of Chicago, 1972.

Johnson, Marilynn S. *Street Justice: A History of Police Violence in New York City*. Boston: Beacon, 2003.

Johnston, Norman. *Eastern State Penitentiary: Crucible of Good Intentions*. Philadelphia: Philadelphia Museum of Art, 1994.

Keels, Thomas H. *Forgotten Philadelphia: Lost Architecture of the Quaker City*. Philadelphia: Temple University Press, 2007.

Kessner, Thomas. *Capital City: New York City and the Men Behind America's Rise to Economic Dominance, 1860–1900*. New York: Simon & Schuster, 2003.

Keyser, Naaman H., C. Henry Kain, John Palmer Garber, and Horace F. McCann. *History of Old Germantown: With a description of its settlement and some account of its important persons, buildings and places connected with its development*. Germantown: H. F. McCann, 1907.

Kingsdale, Jon. "The 'Poor Man's club': Social Functions of the Urban Working-Class Saloon" *American Quarterly* 25 (Oct 1973): 472–475.

Klein, Marcus. *Easterns, Westerns, and Private Eyes: American Matters, 1870–1900*. Madison: University of Wisconsin Press, 1994.

Lane, Roger. *Violent Death in the City: Suicide, Accident and Murder in Nineteenth-Century Philadelphia*. Cambridge: Harvard Press, 1979.

Levine, Jerald E. "Police, Parties, Polity: the Bureaucratization of the NYC Police 1870–1917." Dissertation. University of Wisconsin at Madison, 1971.

Looney, Robert F. *Old Philadelphia in Early Photographs: 1839–1914*. New York: Dover Publication, 1976.

Marshall, Leon S. "The English and American Industrial City." *Essays in Comparative History: Economy, Politics and Society in Britain and America*. Clive Emsley, ed. Philadelphia: Open University Press/Milton Keynes, 1984. 199-207.

McCabe, James D. *Lights and Shadows of New York Life*. 1872. I accessed this through Project Gutenberg—www.gutenberg.org/ebooks/19742.

McCormick, Richard. "The Party Paved in Public Policy." In *Essays in Comparative History: Economy, Politics and Society in Britain and America*. Clive Emsley, ed. Philadelphia: Open University Press/Milton Keynes, 1984. 29–46.

Mendte, J. Robert. *The Union League of Philadelphia Celebrates 125 Years, 1862–1987*. Devon, PA: William T. Cooke, 1987.

Miller, Arthur P., Jr., and Marjorie L. Miller. *Pennsylvania Battlefields and Military Landmarks*. Mechanicsburg, PA: Stackpole Books, 2000.

Miller, Wilbur R. "Police Authority in London and New York City: 1830–1870." In *Journal of Social History* (Winter 1975): 81–95. Rpt. in *Essays in Comparative History: Economy, Politics and Society in Britain and America*. Clive Emsley, ed. Philadelphia: Open University Press/Milton Keynes, 1984. 209–224.

Mintz, Steven. *Huck's Raft. A History of American Childhood*. Cambridge, MA: Harvard University Press, 2004.

Monkkonen, Eric H. *Police in Urban America 1860–1920*. Cambridge, U.K.: Cambridge University Press, 1981.

Moss, Frank. 'The American Metropolis.' New York: P. F. Collier, 1897. Vol. 3: 106.

O'Toole, G. J. A. *Honorable Treachery: A History of U.S. Intelligence, Espionage, and Court Action from the American Revolution to the CIA*. New York: Atlantic Monthly Press, 1991.

Paist, Joseph H., ed. Manual of the Councils of the City of Philadelphia for the year 1874. 1874-1876. Philadelphia: E.C. Markley and Son Printers, 1874.

Photograph of Christian Ross. Photo Box 3, Envelope 1, Sheet K. Germantown Historical Society.

Photograph of the Ross House, East Washington Lane. Photo Box 24, Envelope 2.

Photograph of Germantown's Town Hall. Photo Box E, Envelope 6. Photo Box F, Envelope 4.

Pinkerton Detective Agency Files, Library of Congress. Box 163, Folder 12; Box 47, Folder 9.

Police Department of Philadelphia. Inventory Part 4. 79. Philadelphia City Archives. Accessions.

Powers, Fred Perry. Lecture. "Site and Relic Society of Germantown." March 17, 1911. Historical Addresses No 8. La Salle University Library.

Richardson, James F. *The New York Police: Colonial Times to 1901*. New York: Oxford University Press, 1970.

Riis, Jacob A. *How the Other Half Lives: Studies Among the Tenements of New York*. Dover Publishing, 1991.

Ross, Christian K. File, Historical Society of Pennsylvania. Letter to ELH, Pinkerton, August 22, 1874; Letter to Mr. Morrison, December 17, 1874.

Ross, Christian K. *The Father's Story of Charley Ross, the Kidnapped Child*. Philadelphia: John E. Potter and Company, 1876.

Ryan, Mary P. *Civic Wars, Democracy, and Public Life in the American City during the Nineteenth Century*. Berkeley: University of California Press, 1997.

Rydell, Robert W. *World of Fairs*. Chicago: University of Chicago Press, 1993.

Rydell, Robert W., John E. Findling, and Kimberly D. Pelle. *Fair America: World's Fairs in the United States*. Washington: Smithsonian Institution Press, 2000.

Sargent, Epes. *The Proof Palpable of Immortality*. Boston: Colby and Rich, 1875.

Schlereth, Thomas J. *Victorian America: Transformations in Everyday Life 1876–1915*. New York: Harper Collins, 1991.

Simon, Grant Miles, and Margaret B. and Harry M. Tinkcom. *Historic Germantown: from the Founding to the Early Part of the Nineteenth Century*. Lancaster, PA: American Philosophical Society/ Lancaster Press, 1955. LaSalle University Library.

Sprogle, Howard O. *The Philadelphia Police, Past and Present*. Philadelphia: Howard O. Sprogle, 1887.

Stauffer, John. "Embattled Manhood and New England Writers, 1860–1870." Anthologized in *Battle Scars: Gender and Sexuality in the American Civil War*, edited by Catherine B. Clinton and Nina Silber. New York: Oxford University Press, 2006. 120–139.

Summers, Mark Wahlgren. *The Era of Good Stealings*. New York: Oxford University Press, 1993.

———— *The Press Gang: Newspapers and Politics, 1865–1878*. Chapel Hill: University of North Carolina Press, 1994.

Switala, William J. *Underground Railroad in Pennsylvania*. Mechanicsburg, PA: Stackpole Books, 2001.

Teeters, Negley K. and John D. Shearer. *The Prison at Philadelphia, Cherry Hill: The Separate System of Penal Discipline: 1829–1913*. New York: Columbia University Press, 1957.

"The Bride of a Pirate." *The Youth's Companion (1827–1929)*. April 23, 1874. 47: 17. 134. APS Online.

"The History of the Department of State: VIII." *The American Journal of International Law* 5:4 (October 1911). 1987–1024.

Tholfsen, Trygve. "Middle Class Hegemony: Working-Class Subculture." *Essays in Comparative History: Economy, Politics and Society in Britain and America*. Clive Emsley, ed. Philadelphia: Open University Press/Milton Keynes, 1984. 93-124.

Vaux, Richard. *Brief Sketch of the Origin and History of the State Penitentiary for the Eastern District of Pennsylvania at Philadelphia*. Philadelphia: McLaughlin Brothers, 1872.

Walling, George W. *Recollections of a New York Chief of Police*. Montclair, NJ: Patterson Smith Publishing Corporation, 1972.

Warden Cassidy on Prisons and Convicts. Addressed to members of societies interested in prison management. Philadelphia: Patterson and White, 1894.

Warner, Sam Bass, Jr. *The Private City: Philadelphia in Three Periods of Its Growth.* First Edition. Philadelphia: University of Pennsylvania Press, 1968.

Weigley, Russell F. *Philadelphia: A 300-Year History.* New York: W. W. Norton, 1982.

Whiteman, Maxwell. *Gentlemen in Crisis: The First Century of the Union League of Philadelphia, 1862–1962.* Philadelphia: The Winchell Company of Philadelphia, 1975.

Winner, Septimus. Diaries and papers. Collection, 1845–1902. Historical Society of Pennsylvania.

Wister, Charles J., Jr. *The Labour of a Long Life: a Memoir of Charles J. Wister.* Volumes I and II. Germantown: Charles J. Wister, Jr. 1886. La Salle University Library Wister Collection.

Wister, Frances Anne. "The Great Road to Germantown." *The Germantown Crier,* 23–24.

Wister, John Caspar. *"Reminiscences of John Caspar Wister" (1887–1982).* La Salle University Library Wister Collection.

Wister, Jones. *Jones Wister's Reminiscences.* Philadelphia: J. B. Lippincott, 1920. (Printed for private circulation.) La Salle University Library Wister Collection.

Wister, Sarah. "Sarah Wister's Civil War Journal." *That I May Tell You: Journals and Letters of the Owen Wister Family.* Wayne, PA: Haverford House, 1979. LaSalle University Library Wister Collection.

Wolf, Edwin. *Philadelphia: Portrait of an American City.* Harrisburg, PA: Stackpole Books, 1975.

Wolf, Stephanie Grauman. *Urban Village: Population, Community, and Family Structure in Germantown, Pennsylvania, 1683–1800.* Princeton, NJ: Princeton University Press, 1976.

Zeirold, Norman. *Little Charley Ross.* Boston: Little, Brown, 1967. All Zierold references come from the Norman Zierold Collection.

——Manuscript draft. Norman Zierold Collection, Boxes 1, Rare Book & Manuscript Library, Columbia University in the City of New York.

Zimmerman, Matthias. Map of Germantown and Creeson Townships. 1746. Copied by Joseph Lehmann, 1824. Germantown Historical Society.

index